A MEASURE FOR MEASURES

A MEASURE FOR MEASURES

a manifesto for
empirical sociology

RAY PAWSON

ROUTLEDGE
London and New York

First published 1989 by Routledge
11 New Fetter Lane, London EC4P 4EE
29 West 35th Street, New York, NY 10001

© 1989 Ray Pawson

Typeset by LaserScript Limited, Mitcham, Surrey
Printed and bound in Great Britain by
Mackays of Chatham PLC, Chatham, Kent

British Library Cataloguing in Publication Data

Pawson, Ray, 1948-
A measure for measures: a manifesto
for empirical sociology. — (International library of sociology.)
1. Social sciences. Empiricism
I. Title II. Series
300

Library of Congress Cataloging in Publication Data

Pawson, Ray, 1948-
A measure for measures: a manifesto for
empirical sociology/Ray Pawson.
p.   cm — (International library of sociology)
Bibliography: p. Includes index.
1. Sociology–Methodology. I. Title. II. Series.
HM24.P335 1989
301–dc19   88-19911   CIP
ISBN 0-415-02870-1   ISBN 0-415-02659-8 Pbk

TO WENDY

CONTENTS

PERMISSIONS

I am grateful to the following authors and publishers for permission to reproduce copyright material:

Oxford University Press for a table from John H. Goldthorpe et.al., *Social Mobility and Class Structure*, (1980);

John Wiley and Sons for tables from R. Boudon, *Education Opportunity and Social Inequality*, (1974);

Open University Press for diagrams from *Instrumentation*, T291, Unit 1, (1975);

Verso for tables and diagrams from E.O.Wright, *Classes*, (1985);

Academic Press and E.O.Wright for a diagram from his *Class Structure and Income Determination*, (1974)

ACKNOWLEDGEMENTS

Putting the real workers first, I would like to thank Margaret Gothelf for her professionalism in the hard and unrewarding slog of typing the majority of the text. This book might have been called 'A Mesaure for Mesaures' had we not done the proof-reading but this is all part of the pleasure of having the services of the fastest fingers in Leeds. I would also like to thank Jude Cohen, Carol Peaker, Gena Lodge, Jane Thompson, Carolyn Weaver and Pattie-Jean Brown who all lent a hand in the processing and re-processing of the text.

Nick Tilley and Roy Todd have been kind enough to read the manuscript from cover to cover and I hope that I will be able to do the same for them both some day. They did manage to query whether I need bother with the first half of the book but apart from this they made many useful suggestions for which I thank them warmly. I would also like to record my gratitude to Routledge's anonymous external reader (some grey-bearded sage, I'm sure) for being so clear-sighted in recognizing what I am up to here.

My colleagues at Leeds covered my teaching for a year during one of those quaint old things they used to have in Universities called sabbaticals. My thanks go to them all, as they do to colleagues at the Nuffield Centre (especially the tea club) who made me feel a welcome lodger during '85-'86.

Ray Pawson

Leeds,
Spring 1988.

Chapter One

SUBSTANTIATING SOCIOLOGY

This book asks, and I trust answers, a direct and seemingly simple question – can sociology be substantiated? What I want to do is referee the fight between those in the red corner for whom sociology is a *substantive* discipline, *substantiated* by valid and reliable *evidence* about the real world versus those in the blue corner, who would have it that sociological knowledge is *discursive*, based on conceptual building blocks and tied together by *convention* and *conviction*.

The chastened times of sociology in the eighties provide an ideal vantage point for some mature reflection on the extent to which sociological knowledge can be subject to empirical confirmation and on the form in which such evidence might be cast. Over the years, different views have prevailed and such has been the rate of change of sociological wisdom on the matter that it is appropriate to begin with a personal view of the background and context to this debate. The opening section of this chapter consists of a pen picture of the rise and fall and rise of the significance of empirical work in modern sociology. To summarize the British experience at least, one can begin by noting an early phase based on essentially positivistic assumptions in which the centrality of empirical evidence was taken for granted. Thereafter in the sixties and seventies came the critique of positivism and ascendency was taken by a whole parade of theoretical perspectives whose concerns were centred on internal conceptual consistency rather than empirical confirmation. Presently, we are witnessing an empiricist backlash, prompted in part by survival instinct during hard economic and political times but also by the failure of the

1

anti-empiricist schools to provide any means of justifying or adjudicating between the theoretical labours on offer.

I will not be claiming any particular originality for such an overview, indeed I almost want to apologize for its brevity and anglocentrism. So, whilst I will be unable to resist a dig at some particularly bizarre lines in this evolution of methodological thought, my main aim will be to establish something about sociological methodology itself. Sociology is marked by an unfortunate preference to attempt to legitimize its methods through the medium of polemical exchange conducted at the metatheoretical level. I will argue that the development of sociological method is not particularly well served by such purely philosophical scrutiny, either in its traditional form in the 'naturalism debate' or in the kind of amateur philosophy that has come to the fore as a result of our internal 'paradigm wars'.

In section two of this chapter I will look forward to the return of confidence in empirical sociology. It is vitally important that this revival is not simply a return to an unreconstituted positivism fuelled by political expediency. What is needed is a much more refined quantitative method which is sensitive to the phenomenological and relativistic critiques of the last two decades but which is self-confident enough not to be led up a thousand garden paths in the belief that our methodological salvation lies with some yet-to-be-discovered epistemological miracle. The main purpose of section two of these introductory remarks is to provide a new focus and a more trustworthy method for assessing the viability of empirical sociology. I will suggest that questions about *measurement* are particularly strategic since they straddle the great dualisms which divide the discipline, most notably that between qualitative and quantitative sociology and that between sociologies which are broadly empirical and those which are primarily theoretical. Four critiques of measurement will be distinguished in some detail. I will suggest that the growth of a genuine empirical sociology rests on the discovery of a resolution to these problems. I will further suggest that any such solution need pay heed to both abstract metatheoretical principles and the detail of research practice.

2

1.1 THE RISE AND FALL AND RISE OF EMPIRICAL SOCIOLOGY.

The two cultures

The origins of the issues discussed in this book are as old as inquiry itself; in one sense it is simply a modern version of the constant sparring between the two cultures of art and science. Throughout history there have been those who have championed ideas such as that claiming that material nature is nothing but inert mass and motion, and regard as the pinnacle of human achievement the ability to set down the exact rational calculus describing such motion. Equally vociferous have been the voices claiming that no number of these equations of mathematical physics can explain the vital, active, intuitive, creative aspects of humankind. Whilst most commentators today would argue that this kind of 'trench warfare' does little justice to either form of understanding, it remains a fine source of inspiration for the polemicist.

Thus, inveterate quantifiers in modern-day sociology might be pleasantly surprised to find apparent support for their number-crunching in one of Plato's adages: 'He who never looks for numbers in anything will not himself be looked for in the number of the famous men' (quoted in Georgescu-Roegen, 1971, p. 79). For an opposing view of scientific calculation one might consider Blake's satirical print of Newton, in which the scientist is portrayed as self-obsessed rational man (see cover). To explain to you philistine sociologists – the satirical cutting edge is not obtained by depicting Newton in the nude; the point is that here is a man trying to come to grips with the majesty of the universe with a pair of compass needles. Blake used the image of the compass in other sketches, one of which illustrates the text: 'He who sees the Infinite in all things sees God. He who sees the Ratio only sees himself . . .' (quoted in Butlin, 1978, p. 62). With a bit of imagination it is possible to see a similar dilemma in the quest for an empirical sociology. Picture Newton as a modern sociologist, with the compass and scroll replaced by computer terminal and interview schedule (though, come to think of it, such an intrepid researcher would look even sillier with no clothes on).

Of all the battlecries on this matter, none is more famous than Kelvin's dictum, 'If you cannot measure, your knowledge is meagre and unsatisfactory', (quoted, with suspicion as to its authenticity, in Kuhn, 1961, p. 161). This idea that measurement is the hallmark of science, that numerical data provide both the source and testbed of scientific laws, so impressed one group of social scientists that it was inscribed on the facade of the Social Research Building at the University of Chicago. As ever in sociology, this statement has not won universal approval, even, I imagine, by those who have been greeted daily by the said inscription. Thus, the received meaning of Kelvin's words in the social disciplines, according to one sceptic, is better rendered. 'If you cannot measure, measure anyhow', (quoted in Kuhn 1961, p. 164). I propose to adapt this little maxim as the text for this book, and after investigation of the principles and practice of research we will be in a better position to know if sociologists 'measure' or 'measure anyhow'.

Naturalism and anti-naturalism

Another backdrop to the question confronted here, which cannot be ignored, is the 'demarcation debate' in the philosophy of science in which philosophers try to adduce those points of method which enable us to distinguish scientific knowledge from other forms of ideology, belief and appreciation. We need to dwell here, at least briefly, since the legitimation of method within sociology is the concern of this book and legitimation of method is very much the business of those concerned with prescriptive philosophy of science. What is interesting about the demarcation debate is the way it has corkscrewed around for years as different criteria are upheld as the touchstone of the scientific practice and how sociology has towed along behind, being periodically promoted and relegated from the fold as alternative 'definitive' scientific protocols come and go.

Originally this involved just a two-cornered fight. For roughly the first half of this century, philosophical orthodoxy (usually identified as positivism or empiricism) more or less squared with the Kelvin view above and thus insisted that scientific knowledge was unique because of its certain, factual basis acquired through rigorous experimentation and measurement. The obvious course

4

of action for sociologists was either to imitate or repudiate these prescriptions, and thus one could neatly divide the 'research' side of the discipline into two camps of naturalism and anti-naturalism. Sociological positivists thus stressed the need for valid and reliable data collection conjoined with sophisticated statistical analysis. Those of the interpretative or hermeneutic school, in stressing the intentionality of human action, were inclined to treat measurement-centred analysis as an irrelevance given the paramount need for meaning-centred understanding. Really at this stage matters had progressed little beyond a 'two-cultures' polarization: as far as science went, sociologists had either to take it or leave it, and a certain package of research activities could be assumed according to the designation preferred.

With the arrival of the Kuhnian revolution in the philosophy of science, sociology became even more curious about, though paradoxically rather less well served by, questions about naturalism (Kuhn, 1970). Science, it was now claimed, could not be grasped as a set of established-procedures-to-be-mechanically-followed; rather it was peopled by interest groups who were trained to pursue particular theories and were massively selective in favouring certain bodies of evidence. Though Kuhn's paradigms brought a glint of recognition to every sociologist's eyes no one was quite sure what to make of their relativistic implications, or more to the point, Feyerbend's (1975) invocation that there is no such thing whatsoever as the scientific method. The discipline as a whole ruminated on whether being against method meant that 'anything goes' or 'everything goes' or 'most-things go' or 'nothing goes' and then quietly but steadfastly got on with what it was doing before, whilst perhaps publicly advocating a 'decent methodological pluralism' – a strange philosophy which no individual ever put into practice but was considered awfully good advice for everyone else (Bell and Roberts, 1984, p. 5). With some justification in such a climate a thousand approaches flourished – theorists still speculated, positivists crunched-on, ethnographers empathized, ethnomethodologists ummed and arrhed, and metatheorists laughed all the way to the bank, whilst the case for empirical sociology, or any other for that matter, drew no clearer to resolution.

More recently the naturalism debate has received fresh impetus with the importation into sociology of a newer wave of post-Kuhnian philosophies of science. Terminology can be a little slippery here, but I am thinking particularly of two epistemologies going under the names of 'realism' and the 'materialist theory of knowledge'. Their philosophical importance lies in their complete redefinition of the nature of scientific investigation. It has become respectable, once again, for philosophers to proclaim the power of science since they no longer have to defend all the errors and contradictions of the classical logical positivist account. The great significance for sociology in all this is that it becomes possible for certain forms of analysis to proclaim themselves as scientific without strangling themselves with the yoke of empiricism or even the burden of constructing a programme of empirical research. When such luxurious pastures became open to invasion it was no surprise to find a little army of texts all proclaiming a new naturalist solution to the problem of sociological method (e.g. Keat and Urry, 1975; Benton, 1977; Bhaskar, 1979). Interestingly, most of these took the same triptych form, declaring a plague on both the houses of vulgar empiricism (for misreading science) and hermeneutic subjectivism (for reading science out of sociology), thus leaving their own approach triumphant in its ability to span science and society.

It is instructive to observe the treatment of 'science' as employed in pursuit of these epistemological shifts. The first step is always an attack upon the first principles of the positivist reconstruction of science. Thus both realists and materialists share in the vilification of notions such as that claiming the existence of a bedrock of objective observational statements upon which science supposedly rests. Realists tend to stop short, however, of dismissing the idea that there is a real world out there in which things happen independently of our perception of them. For this school pure unadulterated sensory data do not exist, but observation is most certainly theory-laden, rather than theory-determined. The materialists pursue a more radical thesis. Having rejected all forms of empiricism on the grounds of their repudiation of 'observational facts', no alternative is seen but to recognize science for what it is, namely a form of 'social' or 'theoretical' practice.

6

The next step is to argue for a replacement set of domain assumptions on the grounds that they are logically sounder and/or a better description of the history of scientific investigation. Realists thus stress that scientific terms take their meaning from a network of definitions, relationships and laws, and it is claimed that it is theoretical programmes as a whole which are assessed for correspondence with the world. In particular great store is set by the idea that science does not operate by simply unearthing patterns and regularities in the occurrence of events, but explains by coming to an understanding of the underlying mechanisms that generate and constitute these regular sequences. Materialists stress that science operates by creating 'unities' or 'logical patterns' formed by the concepts of a theoretical system, with Althusserian Marxists going so far as to claim that the world we see is actually created by the theories (or what they term as the 'problematics') we employ.

The final step is to return to sociology and look for illustrative work which can stand as an exemplar of the newly preferred approach. In some instances this involves giving some long-established sociological tradition a 'new reading'. Thus, to combine our principles, if we can find examples of sociological practice which stress the constructed structure of the meaning of terms and/or reckon to unearth the underlying mechanism which generates the surface order of appearance, then it turns out that these have been doing science all along. I need hardly add that best-suited and best-informed by this style of argument have been various traditions of Marxism, particularly the structuralist versions, which qualify as science, as they see it, on both the prerequisites just discussed.

This, I believe, brings our Cook's tour of the naturalism debate up to date and, despite having been your guide, my next step is to ask was it all worth it? Sad to say, I have to tell you the answer is no. In the first place questions about naturalism and sociology are unsatisfactory simply for the patent lack of finality of a criterion to demarcate science from non-science. For every rationalist demarcation proposal there always lurks a relativist rebuttal and any attempt to admit relativist principles into science effectively abandons the very idea of demarcation. Consider the fate of the Althusserian notion of 'theoretical constitution' in this respect. As Hindess and Hirst chose to express it once upon a time:

> The question of the 'reality of the external world' is not the issue. It is not a question of whether objects *exist* when we do not speak of them. *Objects* of discourse do not exist. The entities discourse refers to are constituted in it and by it. (Hindess and Hirst, 1977, p. 19).

This proved a most useful ploy, especially in certain echelons of Marxism which had never been inclined to let a few facts get in the way of a good theory, since in this case there isn't even the need to rewrite history, one simply ignores it:

> Marxism, as a theoretical and a political practice, gains nothing from its association with historical writing and historical research. The study of history is not only scientifically but also politically valueless. (Hindess and Hirst, 1975, p. 311).

One can only look back at this as an exercise in self-inflicted throat-cutting. The anti-empiricism present at the time channelled many into the easy delights of 'scientific discourse'. Everyone now knows, of course, that such a strategy is fine if one is totally committed to one and only one theory about the world; the problem comes if one recognizes a multiplicity of (or even two) competing theories. In this respect the imperatives suggesting the world is discursively constituted do not help us one jot in sorting the scientific wheat from the ideological chaff.

Specific epistemological nightmares like this should not detract attention from the more important reason for the absurdity of seeking the exoneration of specific research practices in the deliberately reconstructed logic favoured by philosophers. Whatever its merits, prescriptive methodology is not something one can apply in any straightforward sense. Set against the task of defining the ultimate character of the whole history and scope of science, philosophers are faced with a choice of (a) producing a favoured model which is exemplified by certain episodes in certain disciplines but whose very language is so conditioned by this context that one needs some inventive metaphorical extension to make it apply to other forms of inquiry, or (b) trying to give credence to the width of scientific endeavour, in which case they produce prescriptions so broad and bland that even the most *ersatz* of science can say 'we'll drink to that'.

Sociology has suffered at the hands of both tendencies. For instance, the traditional positivist model is committed to empirical corroboration as being the hallmark of science, but it does so via a range of notions such as causal laws, experimental control, replication, etc., all of which ideas are quite alien to, say, ethnographers, who at the same time might feel themselves equally committed to a certain notion of exhaustive empirical inquiry. The result is that though most ethnographers end up by scorning positivism and perhaps a few make a 'secret compact' with it, nearly all would agree that the naturalism debate casts little illumination on their everyday research problems.

By contrast, if one looks to the non-positivistic naturalisms to provide the foundation for sociological method one searches in vain for any clear notion of what such positions would look like in practice. For instance, since the advent of realism into the methodological discourse of sociology, one cannot help but notice a breaking of its own ranks. The notion that the first task of explanation is to provide a possible generative mechanism for an observed pattern of events is such a broad and generous injunction that quite a range of research strategies have been able to claim adherence to it. Thus followers of Bhaskar (1979) have taken generative mechanisms to refer to social structures and formations endemic to capitalism, whilst another founder member of the school, Harré (1978), points to social life as a pattern of skilled performances explained in terms of the underlying mechanisms of people's 'problem-solving' and 'presentational' activities. As well as structural Marxism and the dramaturgical model there is another recognizable clutch of 'realist' texts which might be best identified as 'post-empiricist' (Papineau, 1978; Thomas, 1979; Tudor, 1982). These are somewhat less directive than the other two modes of realism, and go no further than to point out that since it is now a platitude to say there is no such thing as theory-free data, then incorrigible data are therefore unnecessary for objective science and sociology, by this fact alone, can resume its candidature as an empirical science.

9

The blooming, buzzing confusion that is plain to see here is merely the symptom of the real disorder. Sociology has been guilty of enormous naiveté, during this period, in pinning its hopes on the prescriptive power of epistemological discussion. The idea of establishing the authentic first principles of scientific explanation prior to going out and doing research is a gross misconception of the nature of inquiry. Ironically enough, one is hard pressed to think of a less sociological way of understanding method; the get-your-principles-right brigade effectively assume that researchers are 'cultural dopes' and that the researcher's own understanding of how to solve a research puzzle has no effect on method. On this view research is entirely a rule-following activity rather than one which grants that researchers' own understanding of their task has a legitimate place in transforming the rules.

What we are left with from the naturalism debate, I would suggest, are thus not timeless protocols of inquiry but a series of reference points which sociologists can choose to accept, reject or modify. Some of the realist notions of inquiry are potentially instructive in this respect and, despite some of the brasher remarks above, such ideas as 'generative mechanism' and the 'network theory of terms' will be taken up in Parts 2 and 3 of this book. Indeed, you will find me arguing that such strategies (and others) can act as the foundation for a post-empiricist sociology. You will not be able to charge me with self-inconsistency, however, since my purpose will be to talk about the *application* of such ideas to research practice and not to persuade you that I have succeeded, where all other metatheorists have failed, in discovering the real McCoy of sociological realisms. All this awaits us however since my preliminary survey of the recent history of the changing face of sociological research is not yet complete. The thought that researchers are not methodological or cultural dopes tells us where next to look for the rules of research, that is much more directly at the strategies of social investigation.

Perspectivism

It has always struck me as odd (as it may well have struck you) that in teaching sociology we normally choose to treat theory and method as a set of ideas detached from the substance of our discipline. Without doing a survey on the matter, I am prepared to bet that no other discipline goes so far in breaking down and isolating these facets of explanation as a set of 'core' ideas to be contemplated in their own right. Such teaching practices are the medium and outcome of that terrible sociological disease – *perspectivism.* Look at a syllabus from any course in contemporary theory and method and what do you find but hordes of competing paradigms. As theory, we teach phenomenology, symbolic interactionism, ethnomethodology, analysis, existential sociology, structuralism, post-modernism, critical theory, figurational sociology and so forth. As method, we teach surveys, experiments, statistical analysis, comparative analysis, ethnography, ethnomethodology, etc., before getting down to the details of the disputes between parametric and non-parametric statistics, one-shot versus longitudinal surveys, conversational analysis versus ethnomethodological ethnography and so on.

In what follows I am not going to treat you to an analysis of the full fashion parade of sociological paradigms but rather make the point that these 'paradigms wars' have tended to sustain another unproductive vein of methodological thought in sociology. What happens is that method gets set on a course of critique and counter-critique rather than facing its practical limitations directly. Although the debates to which I refer are often fought at relatively technical levels, they too tend to end up in another epistemological goose chase. So whilst the naturalism debate is about following the one true scientific method, perspectivism sets us on the search for another chimera – the truly authentic sociological method.

The battle of the perspectives usually begins with a dig at the so-called positivistic orthodoxy. Really this is another myth of the methodological literature, despite the contentions of writers who, even today, still rail against positivism. Feminist methodology provides a good example of the latest school of thought to have rediscovered the evils of positivism in order to forward its own pet ideas (Roberts, 1981). Silverman is probably nearer the mark, in the British context at least, with his remark:

> Since the 1960s, a story has got about that no good
> sociologist should dirty his hands with numbers. Sometimes
> this story has been supported by sound critiques of the

11

rationale underlying some quantitative analyses (Blumer, 1956; Cicourel, 1964). Even here, however, the story has been better on critique than on the development of positive, alternative strategies. So, many thousands of British sociology students have been encouraged to dismiss quantitative research. More seriously, a generation of young researchers have been thrown out into a sceptical world with their heads full of the standard critiques of positivism but often empty of ideas about how to match exciting theories with rigorous research designs. (Silverman, 1985, p. 138).

For argument's sake, let us accept that long, long ago one could assume that sociological research meant survey research, and that regardless of the problem under investigation the research process would be broken down in stages of defining the problem in terms of the hypothetical relationships between variables, devising scales and measures for those variables, drawing an appropriate sample, analysing the observed relationships between variables, and discussing their relevance to the initial hypothesis. Whilst such a format is still fostered in governmental research and in many American strongholds, the rest of sociology has been engaged in the long search for a more authentically sociological method.

The first breaking of the ranks came in the form of what was known as the phenomenological critique, which drew most notably on the two sources that Silverman cites, namely Blumer's (1956) critique of variable analysis and Cicourel's (1964) critique of measurement. These will be analysed in detail in due course, but for the moment we will let them speak for themselves:

> In my judgement the crucial limit to the successful application of variable analysis to human life is set by the process of interpretation or definition that goes on in human groups. This process, which I believe to be the core of human action, gives a character to human group life that seems to be at variance with the logical premises of variable analysis. (Blumer, 1956, p. 640).

> The literal measurement of social acts . . . requires the use of linguistic and non-linguistic meanings that cannot be taken for granted but which must be viewed as objects of

12

study. In other words measurement pre-supposed a bounded network of shared meanings, i.e., a theory of culture. The physical scientist alone defines his observational field, but in social science the arena of discourse usually begins with the subjects preselected and preinterpreted cultural meanings (Cicourel, 1964, p. 14).

Blumer is saying that social life consists not of events but experience, and thus the same happening can carry totally different meanings for people in different social contexts. However because of the requirement that variables or measures have to have standard meaning across a total sample surveyed, this forces social research into the mistaken assumption that events in the social world are commonly understood within and between different groups and cultures. Cicourel extends this critique in various ways, initially by pointing to the reliance on ordinary language in the construction of sociological data. He argues that the parameters of the sociologist's measures are drawn arbitrarily from the counts, categories and classifications used in everyday descriptions of the social world. This is a blunder, the argument continues, since the everyday descriptions are themselves artful, creative, protean, socially rooted and so forth, and thus in general are permanently subject to reformulation. To locate a measurement system in ordinary language is to create measures based on shifting sands, and is thus incapable of providing the bedrock of objective observation necessary for an empirical theory-testing programme.

To see what became of these critiques the reader will have to sit patiently through the rest of the book. However, if I can for the moment adopt my sternest 'moral-of-the tale' tone, the short answer is that, rather than leading to more refined empirical research, Blumer's and Cicourel's critiques merely opened a battle of programmatic statements which ran and ran and ran. To elaborate a little, firstly on the response from mainstream quantitative survey research, which was rather downbeat. Anyone who had ever piloted a questionnaire through several drafts, they would argue, was fully aware of the vagaries and complexities of meaning and language. Thus the problem, by and large, was seen as a practical one and all a matter of degree to boot. By the latter, I refer to the assumption that there are some aspects of the world whose meaning is highly contextual (e.g. deviance, religious experience) and such concepts would, therefore, not figure in the hard currency of social measurement which would be reserved for those areas of social life whose meaning was more nearly stable and universal (e.g. age, income, education).

This rather lackadaisical approach was deemed sufficient because if really challenged orthodox research could call upon a piece of epistemological lore which would show that there was really no alternative. I am thinking of the various counter-attacks which threatened that if carried to the logical extreme the phenomenological critiques would involve all human inquiry in some form of death by misadventure in the hermeneutic whirlpool of subjectivism, relativism, solipsism and so forth. Thus the ethnomethodological view that social objects have no meaning independently of the processes of practical reasoning whereby meanings are established, can be said to bite its own tail. If we decide instead to investigate the said resources and reasoning process, such a study would depend on the very resources the research was designed to uncover.

Whilst positivism slumbered in these conditions and quantitative research (in Britain) slowly declined, the qualitative paradigms established themselves with a somewhat patchy success. A number of programmatic statements appeared which declared the various phenomenological schools as heirs to the throne of empirical research. Most obviously ethnography and ethnomethodology could claim to attend to the central concerns, as they saw them, of meaning and language, but they also promised a further list of virtues, by way of first-hand and non-intrusive research strategies which would produce social understanding that was grounded in data rather than theoretically pre-ordained. What is interesting in assessing the success or otherwise of these developments, is that what seems to count is not so much the catalogue of successful findings each strategy has accumulated but that the very notion of success depends on how well they have fared in the battle of domain assumptions. Hence the story of qualitative methodology in the last twenty years is the tale of how missiles originally directed at positivism were turned inwardly to face each other.

The first breaking of phenomenological ranks occurred between ethnographers and ethnomethodologists on the matter of 'imposition of meaning'. It had always been argued that survey research was guilty of the pre-organization of data and selectivity of analysis so that the audience of the research was in no position to evaluate any results. However, ethnomethodologists were able to extend this same point in arguing that 'field research' in general, and by its very nature, tends to produce findings which are anecdotal and massively selective in terms of the ratio of events reported to those witnessed. Ethnography, in short, lacks any recognized criteria for what counts as data and in any case it provides for the reader only descriptions of data, and not data itself. The ethnomethodologists' solution, at least in the form of conversational analysis, was to 'democratize data'; that is to say the whole raw data base in the form of recording and transcripts are provided along with the analysis (Atkinson and Drew, 1979, ch. 1). Since the audience now has equal access to the researched material, then both the analysis and the analytic procedures are open for inspection.

This of course was merely the opening shot in a campaign which has since seen the emergence of another strategy, ethnomethodological ethnography, which has in turn taken up the cudgels against conversational analysis. It is not putting it too harshly to say that methodology in this respect has become like a branch of marketing. Any product has a 'natural' market share and after a while the only way to increase product penetration is to repackage or rename and attempt a relaunch. The gullibility of sociology in this respect is demonstrated by what is perhaps the natural terminus of this particular product line, namely the school of 'analysis' or 'theorizing'. The real implication of the fact that social understanding is always interpretative, it argues, is that we are left with no anchorage point in concrete facts or favoured theoretical position and thus the only thing left for us to do is engage in self-reflection on how it is possible to contemplate the world. The idea of empirical sociology goes down the plughole thus:

> Our interest [is] in what we call the grounds or auspices of
> phenomena rather than in the phenomena themselves. . . .
> It is not that something becomes a topic for us by having
> something in common with something else but that we
> produce anything as a topic by dealing with it in terms of

our version of inquiry. Anything can become a topic because anything can be inquired about. . . . Examples in our sense should not be confused with data. They do not refer to the world – they are not descriptions. They are more like icons (McHugh *et al.*, 1974, ch. 1).

And to think quite a number of sociologists bought this one too!

These typical laps of the merry-go-round simply exemplify the real target of my criticism here, which is to point to a flaw in the very way in which debate within sociological methodology has been conducted. In a way it is the reverse of the problem encountered in the naturalism debate. There, over-emphasis on the need for philosophy of science to be prescriptive leads to a rather gruesome sociological model of the researcher. In the case of attempting to purify a distinctly sociological mode of explanation, the opposite occurs: sociology becomes a rather second-rate form of philosophy.

Thus in the wake of the critique of positivism, sociological methodologists were besotted with the task of trying to distil a set of alternative proposals on which to base research and forwarding the case for certain strategies as abiding most faithfully by these newly preferred principles. Too often, however, work stopped well short of the business of putting these principles into practice, for the simple reason that no one was able to discover a set of watertight principles in the first place. It is so much easier to offer convincing criticisms of other approaches than to deploy successfully any given method and, what is more, in the journals, criticism seems to be offered as much, if not more, space than work on technical development. The brief discussion of the variants of qualitative method above, shows how easy it is to undercut the authority of one account from the perspective of another. Above all, the widespread introduction of epistemological arguments in research offered critiques so radical that it was not so much particular techniques that came under threat but the very possibility of sociological investigation was swallowed up if some of these arguments were taken as gospel. In this respect, at least, we can thank Althusserians and analysts for bringing us (unintentionally but literally) *back to our senses.*

The empiricist backlash

Our whirlwind tour of sociological methodology is now up to date save for a description of the current conditions. The present time is best perceived as a period of 'backlash' in which empirical sociology is regaining a position of dominance. The most paradoxical result of this state of affairs is that positivism, having lost every single epistemological battle over the years, seems to have won the war, certainly in terms of research effort and funding. Although empirical researchers have every right to be impatient, indeed bored, with epistemological purists, this does not mean that we can forget the last twenty years and return to an unreconstituted positivism. In Britain, prompted by the leadership of a former Secretary of State for Education, this return to another set of Victorian values (empiricism and pragmatism) seems to be just what we are getting in social science research. Quantitative sociology has returned to the fore; we are dealing with a new set of problems (and variables) concerning unemployment, the decline of the work ethic, training, labour markets, etc., but applying the same old method based on the large-scale survey. My modest suggestion is as follows – it is perfectly justifiable to say that sociology ought to be empirically based and to maintain that survey data will remain a basic source of material because of their potentiality for exactitude and wide coverage. However, though several decades of criticism have failed to establish an obviously superior substitute for this, this does not mean that any of the criticism of sociological measurement and variable analysis have been met.

So what is to be done? We need a much more self-confident empirical method but not one constructed out of the conceit that there is no alternative. We need a much more refined quantitative method which is sensitive to the phenomenological and relativist critiques, but that is developed outside the framework of the perpetual rhetoric about the 'crisis in sociology'. We need an appreciation of the significance of the methodological judgements buried in the simplest decision on choice of techniques and to develop a notion of method which regards researchers neither as judgemental dopes, needful of courses in amateur philosophy, nor indeed as all-seeing artisans, hearing all the requisite methodological wisdom in the form of custom and practice. And how is this to be managed?

1.2   MEASUREMENT AND THE DOUBLE HERMENEUTIC

The second part of the chapter will be concerned with laying down a framework for the resolution of some of these long-standing debates and problems. Basically I shall be attempting to define an arena in which the issues can be discussed manageably. Then I will move into a detailed statement of the problems to be faced in the construction of empirical evidence, before sketching an outline solution to these problems.

So far I have referred rather loosely to the problems of empirical research, observational data, variable analysis, quantification, survey method and measurement. I intend to focus in the remainder of the book on problems of *measurement*. This decision is made not out of any attempt to devalue, say, ethnographic or historical evidence; rather it is because the measurement problem is so strategically placed. The measurement debate falls at the axis of the two greatest methodological divides in sociology (see Fig. 1.1). In the first place it allows us to dissect the debate between those who believe it sensible to treat social events in a quantitative manner versus those who stress the meaningful core of human action and assume that this is only open to qualitative appreciation. Secondly, the possibility of measurement marks a traditional dividing line between those disciplines which are thought of as basically conceptual and theoretical versus those which are deemed to be empirical.

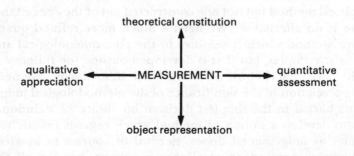

Figure 1.1.   Two tensions in measurement

18

Sociological measurement, then, faces unique problems because it involves an encounter with what Giddens calls the *double hermeneutic*, which, to borrow his own definition, is

The intersection of two frames of meaning as a logically necessary part of social science, the meaningful social world as constituted by lay actors and the metalanguages invented by social scientists (Giddens, 1984, p. 374).

As he constantly stresses, all practice in social science involves the 'slippage' between these two languages. Measurement, of course, is no exception and in fact the would-be quantifier is playing for particularly high stakes, since to measure is to apply a third, numerical language. Thus quantitative sociology does not consist simply of 'pinning numbers on things' but having a knowledge of the precise intersections of lay, sociological and numerical languages.

Taking measurement to be the focus of methodological scrutiny allows us to sharpen up our ideas about the task, as well as the criticisms, of empirical sociology. A good way to think of the critiques of empiricism, positivism and so forth is to see them as pointing to failings in the way in which these three languages are traditionally connected. So what I want to do here is move to a much more detailed review of the phenomenological and radical critiques and, rather than treat them as deadly weapons, see how they can be addressed (and circumvented) in the production of an authentic sociological measurement language.

Discussions of the failures of translations across discursive forms tend only to be found within the anti-quantitative and anti-empirical literature, so first it is necessary to identify the issues within the language of social research. Basically, I am going to be concerned with what I have referred to as the phenomenological critique (associated with the likes of Blumer and Cicourel) and the relativistic critique (associated with Feyerabend and his sociological counterparts). Three basic phenomenological critiques of measurement can be distinguished, all centred on the idea that the language of sociological theory and research needs, but fails to address, the domain of ordinary human meaning. The basic relativist critique of measurement concerns the failure to achieve a proper independence between the languages of theory and evidence.

Add these together and four basic objections can be distinguished as the basis for the present discussion, namely that because of a range of sins of omission and commission in its attention to discursive forms, sociological measurement contrives to be *irrelevant, arbitrary, artificial* and *selective.*

(1) *Irrelevant measurement due to the lack of appreciation of the significance of, and the variation in, cultural meanings and natural discourse*

I would identify this critique as the broadest and best-known objection to sociological naturalism. Sociology is distinctive, the argument goes, because it deals with a universe which is already constituted within the frames of meaning of social actors. Radical interpretations of this state of affairs place the onus on sociological discourse to mirror the linguistic habits of the social group under study. Thus according to Schutz (1962, p. 34):

> Each term in a scientific model of human action must be constructed in such a way that a human act performed within the life-world by an individual actor in the way indicated by the typical construct would be understandable for the actor himself as well as for his fellow-men in terms of common sense interpretations of everyday life.

This provides us with a powerful critique of terminological and measurement conventions in sociology. It is argued that such features as standardization and replicability which are assumed in instruments of measurements can find no natural counterpart in social meaning systems.

The first problem concerns meaning variation across different cultures. The meaning and significance of any event, action, or attitude is dependent on the understanding of that phenomenon within a particular cultural context. This state of affairs applies to all social phenomena, the most quoted in terms of measurement controversy perhaps being our notions of what is suicide, social status and intelligence. What all of these things are and how they are recognized depends on the cultural setting, since it is only in human culture that social phenomena are constituted in the first place. It follows that any attempt to measure a social phenomenon presupposes its common cultural significance. Before we can compare differences in the aforementioned suicide rates, intelligence quotients, occupational prestige scores and so forth, we must assume that there exists a consensual interpretation of the meaning of the underlying concepts within and between populations studied.

These examples are, of course, familiar targets for the claim that there is profound variation in their interpretation and significance even within similar cultures and, depending on the degree of cultural relativism upheld, the expectation is that the same is true of most or all social phenomena. In short, comparing like with like in the social realm is not just a matter of ensuring the use of uniform observational procedures but rests on a more contentious theory of cultural equivalence.

A related body of criticism again starts with the notion that sociological measurement has its root in everyday meaning but goes on to find fault with the lack of understanding of the workings of natural language. This argument rests on the notion of indexicality. Although revisions in its own use prompt the thought that indexicality is an indexical expression without equal, one can say without too much trepidation that it refers to the fact that the meaning of expressions depends on the context of their use. The claim is that the meaning of an utterance (or sometimes its intelligibility, truth or reference) cannot be decided upon without knowledge of the purpose of its user and the particular context of its use. Talk only means something through the social agreement brought to bear to fix meanings on any particular occasion. Although such agreement is routinely reached, the form it takes can vary according to the different experience, knowledge and intent of the participants in any exchange of language. The consequence of this, of course, is that the meaning of any term is indeterminate and permanently open to revision. Furthermore, this implies that the processes of concept application, description and predication in natural language should be treated as work, as accomplishments and not, as it is in sociological measurement, something that can be assumed constant and intersubjective. Relativity of meaning is thus even more tightly envisaged in this version. Not only does the meaning of terms vary from culture to culture, but it does so automatically within the same group of individuals according to the precise context of each occasion of use. We are led to conclude that everyday conceptualization provides only instantial meaning which in turn can only be the source of the most fleeting of measures.

(2) *Arbitrary measurement due to reliance on the vagaries of everyday terminology as the source of formal measurement parameters*

The criticism here is that the numerical parameters of measurement (the so-called levels of measurement) are usually underdetermined in theoretical discourse and researchers have to rely on everyday connotations of terms to arrive at measurement scales. Contrast is drawn between the formal axiomatic properties of measurement systems and the vagueness and adaptive quality of ordinary language. All measurement systems automatically assume that phenomena can be subdivided into parts and that these further parts or objects will stand in certain patterns or equivalence relationships. The type of equivalence relationship operating between objects governs the appropriate formal properties of the measurement system; it determines whether we should use a nominal, ordinal, interval, ratio or other form of scale. The various types of scale are in themselves nothing more than logical relationships or truth statements about abstract properties; they bear no relationship to the empirical world. The key to measurement lies in interpreting them, in establishing their correspondence with the phenomenon under study.

The problem in sociological research is that this correspondence is conventionally achieved by fiat. No theoretical justification is normally forthcoming as to why a given social phenomenon can be conceived as having the numerical properties of a given measurement system. Instead these properties spring directly from research instruments, be they classifications and definitions used in official data, the response categories and coding frames of survey research and so on. These counts, categories and orderings are themselves buried in implicit common-sense assumptions about the social issue in question. They appear to be right and reasonable formal distinctions because they are based in ordinary talk. The argument invoked here is not that everyday speech cannot have a numerical dimension; indeed matters such as wage negotiation provide second decimal place accuracy. Rather the point made is that natural language provides an arbitrary and erratic numerical base. This is so, since by the previous argument the meaning of any term is permanently open to revision, then, likewise, ordinary language numerical predication can have no absolute base. We can and do freely swap from a categorical to an ordinal to a metric language in describing the same phenomenon. Of 'educational status' we might refer to the difference between those with compulsory basic education and those that have gone beyond, or we might argue that level of qualification was more important, or we might differentiate even more narrowly in terms of years and months of education attended. Consequently it is possible to display the information requisite to such a phenomenon by dichotomizing the variable, using any number of ordinal categories, or assuming metric measurement. At best, the argument goes, the choice of measurement scale is arbitrary, at worst it is deliberately manipulated by judicious choice of cutting points etc., so as to maximize the importance and significance of research findings which incorporate these connived measures.

(3) *Artificial measurement due to the creation and imposition of meaning in the communicative process occurring at the point of gathering evidence*

In sociology we cannot produce instrumentation which reduces the final stage of measurement to one of simple observation (i.e. pointer-reading). Instead evidence has always been culled in a process of communication. In general the problem here concerns the extent to which the devices used to extract information from the respondent actually constrain or alter the free expression of first-order meanings. This problem can occur in any number of guises. Does the subjects' behaviour in an experiment resemble how they behave in real-world situations or do they respond to the 'demand characteristics' of the setting? Are responses to questionnaire items free or unfettered or do the questions suggest frames of reference for answers when none may have existed? In such situations phenomenologists argue that the meaning frameworks in operation are those of the sociologist and thus the data produced often tell us more about how subjects make sense of the research context than about their interpretations of those aspects of the social world under investigation.

From the phenomenological perspective, the understanding developed on these occasions is integrally dependent on the social character of language. Social research thus takes place in social situations which demand skilled performances from the participants and which create and constitute separate meaning systems which do not simply correspond to either natural understanding or the theoretical discourse of sociology. Orthodox measurement methodology recognizes the problem without seeing it as a matter of indeterminacy of translation. In the survey manuals, the problem is seen as a technical one – the researcher must not ask leading questions, create new frames of awareness in fixed-choice answers and so forth. This kind of advice appears as a contradiction in terms for the hermeneutician. It calls for prior legislation of that which can only be discovered in the process of communication. Thus, if we regard language as a creative accomplishment which constitutes social activity rather than merely as a response to that activity, there is an irreducible limit to the extent to which social encounters can be anticipated and rehearsed.

(4) *Selective measurement due to the impregnation of observational categories by theoretical notions*

At this point we leave behind problems of the translation between ordinary and sociological discourse and confront a quite separate problem concerning the justification of sociological accounts of the world. At issue here is none other than the classical puzzle facing *all* empirical science, stemming from the truism that 'percepts without concepts are blind'. We have no direct access to the empirical world; our sensory capacities require preparation and guidance in order to operate. And just as observations do not speak for themselves, nor can scientific instruments and the techniques of measurement be constructed in innocence of any theoretical commitment. This presents every scientific discipline with a different kind of hermeneutic problem; if all terms (including those supposedly derived in controlled observation) take their meaning internally within the accepted reasoning processes of that discipline, then no terms

24

would appear to be available to form a neutral testing ground for ideas within that theoretical orthodoxy. It is a short step from these notions to the possibility that a researcher can always be selective in the matter of what constitutes evidence (and counter-evidence) in order to protect some favoured theory.

All these consequences of the theory-ladenness of observation have obvious relevance to the phenomenon of 'selective attention to data' in sociological research. It leads to the position where there can always be an interpretative challenge to any datum. One sociologist sees the official statistics showing the dwindling levels of ownership for the top percentage of wealth holders as an indicator of a trend towards class equalization. Another discounts this information on the grounds that wealth holders are able to disguise exact levels of ownership from the data gathering bodies, one such tactic being to spread wealth holdings amongst their immediate family, thus creating the erroneous impression of more equality in distribution. On this problem more generally, one only needs to think of the diverse concoction of definitions and measures used in studies of the evolution of class positions and places. The class structure can be simultaneously pronounced simplifying or fragmenting or seething with contradictions according to one's preferred body of evidence. In short, the hermeneutic problems involved in measurement redouble soon as one recognizes this 'spectre of relativism' which haunts all theoretical and scientific discourse.

The defence of sociological measurement – an outline.

These are the real issues which confront the production of evidence in sociological research and they require solution, or at least careful circumvention, if we are to operate as an empirical science. What they have in common is the specification of the measurement problem as one of establishing meaning within a discourse and attempting to preserve meaning in translating between discourses. A more formidable clutch of problems is hard to imagine and, because of the manner of methodological discussion in sociology which I have described earlier, *they remain largely unresolved.* What I want to do here is make a preliminary sketch of the arguments of this book which will show how we can accommodate these problems and still provide empirical data to

25

substantiate sociology. Methodologists, I am afraid, cannot escape the need to explain what is wrong before putting matters right, so I find myself working in that irresistible organizational framework of the triptych. Accordingly Part 1, *Desperate Measures* consists of a critique of current measurement practice and is followed by Part 2, *A Measure of Realism*, in which some alternative measurement principles are established, which are then examined for their applicability to sociological research in Part 3, *Practical Measures*. As I have indicated, this kind of formula caters rather too often for some of the less admirable features of methodological writing in sociology, namely that it produces literature which is long on critique, short on positive alternatives, and shows a high regard for principles and a low esteem for applications. To counteract such tendencies I have attempted to make Part 1 a constructive critique, to ensure that the new model in Part 2 is developed from working examples of natural science measurement, and to devote the longest section of the book to Part 3, in which much current research from class and stratification is examined in great detail.

For the purposes of this introduction the flow of my argument is best followed by attending to the interplay between a set of problems (identified in parentheses), a set of alternative proposals [identified in square brackets], and a set of applications {identified in braces}. Chapter 2, *Against variable analysis* and Chapter 3, *Against scaling,* contain a review of the main objectives and techniques of current measurement. Here we shall be speaking the language of variables, scales, indicator selection, levels of measurement, unidimensionality, reliability, validity and all the rest. I will concur with the phenomenological and relativist critiques, on the grounds already specified, in their claim that sociological measurement is indeed (1) *irrelevant* in the face of changes in social meaning, (2) *arbitrary* in its choice of numerical scales, (3) *artificial* due to its production in contrived social conditions and (4) *selective* in its attention to preferred theories and hypotheses.

What is new and constructive about this assessment is my attempt to drive a wedge between these critiques. The crucial mistake made in both empiricist measurement practice and the phenomenological critiques is the reduction, somewhere along the line, of the theoretical terms of sociology to ordinary language. For empiricists this is all a matter of expediency. They assume that the world can be identified and measured directly. Since, however, direct perception of the world is impossible (problem 4), they opt, often quite unwittingly, for the nearest equivalent which involves the use of ordinary language descriptions, in the form of 'indicators' of our chosen concepts. It is this manoeuvre and this manoeuvre only which opens up sociology to the phenomenological critiques. Phenomenologists themselves are not unhappy about the idea of understanding the world by attaching common-sense labels to the different aspects of our experience. They merely disagree utterly and flatly with the empiricist version with regard to the possibility of stability and exactitude of such social definitions.

The way out of the impasse is to by-pass it altogether and seek a fresh basis for sociological measurement. We need to discount altogether the notion that evidence emerges from direct observation of the social world. We need to emphasize that we are in the business of testing *sociological theories* and not everyday descriptions. Thus if one recognizes that it is our theories of the social processes into which social properties are embedded which are the appropriate source of understanding of the nature of social variables, then we sidestep completely all the problems of the changeability and contextuality of everyday meaning. This leaves us in a position to reject the phenomenological critiques and there remains unsolved the relativist critique in its original sense concerning the problem of the impregnation of theoretical discourse into observational language. Our 'score' at the end of Part 1 is thus (1), (2), (3), with problem (4) left to crack.

Part 2, *A Measure of Realism*, begins the process of the rehabilitation of the empirical method by taking on the remaining and most powerful of the criticisms of measurement (no. 4), that concerning the interdependence of theory and evidence. Chapter 4, *Theory and observation*, looks at how these issues are routinely solved in natural sciences. What one finds is that all the familiar measurement techniques in physical science harness and embody dozens of theories and laws. There is, however, no circularity involved in the use of theory-laden measurement provided that theories drawn upon in the construction of the instrument are not the same as those tested in the application of the instrument.

27

This solution to the relativist critique is embodied particularly in two research strategies which I refer to as [A] *the transduction process* and [B] *the intersection process.* The first of these refers to the process whereby the property to be measured is converted into another energy form (usually an electrical system). This allows a test of our theories about a given property against the quite independent theories concerning that further property into which it had been transformed. The second strategy provides a means of adjudicating between alternative theories. Once it is understood that a vast network of theories is involved in the construction of even the simplest experimental test, then one can construe empirical testing as being made at the point of intersection of rival theories. It is by building upon common assumptions of rival theories, and not by an withdrawal to neutral observation, that one can construct crucial empirical tests.

Far from the interdependence of theory and observation causing a problem in physical science, it is the very structure of theoretical reasoning that provides the platform for the construction of empirical evidence. Chapter 5, *On being 'empirical' without being 'empiricist',* develops a model of how explanatory structures provide the prerequisites of measurement, based on a reading of contemporary realist or post-empiricist philosophies of science. The key aspects of scientific explanation in this regard are, [C] *generative reasoning* in the form of models of the underlying mechanisms controlling a system of properties, [D] *closed systems,* i.e. experimental systems which enable researchers to isolate and test for the action of vital generative mechanisms and [E] *explanatory networks,* through which concepts are linked to a whole range of theories, thus allowing research in the form of making connections between the relatively speculative knowledge of part of this network and certain other parts which are understood well enough for their control and regularization.

By the end of Part 2, we will have thus dispensed with problem (4) and in so doing travelled a long way from the 'observations-as-facts' assumptions of the empiricist account. These alternative proposals can be considered as laying the foundations for a *realist model of measurement* in the form of the strategies [A], [B], [C], [D], [E].

Part 3, *Practical Measures*, evaluates the strategies and tactics of realist measurement in terms of their applicability to sociological investigation. Social research cannot adopt the instrumentation, the experimentation, the sheer physical manipulation which is assumed in the creation of evidence in natural science. I do believe, however, that it is perfectly possible to imitate the logic of the process, in particular the notion of having to traverse whole bodies of theory in the construction of empirical data. A chapter is devoted to each of the five phases of the realist strategy and I will scour sociological research, particularly in the area of class and mobility, for examples of analogous forms of reasoning. No single piece of empirical research in sociology has ever been conducted with reference to such a realist strategy. I will be able to show, however, that, in certain aspects of their work, authors as theoretically and politically divergent as Boudon (1973), Goldthorpe *et al.* (1980) and Wright (1985) have signalled a new phase of sophistication in understanding the role of empirical evidence in sociology.

Chapter 6, *From variables to mechanisms*, provides examples of *generative reasoning* {C} in sociological explanation in which research hypotheses are stated explicitly enough as to create a non-arbitrary choice of measurement parameters. Chapter 7, *Closure*, argues for a replacement of statistical control as the method of achieving closed-system inquiry by *contextual control* {D} in the form of longitudinal and comparative investigations. Chapter 8, *Explanatory networks*, argues for the development of sociological concepts within *formal models* {E} so that they can be linked to a network of other concepts rather then forever remaining contested. Chapter 9, *Choosing class concepts*, argues that we cannot verify theories directly against 'real world data' but we can use an *adjudicatory strategy* {B} to choose between theories by identifying their points of intersection. Chapter 10, *Constructing class data*, attempts to build an alternative model of the interview process which avoids imposing meaning onto the subjects. The *teaching strategy* {A} of interviewing works by restricting sociological data to 'external' institutional knowledge and by revealing only the conceptual structure of the theory under test but not its propositional structure. Between them, {A}, {B}, {C}, {D} and {E} represent the new rules of sociological measurement.

The role of methodology

The question of a role-model for methodology is, of course, much debated and metaphors for the deeds of philosophy of science abound – is it 'master-science' or 'hand-maiden', 'rule-maker' or 'under-labourer'? My preferred designation, in this style, would have to be 'go-between', for I think it behoves sociological methodology above all to come to an understanding of method which strikes a balance between principle and practice, voluntarism and determinism, structure and agency. The limitations of prescriptive methodology have already been discussed in some detail, in particular the point that no one set of ordinances can capture the richness and diversity of scientific practice. Such reasoning has driven some methodologists to argue that we must study the day-to-day reasoning process of actual researchers since it is this 'logic-in-use' which steers the real course of inquiry (Kaplan, 1973). Sociological methodology in particular has flirted with this approach in a series of texts which choose to teach method as a personal learning process in which authors 'confess' about how practical, ideological and circumstantial influences shape how research really gets done (Hammond, 1964; Bell and Newby, 1977; Bell and Roberts, 1984).

This it-ain't-what-you-do-it's-the-way-that-you-do-it school has proved a valuable corrective to the determinism implicit in much prescriptive methodology. However, in such cases, the opposite error of voluntarism often lurks and there seems nothing to prevent this kind of descriptive methodology being endlessly stretched to give an account of any activity whatsoever of whomsoever chooses to designate his or her activities as science/sociology. What is especially overlooked in these local, personal accounts of inquiry is the collective and emergent processes whereby rules and standards are laid down as soon as any group forms in the furtherance of a particular activity. Even in the confessional pieces referred to above, there is a tendency to justify preferred alternatives by virtue of their ability to deliver what other methods cannot. Thus it is obvious that researchers do raise their noses beyond the problem-at-hand and always work with embryonic notions of the goals and standards of inquiry. These evaluative criteria become further externalized every time the researcher adapts a technique, criticizes the work of others, teaches what is good practice, referees someone else's contribution and so on. So the principles are there, even if they are locked away in a range of institutional and historical processes which will always prevent any singular once-and-for-all enunciation of them in the manner of prescriptive methodology. One concludes from all this that if the secret of science is not to be found exclusively at the level of principle or practice, then one has no choice but to go-between.

This implies a series of close parallels between methodologists who seek to integrate an understanding of principle and practice in the making of method and sociologists who seek to synthesize the working of structure and agency in the constitution of society. Science is much like any other institution in that it can be seen as a set of rules and resources reproduced across time. These rules and resources are not simply determined by organizational structures, nor are they entirely matters of decision for the individual scientist. Rather, both elements conjoin in what Giddens calls the duality of structure, which he defines as follows:

> Structure [is] the medium and outcome of the conduct it
> recursively organises; the structural properties of social
> systems do not exist outside of action but are chronically
> implicated in its production and reproduction (Giddens,
> 1984, p. 374).

Of method, we do not have to put too many words into his mouth to make him say,

> Method is the medium and outcome of the research it
> recursively organises; the institutional features and
> principles of science do not exist outside of research
> practice but are chronically implicated in its production and
> reproduction.

The implications of all this for the philosophy and sociology of science are potentially enormous. Here, I only wish to follow some direct consequences. It is obvious that scientific inquiry reproduces and changes itself without the assistance of self-appointed methodological overseers. Science itself goes between practice and principle whenever innovatory research examples are turned into textbook exemplars, whenever a strategy is borrowed or adapted, whenever a line of inquiry is forsaken. Such a rule-generating, self-monitoring model of science might seem to offer scope only for the sociologist or historian to describe the structuration process whereby existing rules have come into being. However it does leave a little elbow room for the methodologist. Although research principles are ultimately constituted in practice, it is rarely the case that practitioners are practised in the articulation of high-level justificatory claims for their work. Research, as with most other modern social institutions, evolves a detailed division of labour. Indeed, to parade a bit more Giddens glossography, there will always be a limit to the researcher's 'discursive penetration'; research practice may depend on certain unacknowledged conditions and produce unintended consequences. Hence the charting of the development of the rules and resources of method may be carried a step beyond past and present strategies. The rules of inquiry are both constraining and enabling, one does not have to be hopelessly pluralistic and accept at face value every strategy that comes along. One doesn't have to await the demise of a school of thought to argue that it has unintended and inconsistent consequences. One doesn't have to await the public sanctification of a new paradigm to chart the potential developments and applications of existing principles. The only limitation is that such arguments must be carried out in the language of the practitioner rather than in debate with other philosophers.

It remains to practise what I preach. The whole course of the book from (1), (2), (3), (4) to [A], [B], [C], [D], [E] and onto {A}, {B}, {C}, {D}, {E}, is nothing other than an exemplification of going between principle and practice. This does not involve the thankless task of trying to serve two masters at once but articulates these rarely examined emergent processes which trace the course of science. In what follows I will attempt to close off more than a few dead ends, chart the direction of the most important future strategies and above all inject a bit of self-confidence into the enterprise of empirical sociology.

Part One

DESPERATE MESURES

Part 1 is devoted to an analysis of some of the misadventures in current measurement practice in sociology. Critiques of quantitative method already abound, of course, but we need to go back and spend some time at square one since my objective is to amend both the existing approaches and their critiques. Measurement methodology is one of the more statistically sophisticated areas of sociological research. However, I should emphasize that although this will involve us in a passing acquaintance with such approaches as multiple indicator measurement and individual differences scaling, my aim is to extract the prevailing core ideas on the nature and purpose of measurement. One vital distinction in this respect is that between the two main families of measurement methods in sociology – *indicator selection* and *scaling*. In the former, the researcher utilizes some ready-made classification system, scale or counting device to stand for the concept under investigation. In the latter the rankings and categories used in the measure are founded on some prior investigation of the public perception of the concept under research. I intend to devote a chapter apiece to each of these approaches. Since the two techniques themselves make rather different assumptions about the significance of people's meanings and perceptual frameworks, this gives a clear opportunity to differentiate (and repudiate) the three themes which make up the phenomenological critique.

Chapter Two

AGAINST VARIABLE ANALYSIS: THIRTY YEARS ON

In 1956 Herbert Blumer wrote a devastating critique of 'variable analysis'. He poured scorn on that research strategy which, regardless of the issue at hand, reduces social inquiry to the task of identifying the crucial variables which constitute that issue and goes on to investigate the patterns of statistical associations between the said variables. Many, many others have followed in his wake and by now we have reached the stage, in some quarters, where more sociologists can be relied upon to argue his case than might be expected to know the difference between an independent and a dependent variable.

I have already justified this review of the issue by promising a constructive critique of the usage of the language of indicators and variables. It thus behoves me from the outset to make clear the difference between my approach and that of Blumer and his successors. To put the matter very schematically one might say that Blumer and the phenomenologists object to the 'variables' in 'variable analysis', whilst I seek to repudiate the 'analysis'. The interpretative critique objects to the very notion that the social world can be broken down into a set of stable, identifiable elements. I assume that it is useful to treat the world as having separate components and argue that sociologists should be out there attempting to measure them. Where most quantitative analysis really goes wrong is with the understanding of the nature of the relationship between these measurable components.

To develop this point a little one only has to recall Blumer's central thesis, which I quoted in Chapter 1, to the effect that the crucial limitation of variable analysis was that human action is intentional and thus, in essence, sociology must deal with experiences rather than events. From this idea flows the more practical criticism of measurement, namely that sociological concepts cannot be equated with variables for the simple reason that sociological concepts have to reflect a world that is already constituted in everyday language and meaning. Ordinary discourse is itself so flexible and changeable that one cannot hope to represent its concepts through standard, constant measures. The consequence of this, according to the phenomenological critique, is that variables are constructed quite arbitrarily according to one potential usage of a given term and this imposes a spurious uniformity on the human interpretative process.

I do not object to any of this as a description of the symptoms besetting most quantitative work – indeed arbitrary measurement is exactly the phrase for what is typically produced. However, the interpretative critique is rather poor as a diagnosis of the underlying ills, for it fails to ask the prior question of why sociologists are driven to use ordinary language *at all* as the source of their measures. The thesis of this chapter is that the key problems of measurement occur prior to ordinary language operationalization, and are due to the atheoretical forms of analysis into which variables are customarily pitched. For instance, survey research orthodoxy teaches us to begin analysis by splitting the world into the dependent variable (the issue to be explained) and the potential independent variables (the likely explanatory factors shaping the issue under study). This conceptual stage of hypothesis-making often ventures no further than such selection and naming of variables. Conceptualization is thus a matter of separating out the crucial components of the world and variables, once designated in this manner, are treated as the labels corresponding to each individual item or event. What is not anticipated in all this is that our theories of the social processes into which these items are embedded should be the real source of our understanding of their properties. I will argue in due course that it is this under-identification of explanatory concepts which propels researchers into ordinary language usage for the purposes of operationalizing their concepts and thus to the ensuing perils of vagueness and ambiguity.

My secondary thesis is that the basic phenomenological critique joins positivism in this complicity to regard concepts as free-floating labels which we attach to the different aspects of the world (or as they might put it – to the different aspects of our experience). So when phenomenologists say that social processes are crucial in giving meaning to social concepts, what they have in mind is essentially the process of definition. What is at issue is simply the matter of the stability and exactitude of social definitions. The criticism boils down to the point that people register and interpret things in different ways: that a deviant act in one society is normal practice in another, that one person's pin-money would be a considerable salary for another and so on. Thus although the two are customarily considered to stand in total opposition, we find this perverse little agreement between labelling theory and operationalism that the basic unit of analysis in sociology is to be found at the level of the singular definition/variable.

Ultimately this idea will be the source of my criticisms of variable analysis and my critique of the existing critiques. If one allows that measurement in sociology is more than a glorified labelling process, and if one grants that the labelling process itself is but a part of the way in which social meanings are generated then one can transcend arguments about the stability, arbitrariness or otherwise of our definitions and variables. By this stage, I am in danger of getting the cart well before the horse, so I must return to an analysis of the basic principles of variable analysis.

The making of a variable

Let us take Kuhn's advice and go in search of paradigmatic principles by opening the 'typical' research methods text at the chapter on measurement. What we might find first is a little homily on the importance of measurement, it being the hallmark of true science (e.g. Blalock, 1970). Then there is often a passage on the relationships between concepts and measures. This will often note the distressing gap between theoretical ideas and empirical data (e.g. Phillips, 1985). Next will come a section on the foundations or principles of measurement. These are often presented as a set of criteria to which the variable should conform if it is to be considered an objective source of evidence. (e.g. Open University, 1979). Then will come an explanation of

37

the actual methods of measurement, concentrating on either indicator selection (e.g. Carley, 1981), or scaling (e.g. Smith, 1975). Finally there might be consideration of some of the interpretative critiques, either sympathetic (e.g. Hughes, 1976), or dismissive (e.g. Blalock, 1984).

In such texts and in dozens of similar ones a basic vocabulary is laid down dealing with such matters as reliability, validity, scales (levels) of measurement, unidimensionality, reproducibility and so forth. There are of course a range of more advanced and more specifically technical key texts (Blalock (ed)., 1975; Bohrnstedt and Borgatta, 1981; Blalock, 1982), but by and large these do not depart from, but merely add to, the speech community with such notions as 'auxiliary measurement theory', 'simplicity', 'precision', etc.

It would be impossible here for me to try to explicate the complete ontology and epistemology assumed in all this, and so I intend to concentrate initially on just one desideratum of sound measurement practice as perceived in this literature. This is the notion that the correct level of measurement must be chosen for all variables. I will show that there can be no such thing as a coherent decision made on the level of measurement of a given property because of the truncated sense of theory and explanation which pervades variable analysis. I will not dispute the primitive notion that measurement should reflect the way properties under investigation are constituted and internally organized but I will show that variable analysis is incapable of providing the information upon which decisions on levels of measurement can be made. Having identified the real weakness of the strategy at the level of theoretical discourse, I will move in the second half of the chapter to a more systematic discussion of how theoretical imagery is supposed to work in variable analysis. The general idea that prevails is to be found in the distinction between concepts and observables, with 'theory' being identified with the job of postulating regularities between concepts. This is another incoherent distinction which ultimately reduces theory to a series of technical decisions. All of this leaves us short of any true apparatus for applying theoretical knowledge to decisions on measurement properties, which is precisely how the reputation for arbitrary measurement in sociology was achieved.

2:1   ON THE LEVEL : MEASUREMENT SCALES AND SOCIOLOGICAL THEORY

Empiricist inclinations

Most commentaries on the idea of level measurement begin with some version or the other of Stevens' (1946) typology of measurement scales and thus to the proposal that the first task of sociological measurement is the identification of a nominal, ordinal, interval or ratio scale as the level appropriate to the particular property under investigation. This scale once imputed is said to act as prerequisite to all subsequent investigation; data collection and analysis procedures will ultimately need to be harmonized so as to operate at the appropriate level of measurement.

Despite widespread recognition of the utility of distinguishing the different measurement levels, a debate has rumbled on, almost since their inception into the research vocabulary, concerning, at the general level, which scale type should express the thrust of research effort and, at the particular, what is the surest means of identifying the level of measurement appropriate to any particular item under investigation. The basic inclination of much of the research community in posing and examining these questions, to date, is that all parameters of an object, and thus evidently its level of measurement, are given in the object itself. Thus we are dealing with what is conceived of as the purely analytic matter of how an object is internally composed and organized. We can perhaps best recognize this guiding empiricist impulse through the very manner in which the notion of level of measurement is introduced to the student. One need only examine the main textbooks, and perhaps not a few lecture notes, to assimilate the idea that scale types simply represent natural internal arrangements. We teach from examples; gender and income, we intone, require different forms of measurement to reflect differences in their composition. Viewing what is manifestly a range of different incomes leads us to naturally perceive that it will take on some form of continuous measurement, whereas sexes come in two types and thus a categorical measure suffices.

Although this disposition to think of scales of measurement as replicas of sense impressions is recognizable enough, the charge that simple-minded empiricist theory of meaning controls research practice in the field of measurement will just not stick. What we have in practice is a much more muted empiricism, marked by continuous debate on how to assign a level of measurement. The proliferation of a wide range of instruments of data collection and analysis in most areas of substantive research affirms that, though the notion of the differentiation of measurement levels is firmly fixed in the research mentality, the rules for its application have yet to be resolved.

I would suggest that the reason why these debates remain unresolved and grow markedly more senile on each re-appearance is that they are played out within a deliberately restricted epistemological terrain. The very possibility of debate on level of measurement arises because measurement is not simply a matter of observation but also of conceptualization. Clearly when confronted with an infinitely complex world, an observer has to apply an element of selection and thus some expectation, some minimal form of conceptualization is required to focus attention in order to guide observation. This role for conceptualization has long been recognized in the dual language models of measurement and is expressed in many distinctions such as Lazarsfeld's (1977) separation of images and indicators, and Blalocks's (1968) utilization of main and auxiliary theories in model construction. However, it should be noted that the stronger interpretations of the theory-ladenness of observation, which suggests the sensory systems are completely plastic with respect of the assumptions which are built into them, are studiously avoided.

The epistemological presumptions of most workers in the dual language school are epitomized in the following assertion from Borgatta and Bohrnstedt:

> The variables of greatest interest to social scientists are latent unobserved constructs rather than constructs that are operationally defined. And most of these constructs are conceptualized to be continuous at the latent level, even though they are usually manifestly measured as discrete variables. Examples of this include the constructs of industrialization, social status, power, authoritarianism and self-esteem (Borgatta and Bohrnstedt, 1981, p. 28).

The use of language here is particularly adroit and most instructive. Concepts and indicators, as we are coming to understand, are both regarded as variables; in fact here they are referred to interchangeably by the ubiquitous term 'construct'. Basically there are perceived to be two ways to gain knowledge of these constructs, either through the exercise of some initial imagery which is required to break down the world into its component parts, or through the partial and incomplete opportunities we sometimes possess for direct observation of these elements.

The important point is that on either view constructs are very much singular terms which take their meaning in terms of mappings or representations of the world rather than as part of a theoretical discourse. Hence it is appropriate to see industrialization, social status and the rest as singular items to be measured rather than as evolutionary processes, social relationships and so forth, and thus even in their most abstract and latent interpretation it is right and proper to conceive that such constructs possess a fixed and intrinsic level of measurement.

It thus becomes apparent that the departure from the empiricist, 'direct measurement' position is largely pragmatic; the argument is essentially that because of our limited powers of discrimination we may struggle to resolve with certainty the internal construction of the more abstract building blocks of social investigation. This being the case we then have the decision to let our instinctive conceptualizations or immediate data collection potentialities dictate the scale types to be used. Borgatta and Bohrnstedt clearly favour the former as when they continue their above claims as follows:

> Most of the central constructs in the social sciences are
> conceptualized as continuous and their distributions are
> such that the application of parametric statistics to their
> analysis will not result in seriously biased estimates (Borgatta
> and Bohrnstedt, 1981, p. 29).

Note again the lack of any perceived ontological distinction between concepts and indicators; no contradiction whatsoever is seen in the idea of applying statistical analysis to theoretical terms or in the notion that ideas have distributions.

Such terminological confusions and contradictions result in the possibility of discrepancies of meaning between concepts and indicators. It might often be the case, as in Borgatta and Bohrnstedt's first quotation above, that we receive different messages about level of measurement from the alternative sources. In such cases we need to know which to stick with when conflict arises; we need some principle to decide whether conceptualization or partial indicators best ascribe meaning to the world. Borgatta and Bohrnstedt's second quotation, as we have seen, offers us an apparently clear guideline which can be generalized as the advice to measure according to the way the construct is conceptualized. The tactic, whilst properly recognizing the loss of certainty previously attached to direct observation, only manages to shift our attention to even less secure beginnings. Whilst constructs remain understood as predicates of objects rather than taking their meaning discursively, the whole business of conceptualization must remain virtually instinctive; it is reduced to the business of making one-off judgements. We cannot intuitively grasp the most appropriate scale for a given property any more than we can see it. I will suggest in due course how properly constituted theory can rectify the situation but for the moment let us look at some of the consequences of viewing conceptualization (or should it be constructualization) as the business of making *a priori* judgements.

The ambiguity of the a priori

A quick perusal of the literature reveals direct opposition to Borgatta and Bohrnstedt's advice and even more perversely one can find examples where apparent adherence to their principles leads to arguments for a contrary practice. All this goes to show of course that the underlying reasoning is so flexible as to be empty. A first example comes from Carter in a discussion of the utility of the seemingly uncontroversial conceptualization and measurement of 'age' on a metric scale. He argues,

> For biological purposes, age in years may be useful but for sociological purposes, the early anthropologist's preference for 'life stage' is worthy of consideration. Few sociologists

would seriously argue the equivalence in social consequences of an age difference from 38 to 39 and a difference from 20 to 21 (Carter, 1971, p. 24).

He subsequently refers to the ordered categories 'infancy', 'childhood', 'adolescence', 'young adulthood', 'old age', as offering a better reflection of age-related social distinctions in a modern society as might the categories 'child', 'warrior', 'elder' in certain primitive societies.

Ford pursues a similar line of reasoning with respect to the other time-honoured metric scale – 'income'.

It may appear at first that £3000 p.a. after tax is an income which can be legitimately regarded as three times £1000 p.a. after tax – but *is* it? The sociologist is not interested in first order happenings like pound notes; he is interested in first order meanings; does a man value three-thousand-a-year three times as much as one-thousand-a-year (Ford, 1975, p. 183).

This train of thought, and similar examples, drives Ford and many others to oppose flatly a general rule that cardinality should be the order of the day,

Clearly then, *most* sociological measurement must be limited to nominal and ordinal scaling, for only with these minimal assumptions can the second order yardstick be imposed upon first order meanings without doing too much violence to the integrity of the latter (Ford, 1975, p. 183).

Yet another variation on the theme is pursued by Gilbert, this time contemplating the task of measuring 'education'.

Sometimes there are theoretically based reasons for regarding a measure as ordinal or categorical even though, at first sight, it appears to have been measured at the interval level. This is the case when a measurement is used as an indicator of a more fundamental, but difficult to measure concept. For instance, education is difficult to measure directly, if by 'education' one means the quantity and quality of knowledge and skill people have acquired. We may be prepared to use the number of years that respondents have attended school and other educational establishments as an indicator of education, and 'years of schooling' is obviously easy to measure at the interval level. But even so, the underlying concept, education, should be regarded as having been measured only at the ordinal level. Although the longer one stays at school, the more one may be assumed to have learnt, the relationship between years of schooling and education cannot be made more precise than this. At present, few of the most important and fundamental concepts in sociology can be measured at the interval level – even though some common indicators of those concepts can be (Gilbert, 1981, p. 16).

Wondrous twists in reasoning here manage to deny both viewpoints hitherto. Concept/indicator ambiguities in this case drive the author to the rule of thumb – 'play safe on the quality of the information that data will yield'. Thus although theoretical construct and index are both ultimately interval, since the indicator poorly reflects the meaning of the basic construct we are advised to retreat to the safety of a less precise discontinuous scale.

Finally, and just to compound the confusion, even supposing we remain content with the original restriction of being faithful to metric measurement, we have to confront the possibility that non-linear scale transformations still render an infinite choice of potential measures. If we regard indicators as merely partial glimpses of the essential properties under investigation, then evidently another of their potential shortcomings is that seemingly ready-made metric scales may vary in their powers of discrimination throughout their range. It is not difficult to imagine arguments that a certain ready-to-hand scale distorts its underlying construct by utilizing an overly compressed or extended numerical scale across certain sections in its span. Carter, in an early paper recognizing that such a problematic concerns us with nothing less than 'inadvertent sociological theory', gives many valuable examples of the different empirical findings that can result by treating the construct/indicator link as mediated by logarithmic and other non-linear functions. For instance, on the basis of a more socially oriented understanding of its impact he recommends a possible revision to the standard metric for 'age'. Instead of the literal age-of-your-bones scale he submits,

> An argument can be constructed supporting the notion that the interval-level assumptions are more realistically satisfied by constantly separated integers being applied to the categories 'infancy', 'childhood', 'adulthood', and 'old age' (Carter, 1971, p. 24).

The problem here, as ever, is to elucidate by what standards we are to sanction such a choice as 'realistic'. One answer pertinent in the case of metric measurement is to utilize a transformation which adjusts the units of the scale so as to produce a normal distribution of individual scores in any population inspected. Although such a procedure ought to be virtually standard practice by the lights of many current parametric techniques, to do so would be, as even Stevens (1966, p. 28) has recognized, a 'gratuitous' expression of statistical expedience. It would only serve to reinforce the idea that technical conventions govern measurement practice and drive us further from the task of attempting to recognize the role of conceptualization in measurement. However, the only alternative to such technical protocols seems to be this rather vague notion of the intuitive grasps at the essence of phenomena or, as Carter puts it, 'making intelligent guesses about the assumed nature of our constructs and how our indices can be made to correspond more closely to them' (Carter, 1971, p. 13). The problem as we have seen is that such guesswork leaves us with no court of appeal when faced with the apparently commonplace diversity of opinion on measurement properties of social concepts.

It should be clear by now that, on the basis of arguments from more or less the same premise, there is a diversity of opinion on measurement parameters which not only spans the full range of scale types but which operates as contentiously within any chosen level. The overall position is such that the novice empirical researcher entering the measurement field and looking for guidance on even this initial phase of the procedure could be excused for speculating that a Kuhnian pre-paradigmatic confusion reigned. The more cynical amongst us might see more purpose in all this diversity and point out that the pragmatism engendered by the 'measurement-as-guesswork' school has the greatest advantage for those who have invested time in the development or mastery of a popular mode of statistical analysis which will, of course, place given demands on data forms. On the above logic, such requirements can somehow always be obliged and justified.

Measurement scales and ordinary language

Waiting in the wings to explain this typical lack of certainty that besets conventional sociological measurement are the phenomenological critiques, and it is high time we let them have their say on this matter. Blumer, Cicourel and friends would no doubt be scornful of the half-hearted understanding of the role of conceptualization in measurement discussed to this point; particularly admonished would be the futile attempt to separate the notion of facts from the linguistic expression of facts. On this view, language is everything, and this allows a totally different understanding of the conceptual underpinnings of measurement. Conceptualization is not the insightful image-making of the empiricist model but simply the way we routinely talk about the world. Given that such human descriptive resources are infinite and indefinite we have a ready-made explanation for the seemingly endless diversity of sociological measurement.

Sociological concepts are thus deemed to be crafted in ordinary language and like all concepts their meaning is taken to be indexical and reflexive. The mutability of languages does not stop with everyday discourse, the same analysis can be applied to the apparently more formal properties of sociological concepts such as their level of measurement. The argument in this context would be that sociological concepts have no natural level of measurement at all and that with a little ingenuity can always be redescribed in a linguistic structure carrying different formal or numerical arrangements. Returning to the two stock-in-trade examples of concepts with 'self-evident' scales provides a convenient illustration. We can and do swap freely from a categorical to an ordinal to a metric language in describing a concept like wealth or income. Thus we might speak virtually in the same breath of 'the rich and the poor', 'those further up the pay ladder', and 'those fighting to maintain pay differentials'.

Consequently we can claim with equal justification that the 'natural' organization of the concept was reflected by using a dichotomous classificatory or by the use of a series of ordinal categories, or assuming metric measurement was apposite.

The same applies to the concept 'gender'. First inclinations may indeed be that a binary discrimination is sufficient to make sexual identification. However, even at the level of physiological characteristics, classificatory problems can arise and in certain contexts more 'precise' distinctions concerning chromosome arrangements, hormone balance and so forth can be utilized in the measurement of gender characteristics. More radically, if we allow for a sociological understanding of gender-typing then a whole host of indicators becomes pertinent. Male and female identification could be made in terms of dress, mannerisms, attitudinal patterns, interactional styles, occupational and educational histories and so forth. Each of these might be subject to finer or rougher discrimination according to one or other of the scale types. Once again the property to be measured can be seen to invite everything from simple binary classification to the construction of multiple-measure metric scales.

Particular examples, such as the latter, could well call forth the objection that the proliferation of measures and scale types demonstrated arises since the point of reference is not the single concept but in fact a range of related but ultimately different concepts. Hence one could continue the empiricist counter-argument by insisting that there is an appropriate level of measurement for each separate notion. However, it is not difficult to see that this line of attack cuts both ways. If it is implied that a variety of meanings and measures are appropriate to different contexts then we need to say on what basis we gain knowledge of that context to make the correct assignment. Unless we make the assumption that the contexts for making the appropriate identifications are also self-evident, we seem inexorably drawn to the path which allows theory and conceptualization, rather than the immutable organization of 'what-is-there', to determine what we see.

We thus arrive, by the lights of ethnomethodology and phenomenological sociology, at a completely different characterization of measurement scales, namely that the ascription of level of measurement to various objects is completely arbitrary. On this view the above sample of declarations on the generally appropriate measurement scales for sociology can be seen as attempts to establish conventions rather than to mirror some existing state of the social world. As to the more particular substantive claims when authors like Borgatta and Bohrnstedt stipulate that cardinal measures are appropriate for constructs like industrialization, social status, power, authoritarianism and so forth, ethnomethodologists would conclude that the basis of their reasoning is custom. They would say that usage is borrowed from previous practices with those concepts within the particular language community. As always, there are alternatives within language and thus the sociological community as a whole. For instance, industrialization can indeed be conceived and summarized in terms of counts of the value of production; but another perspective within developmental sociology tries to map industrialization in terms of ordinal 'stages of growth'; and yet another sees the issue as one of the exploitations between two roughly drawn categories representing the North and the South. Measurement parameters for this school then, are entirely a matter for our linguistic resources and total flexibility can be the only rule.

Measurement scales and scientific discourse

Pursuing the arguments so far leaves us with two rather sorry-looking alternatives. One either assumes that it is legitimate to assign a level of measurement to a given concept which one subsequently admits is all a matter of guesswork; or one takes up the critical position and says that our conceptual resources are so adaptable that any such designation is arbitrary. In fact, the options do not rest with these two and I want to suggest that rescue is at hand in the form of 'scientific discourse'. Here, I only want to give an example of an alternative position before developing it more fully in Part 2.

The problem underlying the present confusion is the limited interpretation of the way theory is understood to underpin measurement decisions. What we have so far is a view which quite properly recognizes the limitations of direct sensory perceptions but, having made this curtsey to conceptualization, returns, as if by conditioning, to a language of measurement appealing to such notions as the 'essence', the 'efficacy', or the 'integrity' of the phenomenon to be investigated. The very attempts to make pronouncements on the scale properties of a whole batch of concepts in the manner of Borgatta and Bohrnstedt rests on a willingness to suspend any understanding that concepts take their meaning as part of theoretical discourse and instead clings to the view of a world of objects 'out there', waiting to be discovered, if only through their shadowy images in our consciousness. A sharp boundary is drawn delimiting the theoretical impregnation of measurement which can be simply expressed as follows. The instinct that governs measurement practice within this revised empiricism is that we measure properties in order to discover their relationships with other properties; what is not anticipated is that our theories of their interrelationships can inform us how to measure the properties in the first place.

Somewhat more surprising, perhaps, is that the phenomenological/ ordinary language *critique* makes a similar error in emphasizing the singularity of concepts at the expense of the contextuality afforded by discourse. Thus whilst ideas on indexicality have led sociological analysis of everyday language to take positive steps into 'discourse analysis'; used as a critical weapon, these same ideas treat concepts as though they can be plucked out of thin air. So, rather as in the discussion above on the scales appropriate to 'income' or 'gender', the tactic is to simply start with the word itself, delve into a kind of mental thesaurus of associated ideas and watch the meanings accumulate. Such a procedure would work just as well, if rather bogusly, with the terms of natural scientific discourse like 'heat' or 'temperature'. If we treat them as singular terms they too are quite open-ended; 'heat' for instance being a term applied, in some circles, to your friendly neighbourhood policeman as well as the stuff that comes out of fires. The reason why no one would claim that natural science concepts cannot be assigned a level of measurement is that scientific language is not the same as ordinary language, and moreover, it is scientific discourse which gives a concept meaning, context, indeed a history.

It seems sensible, then, to investigate what makes scientific discourse extraordinary, if I can put it thus, since here lies the solution to our more mundane problem of understanding the status of the concept 'level of measurement'. One illustration will have to suffice here, namely the measurement of length, since even a potted history of the development of its measurement tells quite a different tale from the strictures of orthodox measurement theory. We have seen that, in much sociological research, the notion of level of measurement is seen as one of the authentications that can be bestowed on a measure, prior to it being launched into investigation. So it is assumed that we can know the numerical properties of a measure in advance of, and independently from, any investigations in which we use that measure. Such a belief is reminiscent of some of the early empiricist theories of measurement in natural science. Consider, for example, Campbell's (1928) classic formulation of the criteria for fundamental cardinal measurement. Even today these are usually read as a summons to construct measures by the discovery of operations on a property which are analogous to the criterion that numbers must meet if they are to permit the operations of algebra. Thus the method of *comparison* and *combination* of objects allows us to observe and verify that relationships between a set of objects are transitive, commutative, associative, incremental and so forth and thus possess the properties we identify with cardinal measurement. To remind the reader, transitivity between three objects (a,b,c) requires that if a is greater than b, and b is greater than c, it should follow that a is greater than c. We know that length obeys this criterion since if we *compare* three sticks of unequal length they will always meet this formula. A variety of further such comparison and combination operations are particularly well exemplified in such instruments as the ruler, and this fact is often taken as sufficient to assign length with its time-honoured status as a property capable of fundamental measurement.

Such a chain of reasoning needs careful interpretation. The comparison and combination operations are not sufficient to warrant any universal statement about the measurement of properties which comply with the cardinality criterion because they only refer to specific manipulations with a particular instrument and not the property in general. Thus not only do the operations which exemplify cardinality fail to tell us how to understand and indeed measure the concept in other contexts but it is in fact knowledge of these contextual features that tells us how to operate the comparison and combination operations legitimately in the first place.

Consider, briefly, the measurement of length in this respect. Our familiarity with the basic measuring device leads to a situation in which our notion of the property becomes almost synonymous with the instrument used to measure it. The fact that usage of the yardstick exemplifies cardinal measurement has bestowed disproportionate significance on this particular instrument. However, in practice, of course, the yardstick covers only a part of our understanding of matters of length and distance. We use a range of different instruments for the measurement of length in different contexts: a flexible measure for measuring curved surfaces; a wheel of known circumference for measuring curved lines; triangulation devices for measuring longish distances and so on. Even these simple alternatives presume and, we might even say, were developed as a result of prior knowledge of discourses in which the concept of length or distance is embedded. In other words, even these elementary ways of measuring length assume knowledge of a mathematical language, namely the formal propositions of geometry and trigonometry.

Not only do Campbell's criteria carry little by way of a general understanding of the nature and purpose of measurement since the requisite operations are so bound to a particular context, but their utility is further limited as soon as we recognize that we need prior understanding of that context to perform the operations in the first place. That is to say the comparison and combination operations cannot and should not be regarded as a kind of experimental procedure for the discovery of those properties which happen to exhibit the regularity of composition required for cardinal measurement. Campbell's criteria cannot be regarded as an inferential tool in this manner simply because we need a theory to appreciate that the various stages in the operation are being carried out legitimately. What counts as an operation of comparison or combination of a particular property is never a self-explanatory matter, rather it is necessary to operate in the opposite direction, in that knowledge of the context instructs us how the operations are to be managed, which in turn inform us about the nature of the object or event studied.

Consider in this respect just part of the combination operation in the validation of length measurement. Following Campbell's procedure would have us perform an operation in which we take two lines which have been visually compared side by side and found equal, combining them and then placing them alongside another line and again visually comparing the two. In such a manner we begin to establish equivalences appropriate to metric measurement. However to perform even this simple sequence correctly depends on the successful application of a host of unwritten rules which we can bring to the analysis in an unremarkable way because we understand the context required for the operation to produce the appropriate results. For instance we do not use curved lines in this operation, we attach the yardsticks in a straight line, we combine them end to end and so forth. One sticks to such procedure out of deference to known principles of Euclidean geometry. One could, of course, perform calculations and make comparisons on surfaces other than flat ones, in which case the prerequisite would be to understand the role that length plays in different geometrical systems. In short, it is the knowledge of the laws expected to govern a particular context which makes sense of and guides the measurement operations. We simply cannot perform the business the other way round; it is naive in the extreme to imagine that we establish a measurement system from scratch simply by observing the results of certain comparison and combination operations.

I conclude that it is high time we removed the notion of level of measurement from the lexicon of social research practice and assigned it to some suitably abstract domain of metamathematics. Abandoning the idea of intrinsic levels of measurement would leave our minds clear to ponder the consequences of the rather awesome alternative that measurement parameters are a function of the discourse in which they are embedded and that metric measurement is *de rigueur* in natural science because theoretical discourse is synonymous with the use of mathematical languages.

2.2 CONCEPTS AND OBSERVABLES (CHICKENS AND EGGS)

The bewilderment of sociology on the issue of measurement scales supports strongly my thesis that conventional measurement and the conventional critiques both make the mistake of ignoring the role of theoretical discourse in establishing measurement properties. Mainstream quantitative researchers might still be quite mystified by this stress on theory in my account since they would take it that orthodox measurement methodology has been transformed over recent years by the attempt to systematically incorporate a role for theoretical concepts in the measurement process. What I am referring to here, of course, are the measurement models of the American sociometric school. Blalock, for instance, hardly sounds like the last champion of positivism when he makes the following assertion.

> unless very careful attention is paid to one's *theoretical* assumptions and conceptual apparatus, no array of statistical techniques will suffice. Nor can a series of ad hoc empirical studies produce truly cumulative knowledge, except in the sense of producing dated and situation-specific findings (Blalock, 1982, p. 9).

What I am going to show, however, is that whilst this school makes great play about the incorporation of 'theoretical imagery', 'abstract levels', and so forth into statistical modelling, this is always managed in such a way as to reduce theorizing to a series of technical decisions. The end result is that the basis of measurement remains in arbitrary everyday description and all the auxiliary statistical measurement models do is perform an arbitrary juggling act on the flawed raw materials.

Images and indicators

Having agreed that mainstream measurement methodology is not wantonly 'empiricist' or 'operationalist' in that it recognizes a distinction between 'concepts' and 'observables', the first thing to do is to understand how the distinction between the two domains is managed. All manner of labels have been used to signify the difference: sometimes these are referred to as T and O concepts, more descriptively they have been labelled as concepts by postulation and concepts by intuition, but the most frequent of all the latterday empiricist characterizations is that between image and indicator. This formulation takes us back to

Lazarsfeld, so it is appropriate to begin with his understanding of the distinction and relationship between the two notions. His first step in measurement is indeed the thinking process. He argues,

> The flow of thought and analysis and work, which ends up with a measuring instrument, usually begins with something which might be called imagery. Out of the analyst's immersion in all the detail of a theoretical problem he creates a rather vague image or construct (Lazarsfeld, 1977, p. 80).

This is not to be confused with the observational level, rather,

> The concept is shown to consist of a complex combination of phenomena rather than a simple and directly observable item (Lazarsfeld, 1977, p. 81).

Thus to take a typical Lazarsfeld example we specify a general image like 'efficiency' as follows. Some aspects, like speed of work, are immediately apparent. Further reflection makes it apparent that speed alone is not the only criterion. Speed allied to a high rate of error or spoilage clearly does not reflect efficiency. Further considerations of this ilk continue until,

> In the end you divide the notion of efficiency into components such as speed, good product, careful handling of machines, and suddenly you have what measurement theory calls a set of dimensions (Lazarsfeld, 1977, p. 81).

The distinctive feature of the new empiricists' concept or image, then, is that it can be broken down into a series of 'aspects' or 'components' or 'dimensions'. This decomposition ultimately allows us to arrive at observations. All the various instances of the general idea are examined for directly observable manifestations. Observables, we note, thus remain objects we can 'directly' sense, objects whose parameters can be defined in observation. For instance, we might observe the 'speed' element in 'efficiency' in terms of some taken-for-granted numerical dimension such as components produced per hour.

Indicators thus locate particular instances of the concept under investigation, and as such they are apt to take on different forms in different social situations. Another one of Lazarsfeld's standard illustrations will give the grounds for this development. He uses the example of the concept 'prudence'. How might we break down our image of a prudent individual? Two indicators we might think up are that a person never bets, and that a person takes out lots of insurance. Such indicators would be open to observation and some simple form of quantification. However, these might be irrelevant indicators in certain contexts, as in his 'denominational college', where 'there is no betting and occasions for taking out insurance are rare' (Lazarsfeld, 1977, p. 82). In such a social context we might reconsider that indicators such as locking doors or not lending books are more appropriate. Hence there is no invariant relationship between images and indicators, and Lazarsfeld argues that this is the typical picture for almost all social science measurement.

In summary, the image/indicator division purports to reflect a thinking/observing distinction but is also formulated in terms of a general/particular dichotomy. We need to make use of general concepts as the starting point and building blocks of knowledge. As such they are not directly amenable to observation since they have different manifestations in different situations. These manifestations, since they comprise singular, individual local instances, actions or events, are observable. We can see and point to the particular, but we can only reconstruct the general, the extensive, the universal. All this, of course, closely fits the empiricist mode of explanation. According to this perspective our task is to sort out the crucial parameters and regularities which underlie and govern the more superficial events and happenings in the world. We would, of course, expect such laws and generalizations to be couched in general terms. So, fundamental relationships are thought likely to concern concepts or images, like efficiency or prudence, rather than specifics, like broken components and locking doors.

Multiple indicator models

The immediate corollary of this general ontology is the need to abandon any notion of a one-to-one correspondence between image and indicator, rather –

> the use of multiple indicators is called for whenever the
> researcher has definite theoretical concepts which he wishes

to relate but for which he is unable to obtain or defend simple, unambiguous, direct operational definitions (Curtis and Jackson, 1962, p. 195).

In other words, occasionally researchers can expect the single observation to act as measure of the concept, as with notions like 'gender' or 'age'. More likely, if they are dealing with useful theoretical concepts like 'class' or 'alienation' or 'social integration', they are dealing with a phenomenon with several aspects and potentially many indicators.

This brings us to the crucial question of which indicator or which combination of indicators one should choose to best represent a concept in any particular investigation. In some of the better-researched fields we are indeed faced with an embarrassment of riches. If I am interested in, say, educational status, it would be possible to create a very large, if not infinite, battery of indicators such as number of years' schooling, examinations passed, type of school attended, measures based on the content of knowledge acquired and so forth. Whilst phenomenologists would be lining up at this point to shout 'we told you so', mainstream measurement methodology has chosen to tackle the problem by generating a further set of principles to attend to the matter of the selection, combination or arbitration between the arrays of available measures. Within this paradigm the measurement problem has been transformed so this becomes the central problem, with more and more sophisticated indicator selection procedures being advanced over the years.

As I have mentioned, I do not want to examine the technical differences between the various measurement models here, but rather to extract the underlying logic assumed in the various methods. One can in fact identify two broad approaches to the problem. The first concentrates on the *selection* of the 'best' indicator, relying on the notion of predictive validity, and the other seeks to *combine* and compare indicators with the purpose of seeking to perfect our understanding of relationships rather than measures *per se*. I shall critically examine some examples of the former strategy in Chapter 9. Here I will concentrate on the second school of thought which begins with Lazarsfeld's (1977, p. 85) doctrine of the 'interchangeability of indices', the justification for which seems to be as follows. Supposing we are interested in a certain relationship between two concepts (general images). If investigations using different indicators for these images produce identical results then one is on much safer ground in asserting that result reflects the true, basic and underlying relationship between the concepts. The central thrust of Lazarsfeld's principle is really a proposal to change our expectations of the role of measurement. In social science, any particular index is going to have 'peculiarities'. No two are ever going to classify a set of individual cases in exactly the same way. Hence rather than searching for the perfection of pure classifications, he suggests our interest should focus on the overall or aggregate findings. Thus he remarks,

> this is the point that needs to be driven home.
> Classifications in social research are mainly used to establish relations between a number of variables. The crucial question, therefore, is whether these relations, the empirical findings we are looking for, are much affected if we interchange one reasonable index for another (Lazarsfeld, 1977, p. 89).

I am going to argue that this principle is basically empty. Since, however, it has been developed, it is necessary to examine amendments from within the paradigm before developing a critical commentary. Perhaps the most revolutionary innovation in multiple indicator methods occurred with the importation of the language and logic of causal modelling. The end product, it must be emphasized, is intended to remain the same, namely to select indicators to 'allow a test of the implications of the abstract model on the abstract plane' (Costner, 1972, p. 304). To secure this it is first necessary to conceive that specific indicators are somehow 'caused' by our abstract general concepts. Although the image/indicator relationship is normally understood as an analytic one, in this view it is treated in an avowedly synthetic manner. I should add that the advantage is perceived, not in terms of the causal representation as such, but in that it allows the image/indicator link the same treatment as any other path relationship in causal modelling. In other words, in treating both image and indicator as variables it becomes possible to bring measurement decisions into the overall technical process of model construction and testing.

The logic-in-use involved in all this can be demonstrated with a very simple image/indicator model as illustrated in Fig. 2.1. Suppose we postulate that at the the abstract level we expect a causal regularity between X and Y as in model A. To test this 'theory' we introduce additional hypotheses about the relationship between these concepts and their indicators. Suppose we are able to devise two indicators per concept, we can then introduce an 'auxiliary measurement theory' to give us a complete model B. Such a two-indicator model allows us to define more than one estimate for the 'unobservable' relationship r_{xy} which makes no assumptions about the perfect measurement of its constituent 'abstract' concepts. This is possible in statistical terms because the system is overidentified, we have six 'bits' of information in the form of observed correlations

$$r_{x_1 x_2}, \quad r_{x_1 y_2}, \quad r_{x_1 y_1}, \quad r_{x_2 y_1}, \quad r_{x_2 y_2}, \quad r_{y_1 y_2},$$

and yet the substantive and measurement theory between them only posit the existence of five relationships as in Fig. 2.1. To turn this into a principle for the selection of indicators simply requires that the different estimates for r_{xy} be identical. Costner calls this the 'consistency criterion', which can be expressed as follows

$$(r_{x_1 y_2})(r_{x_2 y_1}) = (r_{x_1 y_1})(r_{x_2 y_2})$$

Obviously I have not gone into any detail here about the statistical derivation of these ideas. For an account of this see Costner (1972) and for a more technical critique see Pawson (1980). All that needs to be clarified here is the key methodological principle of such measurement models in their

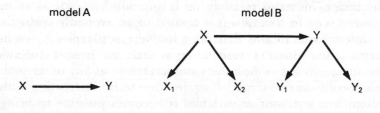

model A   model B

Figure 2.1

rejection of what Costner (1972, p. 300) calls the 'semantic' approach to validity. This approach does not concern itself with what it regards as metaphysical speculations concerning what is involved in embodying ideas in observations. This is most clearly marked in Blalock's approving quotation of Eddington to the effect that a judgement saying that a measure truly reflects the meaning of a concept can never be more than 'pious assumption' (Blalock, 1971, p. 13). Instead Blalock and Costner recommended that with the use of the above apparatus the problem can be transformed into a statistical one of producing overidentified structural equation models. Blalock makes such thinking explicit as follows:

> As a general rule the more indicators one has and the simpler the assumptions the greater the number of excess equations that will be available to test the compatibility of the data with the model (Blalock, 1972, p. 296).

The impoverishment of theory in multiple-indicator models

I want now to argue that the assumptions underlying this whole multiple-indicator strategy are themselves rather pious. The above procedures are wholly futile; they provide more arbitrary measurement rather than sounder measurement. The distinctions introduced above between image and indicator, main and auxiliary theory and so on are put forward in an acknowledgement of the importance of theory in measurement. I want to argue that the various modifications do not in any proper sense introduce the use of theoretical concepts into the measurement process. Theorizing is not the discovery of invention of images or general categories which encapsulate and summarize observational terms. The end product of such strategies is not abstract understanding but summary description.

My critique follows each step in the modification to crude empiricism. Firstly, I want to argue that the image/indicator distinction fails to warrant any sustainable demarcation between observable and theoretical terms. Secondly, I show that the attempt to overlay the general/particular distinction upon the image/indicator pair is incoherent and unstable; not one step is gained in the move to establish knowledge on the 'abstract plane'. Thirdly I point to misconceptions in the idea that multiple-indicator usage can resolve the problem of arbitrary measurement. The rules for the combination of measures produce results every bit as capricious as that for single indicators.

Observable and theoretical terms

Any idea that variables exist 'out there' awaiting direct apprehension on the part of the researcher is apparently scorned with the introduction of the two-language models described above. In fact all that happens is the idea of direct perception of the world is displaced somewhat and resurfaces in the guise of indicators. Blalock can be caught verbalizing the manoeuvre as follows:

> Many 'property' variables that are associated with systems of whatever nature, will be difficult to perceive directly in terms of any of our human senses or of the instruments that we may have constructed to serve as more accurate recording devices. Instead, we often infer these properties in terms of their presumed effects or sometimes their causes or the stimuli we assume produce them. Thus, we do not observe hunger directly but infer it on the basis of food deprivation or certain behavioral responses. We do not 'see' a person's 'loyalty' or a group's 'solidarity', but we infer these by watching the individual or group respond to various stimuli. The physicist postulates a number of elementary particles having certain electrical charges, masses, and spins and then checks up on these assumptions by theorizing how these particles will behave when subjected to various stimuli and how these behaviors, in turn, may impact on other phenomena that may be observed, say, in a bubble chamber. Heat energy is measured in terms of its effects on a column of mercury, and mass is inferred on the basis of pointer readings produced by placing a number of weights on a balance at or near the surface of the earth. . . . In all of these instances, then, a causal theory is needed to link up the postulated property with some indicator that we can observe in a fashion we are willing to refer to as 'direct' (Blalock, 1982, p. 26).

60

This passage is worth quoting at length because it makes the double error of assuming that some (if not all) of the world remains open to direct observation and furthermore that what passes for 'direct observation' in sociology is akin to natural scientists making direct readings from experimental apparatus.

If I can rehearse (for the final time!) the arguments against direct observation, one sees that in order to preserve the priority of 'pure observation', one needs to engage in speculations that are downright metaphysical. The first of these assumptions is of the so-called 'picture theory' of language (Wittgenstein, 1961). This requires 'there is a language of elementary propositions whose distinct constants "point to" different elements in the world and whose logical grammar reproduces the structure of the world' (Hindess, 1977, p. 135). The second presupposition is that 'the essential structures of experience are inter-subjectively valid and that the knowing subjects are also endowed with language and the capacity to communicate facts' (Hindess, 1977, p. 139). In other words, it is necessary that we all experience the world in exactly the same way and are thus able to share knowledge of it through this picture language. All in all, to retain the notion of an observational realm that is independent of us yet knowable, we need to propose some automatic, pre-established harmony between subject, language and world.

So to go back to Blalock's examples, if indeed there existed a direct indicator of 'solidarity', every one of us would have to know it when we see it and furthermore to know what to call it once we had seen it. Blalock does not tell us which indicator would allow this state of affairs to pertain because, of course, such a decision would be to call into play his own common-sense ideas about the significance of certain actions in particular social situations. Let us do the job for him and imagine what such indicators might be. An indication of the 'solidarity' of the positivist school of US sociology might be the number of references it makes to its own writings as opposed to those of other perspectives. An indication of 'solidarity' of the rivals at times of war might be their respective rates of acquiring voluntary recruits. An indication of 'solidarity' of a group at times of extreme danger might be the suicide of the weaker brethren to promote the chances of the remainder. Thus we might have ready made indicators in the form of citation, joining-up and suicide rates but no one can doubt the phenomenologist assertion that these are necessarily generated in bodies of mercurial, common-sense theory. The fact that sociology deals with issues and concepts that have everyday relevance does indeed allow us to summon up seemingly instantaneous measures, but this is a testament to our *powers of imagination* rather than the *immediacy of observation.*

In passing it is worth noting the second confusion in the passage from Blalock – that identifying observation using laboratory instruments as 'direct' observation. He seems to assume that the capacity for instantaneous visual read-out from such apparatus amounts to some immediate contact with the world. Nothing could be further from the case; the construction of a piece of apparatus like a bubble chamber calls on a whole army of assumptions, laws and theories, and similarly, although we can read a modern thermometer at the flick of an eye, our facility for doing so rests on centuries of conceptual and theoretical development. Thus it is not direct apprehension but their deep roots in networks of laws and theories which gives us faith in the evidence obtained with these standard instruments. In maintaining the notion of direct apprehension as part of the measuring process, he is seeking the futile goal of something which is not obtainable nor even required.

Having settled the hash of the notion of indicators as direct observation, it is necessary to examine the conceptual side of the new empiricism. It is apparent that on these measurement models there are a host of terminological and procedural differences separating image from indicator, main from auxiliary theory and so on. However, no ontological basis is ever suggested for distinguishing the theoretical and the observable. Recall that according to Lazarsfeld a concept begins life as a vaguely conceived entity born out of theoretical immersion in the chosen problem. We can have no dispute here, it is certainly true to say that no one can specify much more about the initial leap of imagination which allows the invention of potential explanatory concepts. Unfortunately this primary speculation marks the total extent of theorizing on the revised empiricist model.

After this point the theoretical image is separated into aspects or components, vague thoughts are concretized by reducing them to observable indicators. The 'theoretical' plane is attained once more after the reprocessing and combination of observables according to a consistency rule. Thus, by the time results emerge, the original theoretical concept becomes composed of nothing but observational information and is defined entirely on the basis of observational terms. The surest sign of the ontological equivalence of concepts and observables in these measurement strategies is Costner's (1972, p. 301) notion of 'epistemological correlation' or 'epistemic coefficient' as a way of expressing the relationship between the two levels. No contradiction is seen in the idea of deriving expressions for the correlation between observational and theoretical terms. The assumption is simply that, 'indicators are 'reflectors' of the abstract variable, that is a change in the abstract variable will lead to a change in its own indicator' (Costner, 1971, p. 300). The connection is in terms of constant conjunction; it is thus reduced to the standard empirical connection between objects.

We are safe, therefore, in the claim that there is no ontological difference between the various levels of operation in the measurement models. Attempts to distinguish images and indicators are rather like attempts to solve the old question of the precedence of chicken or eggs. Theoretical concepts and observables have the same status, the first merely summarizes one or more of the second. The thinking/perceiving distinction cannot be maintained. Observational terms are firmly rooted in particular everyday theories about the composition of the social world. As such no level of research operation is free of theoretical conjecture, we have no level of observational primacy to act as the building block and testing bed of knowledge. But equally, according to this model, it seems there are no theoretical concepts which are 'observation-free'. Theoretical constructs merely summarize observations made, they have no meaning outside observations made.

The general and the particular

It is just about conceivable that the empiricist would be content with the above reconstruction of image/indicator terminology and agree that here, as in science generally, the conceptual and the observable do tend to run together. Thus it might be agreed that these measurement models are based on partial, theory-laden descriptions, but argued that these are at least descriptions of something and that by building up a many-sided picture based on such observation an overall pattern might emerge, perhaps forming the basis for a broad generalization. In other words, the claim would be that movement from the observable to the 'conceptual' did not concern abstraction or theorizing in any strong sense, but simply the production of more-general categories. On this view, the difference between concept and observable really boils down to the difference between the general and the particular, the whole and its parts.

This simpler distinction is, none the less, vital because it reflects empiricist views of how the world is organized and the way the search for knowledge ought to mirror it. As we have seen, the empiricist perspective presupposes an ordered world of fundamental regularities underlying a surface of disorder and superficial local regularities. The really basic generalizations are going to be concerned not with abstract theoretical notions but broad empirical categories. Superficially the idea seems logical enough. For example, years of schooling, qualifications gained, type of school attended and other such indicators can be thought of as expressing aspects of a more general category which we might label educational status. Parents' income, parents' occupation, housing standards, etc. might reasonably be considered indicators of a broad underlying concept – home background. Consequently a relationship between any two such observational indicators, say, income and years of schooling, quite reasonably seems only a partial expression of a much more general domain concerning the effect of home background on educational status. It is thus at the level of general empirical categories that we are led to expect to find our fundamental causal laws.

This expectation is false. We can stay with the example in order to point to the weakness in the reasoning and then go on to treat the issue more generally. The problem is that the relationship between the two concepts will be influenced by a whole range of contextual features which are quite unrelated to the issue of how we have measured the variables. The most obvious contextual mechanism in this case would be the nature of educational institutions and policies. Suppose we had a society in which education was entirely private and paid for on an individual basis with the expertise of the teaching institutions varying closely with their price. In such cases the home background/educational status relationship would look totally different if estimated with parents' income/school fee indices as opposed to, say, parents' education/years of schooling. The point is that the first pair of indicators would capture the mechanism really at work; whilst seeking to combine the different indicators under some consistency or interchangeability rule would only serve to confuse the issue.

The consequence of this as far as the measurement strategy stands is that the emphasis on the image at the expense of the indicator, the move to attempt to embrace highly general concepts, is probably misplaced. There is no reason at all to expect that laws operate only between variables supposedly expressing more general ideas. Rather we now see that it is possible to locate a law at any level, providing we can spot its appropriate environment and form a theory to justify why the regularity should take on the particular form it does in such a context. So indeed we might argue that the reverse logic is nearer the mark and that genuine laws are more likely to be uncovered, by quite specific indicators. To modify our example again, suppose that we had a meritocratic education system in which only public education was available, taught in identical institutions, to a common curriculum and through which one progressed only by passing an annual exam. In this case the other pair of indicators, parents' education/years of schooling, might give a better indication of how advantage was passed on.

To turn to a more general statement of the issue, the problem is that several features which are necessary to the idea of producing law-like generalizations are not defined and not definable in the empiricist account of the growth of knowledge. The difficulty concerns the manner in which we separate laws from local regularities, or more formally, nomic generalizations from accidental ones. The distinction is of vital importance in assessing the typical findings of causal research. The end product of single- or multiple-indicator models is a coefficient or set of coefficients expressing the relationship between particular properties. The issue is whether such relationships merely represent a description of the particular case studies or whether they provide the foundation for a more universal law claim.

65

To settle the basis for the distinction it is necessary to examine the full statement of a scientific law which typically runs thus, 'There exist environments in which for all X, if X is A, then X is B'. There are other versions and notations used in law statements but the important point to note is that every law has associated with it a set of 'boundary conditions' restricting its scope. Hence the first point to be noted is that, paradoxical as it may sound, a universal law is not necessarily one that applies in all time and space. This is the case only in an 'all other things being equal' sense. In other words, a law is universal in as much as it always applies in the appropriate context. This is the case for all the major laws of science. For instance, Newton's laws are not universal but only apply in a vacuum, at low speeds, without significant light-pressure and so on.

This construction has the unfortunate consequence that it brings law statements, superficially at least, very close in form to descriptions of local regularities. Both have the form, 'this relationship holds in this context'. Indeed it is this very similarity which has probably led Costner and Blalock to believe that causal modelling methods can be used to derive 'abstract regularities', 'if-then laws' and so forth. However, there is a way of distinguishing the two types of statement. To this end Kaplan, amongst others, introduced the notions 'content' and 'context' to distinguish the two parts of any law statement (Kaplan, 1964, Ch. 3). The content refers to the unit of analysis (individuals, groups, actions), the variables (the substantive issues) and the form of the relationship (exact, stochastic, linear, non-linear, etc.). The context delimits the area of application of the law, it is the social space within which the law holds. Crucially it is only knowledge of the context of its occurrence that allows us to explicate the content of any law. As Kaplan tersely puts it, 'content depends on context' (Kaplan, 1964, p. 95).

This provides us with a device for separating laws from local regularities. The vital difference is that in a nomic generalization we have a theory about the context, whereas in an accidental generalization we can only name the context. So in an accidental generalization the evidence for the regularity coincides exactly with the range of its application. Our reason for asserting it is limited to the particular information that we have observed in a given context. Contrary to this, according to Kaplan, 'a nomic generalization must play a part in a scientific theory' (Kaplan, 1964, p. 92). We need reasons for asserting it other than the evidence of its occurrence alone. We need a theory to interpret why the regularity takes on its particular form. This is the case even if the law is stated in the 'ceteris paribus' form. As Stinchcombe says,

> The more responsible meaning of ceteris paribus is, 'this relation holds, other things being equal, and the rest of the theory tells what these other things are' (Stinchcombe, 1973, p. 6).

Kaplan provides us with a rather exotic example of the difference:

> that the Japanese regard the back of the neck as an erogenous zone may be a matter of fact but it is not a law; that the neck will be so regarded in any culture in which the infant is carried on its mother's back and facing it, might be one (Kaplan, 1964, p. 91).

In short, we conclude that this view of concepts as general/summary indicators is incoherent and that once again the strategy lacks credibility for want of a proper understanding of the role of theory.

Consistency criteria

At the risk of adding insult to injury, it remains to assess the final feature of multiple-indicator methodology, namely the principles for selecting between the rival measures. What scientific protocol is embedded in the consistency criteria and the principle of interchangeability of indicators? Both criteria share the notion that the real business of measurement is to inspect propositions, so that it is relationships founded on measures rather than the measures, *per se*, that are important. The primitive version of this is Lazarsfeld's principle which informs us that if the same results are obtained for the overall relationships after interchanging concomitant indicators, then there is more reason to have confidence that the general relationship is a true regularity. However the important point to note about identical (or near identical) relationships discovered in this manner is that they are equivalent only in an aggregate sense. So in fact as far as classifying individuals is concerned, each single index is totally clear (if arbitrary) as it stands, classification only becomes ambiguous when indices are compared. It seems most odd therefore on the basis of necessarily ambiguous classification at the individual level, that one is willing to claim that relationships built on them are somehow purer. The ambiguity at the individual case level does not disappear just because we are able to express relationships in the aggregate. A composite of the arbitrary remains arbitrary.

This state of affairs has a number of practical consequences which have received much comment. Park (1968, pp. 158–60) provides the standard technical critique in a commentary on some of Lazarsfeld's substantive research which makes use of the interchangeability notion. His first point is that the results required to meet the principle are easily produced using any data dredging technique, since in research of the type Lazarsfeld engages in one is handling large numbers of indicators, so large that one cannot help finding substantial numbers of pairs of variables that share the same numerical relationship with a third. The second point is that many of the general relationships, even though demonstrating the requisite close agreement, produce correlations of the order of 0.30 or less. Such a relationship is, of course, practically useless in terms of its predictive power. As Park rather drily puts it, 'It is difficult to see how the fact that two indices are interchangeable in not being able to relate to a third variable establishes that they measure the same inferential concept' (Park, 1968, p. 160). Lazarsfeld's rule, then, requires ambiguity at the individual level; we might even say that it thrives on it since the looser the general relationship the more easily it is fulfilled. We can thus summarize what Lazarsfeld's principle has to offer. Put bluntly what we get for the effort is proliferation of detail, the promise of description and yet more description. The logic involved is nothing more than the search for an overall arithmetic equivalence. It reflects the naivest level of belief in 'safety in numbers'. What is worse is that the actual form of the principle is quite arbitrarily stated. Lazarsfeld's prescription requires that correlations based on different indicator pairs be equal. In Costner's terminology it requires all epistemic coefficients to be the same; each indicator, therefore, needs to be equally good (or bad). However, the whole point of the method, and the precise difficulty in using indicators, stems from the fact that any index will have some 'idiosyncrasy' that prevents it from acting as the pure measure. The interchangeability rule requires they match each other in the degree of this peculiarity. However if one accepts the image/indicator formulation in the first place there seems no reason why one should shun the use of indicators of uneven quality. The measurement prescription offered then is quite arbitrarily shaped, our basic convention of scientific thought turns out to be nothing more than the principle of *chance coincidence.*

Costner's principle can be dealt with quite summarily. It is based on similar principles to its predecessor and so has the same faults. So whilst it speaks the language of multiple indicators, relationships on the abstract plane, structural equation models, overidentified systems, multiple estimates and so forth, this can be 'decoded' as employing the specious distinction between images and indicators in order to find more than one way to calculate a relationship which, if found to be equal, is pronounced more fundamental than if calculated singly. To see how ludicrous is this faith in *arithmetic equivalence,* imagine, if you will, a physicist with two imperfect thermometers and two idiosyncratic pressure gauges arguing that we will be able to settle on the abstract form of the gas law relating temperature and pressure should both possible estimates of the slope of the regression line relating the two be identical.

Costner's method has, of course, met with a range of technical criticisms which rediscover almost point by point those directed at Lazarsfeld's founding principle (for a summary, see Jacobson and Lalu, 1974). Given an adequate data dredging technique, sufficient potential indicators, lowish 'abstract' associations and generous margins for error in assessing what constitutes equal estimates, it is not difficult to meet the arithmetic requirement in a fairly mechanical way (Althauser and Herberlein, 1971). Though the technique has been further refined and Blalock (1982), in particular, has warned against unquestioning mechanical application of the formula, it is important to realize that such principles are wanting for reasons far more important than technical indiscretions.

The real issue goes right back to our very understanding of what constitutes a variable and how we establish any particular variable as a true representation of part of the world. The principles under discussion here reject the 'direct apprehension' notion of crude empiricism but replace it with alternative suggestions about the nature of validation which can turn out to be equally problematic. Lazarsfeld's principle insists that the validity of indicators is settled at the level of relationships between indicators but our knowledge of what constitutes a true relationship turns out to be just an artefact of the method used to calculate the relationship. Costner's principle says our use of a particular set of variables is justified according to the validity of the model as a whole. But again the notion of the validity of the model as a whole receives an interpretation which is *internal* to the way the model is constructed. That is to say we describe a set of associations between variables via a set of simultaneous equations that is overidentified. This allows us to produce multiple estimates of certain relationships within the model and if these estimates agree the model is said to be exonerated.

So all that is happening in this revised empiricism is that abiding faith in observation as direct representation is replaced with a loyalty to the notion of estimated causal relationships acting as fundamental laws. We end up in yet another version of the chicken and egg problem. Previously, empiricists might have said they had faith that they were uncovering fundamental law-like regularities because they had faith in their basic measures; now the position is reversed, it is the assurance of arithmetic consistency in the observed patterns of relationship which justifies confidence in the validity of the measures. One only needs to ask, of course, from whence springs the information which allows estimation of the consistency of the overall pattern – direct observation, no less? – to see the fatal circularity in the revised logic.

Conclusion

I have shown that variable analysis works with a remarkably commonplace image of measurement in which one gets hold of a bit of the world and assigns it a value. This is exactly how a grocer weighs cheese, a draper measures inside legs, an egg-packer grades eggs and so on. This is a fine model of measurement for the tradesman but a lousy one for the scientist. Treating the social world as though it comes in monadic, discrete, singular lumps omits consideration of the role of theory and conceptualization in the perceptual distinctions we make. Such thoughts have opened the way for the phenomenological critique of measurement, which to continue in the above vein, would say that although we might just about recognize a piece of cheese, a pair of trousers and an egg when we saw them, such a clear observational base does not apply when it comes to consideration of social class, educational attainment, intelligence and most anything else of interest in the social world.

The reason why empiricist measurement is captured in such a critical loop is the lack of any notion of the role theory plays in understanding and justifying a particular regularity or model or law. Although we have seen Blalock at pains to exhort the causal modelling fraternity to pay proper attention to conceptual and theoretical issues, one finds, in fact, that the potential for the development of theory is severely limited by the very format of these models. Basically theory plays two roles in variable analysis. First there is the immediate, intuitive theory involved in specifying the key concepts or variables that comprise the issue under investigation. Thereafter the role for theory is to hypothesize a pattern of causal relationships amongst these variables. The theorist has to suggest which is the independent and dependent variable, whether a relationship is 'direct' or mediated through another variable and so on. Theorizing is quite literally the mental fabrication of path diagrams.

It is this theorizing-as-stipulation-of-causal-sequences that should be recognized as being responsible for the predicament surrounding the status of variables. Empiricist sociology has always made the error of mistaking the categories and distinctions held in everyday language for 'direct observation'. All that happens in these more refined models is that the basic method of making a choice between readily available, if arbitrary, measures, is now buttressed with a whole series of even more arbitrary justifications and pronouncements on the combination and comparison of these observations. Phenomenologists can thus hang in there to the last and argue with justification that sociological measurement now exhibits a 'higher' or 'double' arbitrariness.

What is missing in both accounts is an understanding of quite a different kind of theorizing concerning what Kaplan would call the context lying beneath the content, or modern-day realists would call the *underlying mechanisms* which connect the causal sequences. Rather than simply suggest that one variable forces or causes or influences another we can ask questions about the reason for the connection, and answers to such queries are often better conceived in terms of the internal processes connecting the two. For instance our knowledge of the laws relating gas pressure and temperature are not simply derived as either empirical generalizations calculated on the basis of trusted measures, or on the basis of the arithmetic consistency of a causal model utilizing auxiliary theories connecting the social concepts to partial indicators. Rather any empirical evidence on the relationship we have is treated against independent knowledge of the form of the gas laws derived from our understanding of the behaviour of the underlying mechanisms, namely the kinetic theory of gas molecules. Trying to understand a relationship as part of a whole process in this manner avoids the predicament of having to place undue faith in either direct observation or estimated causal laws.

If one allows that theory should not only posit the existence of a relationship but explain its form, sociological model construction would develop in a quite different fashion. For instance if one started with the typical relationship between parents' social class and children's social class, one would begin by asking about the mechanism of inheritance that advantaged or disadvantaged certain groups in acquiring class (occupational) positions. One would theorize about the credential barriers constructed to serve the interests of particular occupational groups. One could hypothesize how legislation on the inheritance of wealth and property, favoured or disadvantaged particular groups. One could try to understand how the changing patterns of opportunities available with technological and economic change lessened or increased the mobility opportunities of different groups.

Theorizing of this type has many advantages over what passes for theory in variable analysis. Perhaps the most important, from the point of view of the discussion here, is that deliberations about the mechanisms underlying a relationship can inform us of the parameters of the properties that make up the relationship. So rather than depend on separate common-sense theories about social class as the source of its indicators we can anticipate that some of our theories of the mechanisms of class inheritance will identify what are the significant class groupings in the first place. Detailed speculation in the manner above about legal rights, educational advantage, technical change and so forth might enable the development of a measure identifying property owners, credential-based professional groups, technical workers, unskilled workers and so forth as key components. In Part 2 I will show exactly how such theorizing about underlying mechanisms underpins every stage of the measurement process in science and in Part 3 I will consider how this model can be adapted for sociology. Here I rest content in the hope of having convinced the reader of the truth of an amended version of Kelvin's dictum: 'If you cannot theorize, your measurement is meagre and unsatisfactory'.

Chapter Three

AGAINST SCALING: MEANING AND MEASUREMENT

Scaling stands alongside indicator selection techniques as the other major method of measurement in current social research. Unlike the family of variable analysis methods, scaling, perhaps because of its technical complexity, has received little critical attention within sociology. This chapter aims to remedy the situation but not, I hope, in the form of another dire anti-positivist tract of which the discipline has had a bellyfull already. An assessment of scaling techniques is in fact particularly pertinent to this study because its very objectives are formulated in relation to, or one might even say as a defence against, certain of the phenomenological objections to measurement. Thus again the second, though not secondary, purpose of this chapter will be an evaluation of these very criticisms. Since I am going to be involved in deciphering another complicated round of critique and counter-critique, I should begin by informing the reader of the basic argument and the order of proceedings.

Scaling is unlike other measurement techniques in that it is based on the observation of what are claimed to be the common cultural meanings, the shared social interpretations of the public-at-large. Though in fact it wasn't the case, such a strategy could almost have been conceived as a direct counterplot to frustrate those phenomenological critiques which argue that social measurement is impossible because it is based on everyday meanings and language and thus carries no common meaning between, or even within, cultures. One is faced with a flat contradiction here which I shall resolve in favour of the phenomenologists. To do this, it is necessary to examine in much greater detail the combined effect of the different elements in

74

the phenomenological critique outlined in the introduction, namely that the claims to the objectivity of social measurement are undercut because of (1) cultural variation in meaning, (2) the arbitrary assignment of measurement scales, and (3) the imposition of meaning in the research context. It transpires that although scaling does provide some evidence of the stability of meaning in the social realm, it does so in ways which display the said consensus through the arbitrary imposition of numerical values and by way of artificial research contexts. In short, scaling leaps the barrier forward by the first phenomenological critiques only by riding roughshod over the latter two.

I make the case for this thesis in the first part of the chapter by considering the major example of occupational scaling, namely the Hope-Goldthorpe scale of occupational standing (1974). The scale is based upon an examination of the public perception of occupational hierarchy and is constructed by asking respondents to rank a list of occupational titles. Goldthorpe and Hope argue that there is a remarkable degree of consensus in such rankings and that they thus provide a sound base for the measurement of social standing. I argue that their method is artificial and arbitrary and ignores the problem of the incompatibility of natural and numerical languages. In the last analysis it is always the techniques of occupational scaling which bestow the crucial formal measurement properties which are absent in ordinary occupational discourse.

The second half of the chapter looks at some of the consequences of this result. It would appear that I am left siding with the 'opposition', in that these arguments seem to approve at least some of the doctrines of those who have no truck with the possibility of sociological measurement. Once again, this would be too hasty a conclusion, for, in fact, all this battery of propositions sustains is the case that ordinary language can never be the source of measurement parameters. So although this does imply that scaling techniques are worthless as instruments of measurement, it does not even begin to make a general and overall case against sociological measurement. In fact the lesson one should learn from all this is a positive one, namely to give us confidence to look for other sources to reveal the basic parameters of sociological measurement. In short, and perhaps seemingly paradoxically, I believe that a close reading of the phenomenological critique confirms the message of the previous chapter that we have to take seriously the claim that we depend on theoretical discourse as the ultimate context of our knowledge of measurement properties.

3.1 SCALING AND MEANING CONSENSUS

As we have seen in Chapter 1, the conventional defence of sociological measurement against the phenomenological critique is to acknowledge meaning variation to be a problem but to argue that it is all a matter of degree. Empirical sociology can survive quite happily by concentrating on those areas of social life which we experience intersubjectively. Thus it is argued that what counts as suicide, social status and intelligence may well be in the eye of the beholder, but there can be no doubts as to what constitutes birth, marriage, death, income, educational qualifications etc., and so measurement of social facts such as the latter is perfectly legitimate and objective. Although this might sound a most appealing counter-strategy to the pheno-menological critique, even its supporters would recognize that it is not unproblematic, since it pitches us straight into arguments over what constitutes 'consensual' or 'sufficiently similar' cultural interpretations. We have already seen how *a priori* judgements on such matters can be hotly contested; recall what the phenomenologists would have to say about the social significance of the loss of a pound to the beggar as opposed to the millionaire.

Scaling would seem to offer a happy solution in the face of such dissent. Rather than speculate on the unanimity (or otherwise) in the interpretation of concepts and measures, the appropriate course of action is to get out there and investigate directly the amount of variation in the meaning of would-be social indicators. The example of this strategy I will examine selects itself as the major attempt to devise a measure of social standing using occupational scaling techniques. The Hope–Goldthorpe scale (1974) was devised to serve as the measurement basis for the Nuffield inquiry into social mobility in Britain. Although the tools and techniques preferred seem to have changed according to the personnel involved in the various phases of the inquiry, at the initial stage Goldthorpe and Hope chose to devise a measure through re-examination of the long line of occupational grading or prestige scales. Basically they were impressed by the apparent absence of any kind of socially structured discordance about the occupational order typically found in such inquiries. The justification, then, closely follows Goldthorpe's defence of conventional sociology against the early onslaught of ethnomethodology (Goldthorpe, 1973). The normative paradigm can cope, he claimed, because it not unreasonably assumes that there are some significant and common facets of meaning and understanding which go towards creating the social world and which, when discovered, will provide the means of measuring it. For Goldthorpe and Hope then, a well-founded measure is a measure found to express common first-order meaning.

The method they employed followed the typical scaling drill as follows. Twenty 'representative' occupations were chosen to form the standard titles which were ranked initially by all respondents in the grading inquiry. The respondent's task is to rank the titles in terms of their 'social standing'; ties were allowed so that the choice of number of ranks was the respondents'. A secondary ranking task in which respondents had to insert a further twenty assorted titles allowed coverage, by parts, to reach the 860 titles which Goldthorpe and Hope reckoned gave ample coverage of the total range of occupational categories. The final overall scale is obtained by centring and standardizing each respondent's gradings, taking the mean score of the grading of each occupation and adjusting by a common factor to ensure the final scores fall into a given convenient interval.

As well as this main investigation a range of pilot studies were undertaken to test the structure and the substance of the scale so formed. These further inquiries are said to warrant Goldthorpe and Hope's claim that their method provides a measure with the requisite degree of permanence and certainty. They directly confront the first and broadest of the interpretative critiques, namely that variation in social and linguistic settings undermines the uniformity of meaning assumed in measurement. Consequently one pilot investigation examined the rankings obtained by using the basic procedure in different social collectives (subsets using age, sex and four rather raggedly drawn occupational groups). Second, the basic procedures were repeated with variation in the verbal criterion used in occupational judgement, so that scales of respondents' rankings in terms of 'standard of living', 'level of qualification', 'power and influence over people' and 'value to society' were also obtained.

The upshot of these investigations in Goldthorpe and Hope's eyes is a confirmation of their expectation that there is a general and stable public recognition of what can be thought of as as 'general goodness' or 'general desirability' of occupations in our society. Actually, the average correlation of the rankings produced by any two of their graders was only of the order of 0.5, which on the face of it indicates individual discrepancies. Indeed, Goldthorpe and Hope perceive this level of inter-grader agreement as 'modest', but argue, not unreasonably, that the precise value of such a coefficient depends somewhat on the choice of occupational groups and categories selected, (1974, p. 166). Grouping the occupations into collectivities would reveal higher levels of agreement. However this finding pales into insignificance when we examine what is for them the key issue, that different social groups share a common view of the occupational status hierarchy. On this score evidence from their limited inquiry seems good. No marked differences at all between the gradings of the different subsets were discovered, regardless of whether they were constituted in groups by age, sex or occupations (1974, p. 15).

Furthermore, they claim that some of the linguistic discrepancies and variations that have bedevilled 'prestige' scaling in the past are explained and overcome by their experiment in using different ranking criteria. As they point out, it has never been quite clear just what is the criterion respondents use in understanding and performing such tasks. Certainly, there is no reason why the considerations brought to bear by the rankers should concur with many second-order, sociological interpretations of prestige. Goldthorpe and Hope's feeling is that 'most respondents assess the occupations presented to them on the basis of what they know, or think they know, about a variety of more "objective" occupational attributes' (1964, p. 11). Now whilst standard of living, qualifications, power and influence, and value to society are not deemed to exhaust the potential underlying dimensions of occupational desirability, they are very much the notions that Goldthorpe and Hope believe are subject to ready public scrutiny and hence agreement. They are pleased, therefore, to be able to report that the mean rankings of these four assessment criteria correlates almost perfectly (0.98) with the task as carried out on the main inquiry dimension of 'social standing' (1974, p. 16).

This then forms a perfect example of the theory and practice of the conventional defence of sociological measurement. By such internal examination of first-order conceptualization, it is supposed that it is possible to investigate, understand and control the linguistic and social variation that threatens the more simple-minded applications of our scales and measurements.

A critique of the Hope–Goldthorpe scale

Whilst such an approach clearly shows an awareness of the pitfalls that await the unwary in sociological measurement, the answer provided is inadequate. I will argue that the claims made by Goldthorpe and Hope, concerning the justifications provided by their pilot studies for their scale, are unfounded. On the matter of cross-group consensus of rankings, a statistical critique of their assumptions already exists. The much-vaunted cross-national consensus of occupational rankings has been criticized in that the method used to estimate the degree of cross-cultural agreement, because of its own construction, is likely to overstate that consensus (Coxon and Jones, 1978, pp. 38-42; Guppy, 1982). The measure of cross-cultural consensus used is basically a summary of the agreement between two rankings which are themselves summaries. In all this summarizing, discordance is effectively squeezed out. Given a modest level of agreement within a group of individual graders then the mean gradings of any two sub-groups from these, even randomly drawn ones, are likely to be very highly correlated.

Though these considerations could be applied to the efforts to justify the Goldthorpe and Hope scale, I will not pursue them here since this possibility of overstating consensus is in fact only a sign of more deep-seated problems. The issue of how best to state the precise degree of consensus of social meanings rather begs questions about the source and nature of that consensus. The more fundamental problem that confronts investigations of first-order meanings is the inevitability that the method used to extract such knowledge will shape that knowledge. Any attempt to measure consensus of interpretation must first make questionable and unverifiable suppositions about the form of those interpretations. This problem entered Goldthorpe and Hope's inquiry when they pondered on the actual mental processes brought to bear when people perform the tasks associated with grading the social standing of occupations. Several possibilities are evident. Respondents might have a ready-made cardinal scale in their heads which allows the discrete location of occupations on a metric; they might, more simply, make comparative judgements of the relative standing of different occupations; they might operate at a cognitive level that routinely distinguishes occupations but which properly excludes an evaluative element; or they might operate some simpler or intermediate level.

In the light of what they saw at the time as lack of any 'decisive empirical evidence' on this matter, Goldthorpe and Hope plumped for the 'common-sense' view that people make case by case, better/worse judgements when thinking about different occupations and that the ranking exercise as described above would have more 'psychological validity' than any more numerically sophisticated scaling task (1974, p. 47). This is a clear example of a presupposition about everyday cognition that precedes investigation, remains unchallenged through it and thus shapes all subsequent findings. My point is that this particular assumption can easily be challenged, in fact on the basis of material readily available to Goldthorpe and Hope. One needs only to consider the long tradition of research into working-class consciousness (Bulmer, 1975). Empirical study in this field has typically taken the form of presenting different frameworks, different images of the social composition of society to the respondent whose task is to say which one pertains. In a variety of investigations substantial numbers of respondents have indicated that an image of society compatible with graded hierarchy is unlikely to have any salience for them. Hence in answer to a variety of questions, and no doubt for a variety of reasons, certain subjects are generally found who maintain that the social structure is undifferentiated. Other subjects have, in turn, been prepared to identify separate social groups which they do not perceive hierarchically. Such evidence has, of course, since been hardened by Coxon and Jones's research. These Edinburgh studies, to which I will return shortly, unearth many cases which are incompatible with the Goldthorpe and Hope assumption that invidious comparison is a natural operation. A significant number of respondents who were engaged in a task of occupational grouping and categorization failed to perceive that it was appropriate to order their categories in any way (Coxon and Jones, 1978, p. 131).

The conclusion I would draw from this is not a substantive one. I am not trying to argue for some rival mental model of occupational understanding. I am not claiming the existence of some other more instinctive image of society. Rather I am making the methodological point that the image or pattern or scale that emerges from such investigations is necessarily influenced by the research instrument devised to discover it. This, as we shall see, is as true of these counter-examples as it is of the Goldthorpe and Hope scale. What they all have in common is that the questions they pose to ascertain the respondents' notion of societal order are the ultimate source of the categories in which the subjects frame their response. Posed in this way, it is evident that these investigations face a methodological Catch-22. If a specific framework for recording the respondents' viewpoint is provided (such as a rating or ranking task), then one necessarily forgoes knowledge of how pertinent that particular formulation is for the subject. If, on the contrary, one wants to discover an image that is self-originated then there is no clear way of providing the cue that will bring forth responses that are at the same time unprovoked and comparable. There is no escaping from this circularity and it is this feature that leads to the failure of this measurement strategy.

Scaling as a social occasion

This problem of the intrusion of the research instrument in studies of first-order conceptualization allows a radically different interpretation of Goldthorpe and Hope's results. There are reasonable grounds for supposing that people do not go around with rankings of the social standing of occupations in their heads but can quickly produce one if called upon to do so.

To put it bluntly, what Goldthorpe and Hope have investigated is not so much fundamental forms of occupational cognition, but rather subjects' perception of the appropriate mode of taking part in a research exercise requiring them to rank a list of occupational titles.

How subjects come to make a particular description of the occupational structure must be understood in the same light as the application of any human descriptive resource. No description, however detailed, can exhaust the subject or state of affairs it seeks to describe, so we have permanently a problem in organizing any account we wish to make. According to the students of this dilemma, we routinely solve it through the application of 'multiple reflexive interactions between descriptor and described and between descriptions and their contexts' (Heritage, 1978, p. 85). In other words, we don't just utter descriptions as they take our fancy, rather we continually monitor what we have to say about any situation taking into account what has already been said about it and the purpose of the people with whom we were engaged in conversation.

Taking seriously the problem of meaning variation requires that we treat descriptions as social performances to be understood in terms of the practical purposes for which they are produced. This invites us to treat social research as an activity in which the subject actively examines the cues generated in the research process for the appropriate forms of response. Respondents' utterances are made with an eye on what the researcher is 'really after'. This is by now a commonplace observation, but I would submit that its consequences vary markedly with the topic under investigation. If the inquiry is seeking the respondents' own meanings, frames of reference, vectors of mind and so forth, then this hypothesis-seeking behaviour becomes totally damaging. If, on the other hand, our investigation uses categories and concepts predetermined by the researcher, then the problem reduces to a technical one (cf. Hindess, 1973, p. 44). To put it rather figuratively, the latter form of research merely seeks answers whilst the former is committed to find both the answers and the questions.

A brief examination of the subjects' task and instructions in the Goldthorpe and Hope inquiry reveal that it is littered with clues that we might suspect signal the 'appropriate' type of response. Although both the ranking criterion, 'social standing', and the nature of the occupations listed are studiously left undefined and inquiries regarding them are systematically deflected by the interviewer, there is still plenty to go on. The first clue to the nature of the social evaluation required is that the inquiry is carried out on behalf of university academics. This in itself is enough to alert respondents to the likelihood that the inquiry will concern 'public' knowledge about 'society' and 'inequality' rather than their own 'private' hopes and dreams. Secondly, they learn the research is about 'occupational standing' and 'change', and since the pay, skills, qualifications and industrial muscle of different workers are always 'in the news' in these respects, then the diligent subject might rapidly guess that these items might well be the sort of things under investigation. Above all, clues are obtainable in the occupational titles. Since the instructions make it crystal clear that a ranking of occupations is called for ('highest', 'lowest', 'following in order', 'top', 'bottom', 'very bottom' and so on), then it is hard to resist looking for properties which divide the occupations and enable a hierarchical sorting. (1974, p. 182). This would provide useful confirmation that the above dimensions were indeed salient, and closer inspection might reveal the obligatory 'worthy' occupation like nursing, perhaps calling for an additional dimension to take this societal value into account. Since the occupations listed are deliberately chosen in the first place to span these above-mentioned qualities, it is hardly surprising, given the specific nature of their task, that respondents express a degree of uniformity which confirms the professional expectations and hypotheses (1974, p. 46).

In summary, Goldthorpe and Hope are wrong to invest so much significance in the consensus they obtain on those particular views of occupational status. In a world where you can win prizes for ranking the seven most important features of the 'Ford Escort' or the 'Ideal Kitchen', scaling occupations is no trouble at all, and perhaps about as meaningful. My argument does not concern whether social meanings are or are not structured. Human descriptive resources in themselves are infinite and indefinite but become structured in certain contexts, given the particular problem in hand. The rating task performed in these studies is always singular enough so that the variations of social and linguistic contexts that Goldthorpe and Hope do employ are slight enough not to threaten seriously the uniformity of opinion.

Respondents carry out their task on the basis of the totality of cues mentioned above and the actual word affixed to the rating task is but one of them. The overall agreement between the general rating task and those using more specific grading criteria is a token of the whole set of other linguistic constraints common to all the exercises. There is no need to view the widespread agreement (if it can be so named) in this particular episode as part of some inbuilt social predisposition. It is not a sign of some social constant and has no particular significance for measurement.

The miscellaneous manufacture of measurement systems

I have still to come to a consideration of the numerical properties of measurement and it is this that casts final doubt on the validity of measures constructed by scaling first-order meanings. As noted earlier, the issue is that of warranting a correspondence between verbal and numerical formulations of a concept, which in this case involves the words and numbers used to describe occupational standing. No such correspondence is justified in Goldthorpe and Hope's methods. Even if we were to grant that invidious comparison was a self-generated mode of thinking about occupations that did result in some consensus view, this still would not sanction the final numerical form of the scale. The numbers and ranks assigned to the complete list of occupational titles are nowhere to be found in the subjects' judgement, rather they follow entirely from the method used in the aggregation of all the individual judgements.

This problem of the numerical reification of mental categories and distinctions is a longstanding one in attitude scaling dating back to the early days of the Thurstone scale, and it crops up once more in the Goldthorpe and Hope scale. In fact they offer us a fine array of scoring systems, none of them being legitimate. First we have 1–100 metric scale, pinpointing the desirability of occupations to the second decimal place (e.g. jobbing builders = 43.25); then a rank order of 124 occupational groups; a collapsed version of thirty-six groupings; and finally in the first of the empirical work to emerge from the mobility study the scale is virtually crushed out of existence into seven categories (Goldthorpe *et al.*, 1980).

The metric version is clearly out of order, since it involves treating the original rankings as scores quite freely throughout the process of creating scale values. Each individual's rankings are centred and standardized, scores are calculated from mean values, occupations outside the standard twenty are inserted by spacing them in equal intervals between two 'known' scores and so on. Each one of these manipulations erroneously assumes that interval and ratio type distinctions can be superimposed on the subjects' rankings. The care invested in framing the original non-metric ranking task is totally frittered away.

The same criticism applies to rank order versions of the Goldthorpe and Hope scale. Although these preserve the mental operation supposedly at work, they too are illegitimate because of the method of construction. An overall ranking cannot be directly ascertained from those of a group of individuals who employ dissimilar numbers of ranks. These overall rankings are and can only be obtained by inventing 'breaks' and hence sub-categories within the metric scale constructed as above. So again metric distinctions are freely and illegitimately used. What is more the cutting points within the overall scale are chosen according to a set of rules of thumb specifying what Goldthorpe and Hope call 'major employment status divisions' (1974, p. 31). The vital point, however, is that these are the authors' inventions. They beg the question under investigation, since we have no information whatsoever on whether such divisions figured in the respondents' view of the matter.

It must be concluded that the scoring operation and hence the formal properties of the scale bear little or no relation to the judgements originally exercised. Scoring is necessarily a synthetic operation and not a collective representation at all. The choice of scoring system is thus arbitrary, ranks can be collapsed and extended at will, and thus the whole process is open to the charge of being tailored to generate a favoured set of results in any particular empirical inquiry. Measurement is achieved by fiat.

This is the sad irony really; the method which takes trouble to accommodate one part of the interpretative critique ultimately has to fall foul of another aspect. The failure of Goldthorpe and

Hope's measure clearly shows the quite separate force of the three initial critiques. They try to accommodate social and linguistic variation by demonstrating a consensus of first-order opinion. Whatever one's views on the nature of the 'consensus' that emerges it is clear that in itself it offers no solution to the problem of numerical vagueness. It is clear that this consensus does not and cannot display itself. It is the means of specifying the consensus and not the first-order conceptualisations themselves which give the measure its numerical properties.

3.2. WORDS AND THINGS AND NUMBERS

Although the imposition of formal properties onto the subject's perceptions is quite evident in this particular example, there always lurks the suspicion that such findings might be unique to specific studies. The meaning imposition problem in the Hope–Goldthorpe scale is in fact not due to shoddy practice nor technical error on the researchers' part, rather it is the inevitable consequence of trying to engage in the mathematical representation of ordinary language forms. I could try to make this case using further examples of scaling method and indeed, elsewhere (Pawson, 1982), I have extended precisely the above critique to the most sophisticated analysis of occupational cognition (Coxon and Jones, 1978, 1979a, 1979b). These authors invited their respondents to engage in much less directed tasks to do with the sorting of occupational titles and subjected their responses to forms of analysis which made less definite assumptions about the numerical arrangements into which the interpretations fell. However, I demonstrated a general rule in the above paper that such amendments merely change and cannot ever rid scaling methods of the need to impose certain assumptions about how the subject perceives the social world. Readers interested in a fuller and more technical examination of this claim are directed to the above paper, as well as a subsequent exchange on the issue between Coxon (1983) and myself (1983).

Here I want to clinch my thesis in a more fundamental fashion by demonstrating the contradiction that lies at the root of all scaling methods. Scaling is premised on the assumption that it is possible to come to some privileged formal description of ordinary language. I want to argue that the characteristics of ordinary languages and mathematical languages are such that the very task of the direct representation of one in terms of the other is impossible. As long as measurement remains locked in trying to achieve this transition directly, this contradiction is insurmountable. What this problematic omits, however, is a place for a third language, namely sociological theory. Introducing this into the picture will show us a potential path to measurement which takes us beyond the incompatible traditions in which it is normally rooted.

Formal discourse

Taking formal or mathematical languages first, it is customary to think of them as the embodiment of deductive thinking; mathematical systems develop according to the axiomatic method, all the propositions of mathematics being derived from a few basic axioms or postulates that are taken to be true without proof. The mark of the deductive power of mathematics is precisely that the inexhaustibly numerous theorems and propositions that constitute its superstructure rest on a relatively tiny axiomatic base.

A question that bothers the novice more than the working mathematician is why a particular set of propositions is accepted as axiomatic, what principles underlie the selection of primitives in a mathematical system? The fact that they are supposed to be self-evident is often not quite so self-evident to the uninitiated. It turns out that this simple question is the one that concerned a number of mathematical gurus for a century or two. Mathematicians from Hilbert to Russell strove towards the complete axiomatization of mathematical systems. The attempt was made to simplify and strengthen the axiomatic base of mathematics, not by determining the truth of the supposedly self-evident, but by demonstrating the internal consistency of the axioms which are basic to a particular system. Self-consistent axioms should find a logically consistent totality of propositions. This episode itself foundered on all kinds of inconsistencies and was finally rendered redundant with the publication of Godel's Proof in 1931 (Godel, 1931; Nagel and Newman, 1959). Godel proved that it was impossible to demonstrate the internal logical consistency of a very large class of deductive systems, even the propositions of elementary arithmetic. The full implications of the fact that mathematical proof does not coincide impeccably with the doctrines of the axiomatic deductive approach need not detain us here, other than to note the key fact that there is an irreducible level of presupposition built into any mathematical system. The relationships within any formal language will rest on a few basic elements whose structure has to be taken for granted.

Whilst we mere sociologists probably have to take the mathematical proof of mathematics limitations on trust, what we can do is to see how certain taken-for-granted assumptions feature in the formal systems that are familiar to social research. A common theme of data analysis already mentioned is the idea that level of measurement dictates the statistical techniques that can be applied. There are recognizable families of statistical models each based on different assumptions about the measurement properties of the situation studied. However, following the above argument, it can be seen that the notion of level of measurement is by no means the primitive in these particular systems. To make use of a particular level of measurement is to make further assumptions that the world is composed of a set of basic elements which organize themselves into certain given configurations. Higher-level scales assume that there are a set of objects which can be meaningfully related by various mathematical operations and transformations (viz. relationships of transitivity, asymmetry, identity, equality and so forth are applicable). The use of the simpler levels of measurement allows us to shed some of these presuppositions but such a reduction does not lead to an end-point of a measurement system without built-in assumptions. Even the use of the simple nominal scale commits the researcher to a series of formal assumptions. To classify is to make certain unquestioned assumptions about what is being classified.

The formal requirements taken for granted in classification have come under scrutiny in a little-known paper by Reason (1979). He identifies the principal 'logic-substantive presuppositions of set theory' as *identification, atomism, application* and *relevance*. Although it is not possible to go into the derivation of these principles here, I think they will be recognizable enough to anyone who has had to classify or code survey data. The principles of atomism and identification imply that the elements to be classified are logically quite separate from the classifications to be applied. This is the direct equivalent of the rigid separation of the unit of analysis from the variables in a data-matrix in survey research. I exist as a separate entity from the classifications which can be applied such as bespectacled, male, sociologist and so forth. Hence in the formal world of set theory, it is a prerequisite that at least one further analytic distinction must apply which allows for the differentiation of various kinds of objects and different kinds of classifications. The other principles of application and relevance serve to draw boundaries around the objects and classifications in order to facilitate the complete identification of sets. Again the survey equivalent requires us to delimit the population boundary to which the classifications are to be applied (I could appear in a survey of Leeds, British universities and so on). Also rules are required identifying the relevant characteristics of the classifications used (our surveyor would have to know what counts as a spectacle-wearer, as a sociologist and so on). It turns out, then, that the apparently simple and intuitive act of classification embodies a whole series of further assumptions about classification. Although these further principles are quite unremarkable they are quintessential to the idea of classification. Reason summarizes the matter well, 'all formal representatives of "classification" trade on prior classifications which are not formally representable, formally articulable' (Reason, p. 5).

The formal demonstration of the failings of our intuitive grasp of the notion of classifications occurs in Russell's *Principia Mathematica* (1910). His basic task therein was the reduction of mathematics to logic, the elimination of numbers in favour of classes. This objective foundered precisely because the notion of class is not as pellucid as it would seem and that its intuitive usage can drive us into contradiction. The contradiction that Russell discovered was based on the fact that there are two types of classes, those which are members of themselves and those which are not. The paradox that emerges concerns the status of the class of all classes that are not members of themselves. It is by definition an example of both types of class and thus a contradiction. The attempt to solve this antinomy lead Russell to construct a whole new axiomatic base for classification, usually referred to as the theory of types. In other words, further presuppositions, such as the logical separation of objects from their classifications mentioned above, need to be included to buttress the use of any mathematical system grounded on classifications.

To conclude, classification and set theory are more or less the simplest mathematical operation and structure. Even they clearly exhibit this characteristic of all formal languages in that they inevitably presuppose a whole series of conditions in their construction. It is these presuppositions as much as their propositions that require attention in any application of formal languages.

This is, in fact, the ultimate source of difficulty in the formal description of natural language. The underlying formal presupposition of all scaling techniques is that there is this basic set of elements which can be classified, ordered and related in various ways. This principle of identification, the logical separation of any object from relationships or categories it enters into, is inviable. I am going to argue that as a rule no such conditions apply in natural language and that they only pertain in scaling methods because they are realized, quite deliberately but also quite artificially, in the very first stage of the strategy, namely the compilation of the set of items to be scaled by the respondents.

The constituent elements of item pools, of course, vary according to the property being scaled. Here I will continue to make the case in terms of occupational scaling though it should be noted that the point can be extended to any scaling method whatsoever. There are, of course, a variety of tasks and techniques applied within the method of occupational scaling but there is one preliminary stage that is common to all approaches, namely the selection of a specific set of occupational titles. This is such a taken-for-granted step that it hardly ever warrants a mention in technical reports. Coxon and Jones are probably the only researchers ever to verbalize the underlying presupposition.

> a concept is a cognitive structure consisting of a set of components embedded in certain relationships to each other. In the case of occupational concepts the basic components are presumably occupational titles themselves

such as 'diplomat in the US foreign service, joiner, combing jobber' (1979c, p. 124).

Innocuous as it sounds, this statement is in fact completely unwarranted. What is more it is the key to the whole strategy since it realizes the essential formal presuppositions at a stroke. The array of occupational titles chosen defies a set of individual elements as clearly as a set of guards on parade. It is this initial identification of units that regulates the forms of cognition applied more crucially than any other point in the method. It is this initial identification of primitive terms which is quite unknown in ordinary language.

Natural discourse

The structure of natural language stands in complete contrast to the axiomatic, recursive character of formal language. To put it rather generally, the distinctive feature of ordinary language stems from the fact that it is utterances rather than words which we produce and understand, so that utterances have to be the focus of any theoretical discussion of language. We do not possess direct access to the primitive elements of recognition; objects are not endowed with their own terminology which we somehow experience intersubjectively. Rather we come to understand words through the relationships and sentences in which they occur. This situation accounts for the key difference between the two languages – in everyday talk the postulate of identification of basic unit cannot apply. The logical separation of elements and classes required in formal languages has no ordinary language counterpart. There is no bedrock level of self-contained elements which, once recognized, stand as the units awaiting classification or insertion in some further relationship. We cannot study meanings by isolating words and investigating how they are located in relationships because the very usage of a word assumes its place in some relationship. Even the simplest ascription of a predicate in naming and recognizing objects involves the use of further conceptual distinctions. That is to say, we never recognize objects, we recognize them as something. We never directly perceive a chair but we recognize the object upon which you are now sitting as a chair. In the same way the correct attribution of a more abstract predicate (like 'situation' or 'impressionist' or 'occupation') assumes knowledge of a widening circle of relationships between ideas and things. In short, the objects referred to in natural talk are always embedded in some relationship. The ability to use a word is synonymous with the facility to express the relationships in which it enters.

All this has direct relevance for occupational cognition. Again, it is the case that I never perceive occupations as such, I recognize someone as having an occupation or some activity as an occupation being pursued and so on. The crucial point is that the relationships taken for granted in everyday speech have no natural unit, no primitive base. Generally speaking, and contrary to Coxon and Jones's formulation above, there is a whole range of occasions when we are engaged in occupational cognition without a set of occupational titles acting as the basic concept. Occupational talk might first of all turn on the vital distinction of whether you have any occupation or you are unemployed: it could concern itself with matters of boundary and definition, such as whether housework or casual work or voluntary work counts as an occupation; it could concern itself with drawing contrasts between occupational and non-occupational activities, such as that between work and leisure; it could contrast the difference between the formal and informal economy and discuss such matters as 'working on the side', the 'black economy' and so forth; it could concern itself with debates on the very purpose of working or the philosophy of pursuing a career. Pahl has recently drawn the attention of the discipline to such concerns in his *Divisions of Labour* (1984), in which he manages to write a whole book about work containing virtually no mention and certainly no invidious comparison of specific occupational groups. Though his target was undoubtedly wider, he could have been thinking of occupational scaling when he wrote:

A problem with many of the scholarly discussions of work certainly since the time of Adam Smith and Karl Marx, is that too much emphasis has been given to that work narrowly perceived to be connected with a specific conception of production and too little to the other productive work connected with reproduction and consumption. (Pahl, 1984, p. 19).

The point I am making is not simply about shifts in academic focus required by the coming of post-industrial society or such-like. Precisely the same objection applies to imagining that everyday occupational cognition operates along channels emerging from a pool of occupational titles. Think of the specifics which make up our day-to-day occupational discourse – the model chosen for the company car, my lecherous boss, the new shift arrangements, whether to join the breakaway union, the quality of the office carpet, the number of years that must elapse before my next sabbatical comes up, etc. None of these forms of occupational cognition can be captured in a formal language that requires we attend to concepts as a set of components embedded in certain relationships to each other.

Having pinpointed the key property which divides natural and formal discourse, it is useful to say a little more about how they go their separate ways in terms of how meaningful discourse is produced within them. Mathematical discourse, as noted above, is a virtually closed system. Once mathematicians have accepted an in-built level of presuppositions in the axioms of these systems then the meaning of a term is either set by definition or can be deduced according to the rules of derivation of that system. Thus a 'set' in mathematics is defined by simply listing all its elements within braces, e.g. { -1, 0, 1, 2 } or by indicating a characteristic property whereby we can determine whether or not a given object is an element of the set. So if $P(x)$ is a statement concerning x, then the set of all elements x for which the statement $P(x)$ is true is denoted by $\{x/P(x)\}$. The system builds on this base in definition and if, for instance, I know the rules for the 'union', 'intersection' and 'difference' of the two or more sets I can work out the exact membership of further sets so composed (Burton, 1965).

Now unlike these mathematical sets, in natural language no one property, or fixed set of properties, runs through a whole class of objects. The same term can index a variety of characteristics, each characteristic in turn can index a variety of others. Wittgenstein in a famous passage on games describes this ever-changing pattern of properties as 'family resemblance' as follows:

consider for example the proceedings we call 'games'. I mean board games, card games, Olympic games. What is common to them all? Don't say: 'There must be something common or they would not be called 'games'' – but look and see whether there is anything common to all. For if you look at them, you will not see something that is common to all, but similarities, relationships, and a whole series of them at that . . . look for example at board games with their multifarious relationships. Now pass to card games; here you will find many correspondences with the first group, but many common features drop out, and others appear. When we pass to ball games, much that is common is retained, but much is lost – Are they all 'amusing'? Compare chess with noughts and crosses. Or is there always winning and losing, or competition between players? Think of patience. In ball games there is winning and losing, but when a child throws his ball at a wall and catches it again, this feature has disappeared. Look at the parts played by skill and luck; and at the difference between skill in chess and skill in tennis. Think now of games like ring-a-ring-of-roses; here is an element of amusement, but how many other characteristics have disappeared! And we can go through the many, many other groups of games in the same way; and see how similarities crop up and disappear. And the result of this examination is: we see a complicated network of similarities overlapping and criss-crossing; sometimes overall similarities, sometimes similarities of detail (Wittgenstein, 1958, pp. 31-2).

This gives us the first key difference between the two language forms. In mathematics a set is defined in relation to a given property, whereas in natural language we can apply a seemingly limitless range of predicates to a given set of objects. Note, however that the argument has a further vital turn. One can see that to make the point that games possess no single common meaning, Wittgenstein has, in fact, to supply us with a list of objects which qualify as a game. Being mischievous we might say the common feature of his sample is the fact that Wittgenstein recognizes them as games. So somewhat perversely it seems that both propositions, one claiming to uncover a specific pattern or order between a set of terms, and one claiming there is no common denominator of meaning, presupposes that we do in fact naturally possess general samples of such objects. The point, however, is that such samples just do not exist independently of discourse, but they are continually constructed and reconstructed within language. This is precisely the case that Wittgenstein wishes to make, and having formulated the family resemblance argument from the point of view of the specific illustration, he characteristically proceeds to kick that ladder from beneath himself. It is a mistake, he argues, to think that 'family resemblance' implies that we are dealing with a set of objects or cases which naturally belong to a given type of set. Rather we are dealing with concepts and it is only by recognizing how we refer to a particular case that we provide a frame of reference through which we decide what further items might be related as part of the family. Wittgenstein constructs this version of the argument in a discussion of what a natural representative sample of 'green' would look like:

> Ask yourself what shape must the sample of the colour green be? Should it be rectangular? Or would it then be the sample of a green rectangle? So should it be 'irregular' in shape? And what is to prevent us from regarding it – that is, using it – only as a sample of irregularity of shape (Wittgenstein, 1958, p. 35).

We can now set down the full range of problems facing anyone set on producing a mathematical representation of ordinary language. Natural discourse operates without sets of primitive terms and the open texture of ordinary talk is demonstrated not only in our startling ability to apply a countless range of predicates to a given set of objects but in the manner in which these basic objects of discourse are circumscribed and recircumscribed in every utterance. Objects (or terms) have no automatic membership within any particular set, it is only when an utterance is constructed that we understand what is the object of discourse, and only then can we identify the potential families to which such an object might belong.

Scaling, of course, can never come to terms with such a language structure. It is premised on the astonishing assumption that our perceptions begin with a given set of objects which then mentally organize into hierarchies, subgroups, groups, etc., and it is the task of scaling to uncover the particular configuration involved. I have shown that there are no such permanent objects of discourse and that respondents accept the limitations of such an imposition because they are very tolerant of the games sociologists play. One concludes that, in linguistic terms, scaling is doomed to failure since it is an attempt to marry off the incompatible.

Sociological discourse

What is the significance of the above discussion for the prospects of sociological measurement? The fact that scaling provides us with arbitrary and contrived quantification does not mean that we can never represent the elements of the social world formally. I want to insist that these arguments which are fatal to scaling are not at all damaging to other strategies of sociological measurement. I will set down the prospectus for a more authentically sociological measurement in the next chapters but there is a need for a bit of preparatory ground-clearing, by way of disentangling the objectives of measurement from the objections voiced in the present chapter.

Measurement is not a modest enterprise; to measure is to lay claim to providing an objective and therefore privileged description of the elements of the social world. Given this it should be clear that no amount of inspecting first-order meanings will provide such a definitive measurement base for social research. For those interested in substantiating sociology there is no alternative but to locate an entirely fresh basis for grounding measurement statements and the prerequisite is the radical disengagement of the language of measurement from ordinary language.

Thus my suggestion is to throw out the bathwater with the baby. In rejecting the premise of scaling – that social measurement has to be faithful to the workings of ordinary language – I also repudiate the corresponding linguistically-based critique of measurement to which scaling is a response. In particular, there is a need to dismiss Schutz's postulate of adequacy, which in its strong form as defined earlier required that *each term* in sociological discourse should correspond to an equivalent item of meaning or action on the part of actors. Such a proposition amounts to highly contestable sociology but perhaps more surprisingly a profoundly mistaken piece of linguistics.

In terms of sociology involved, we have become very familiar with alternative interpretations which lay stress on the 'escape' of meaning from individual action. Simply because of the phenomena of the 'unanticipated conditions', and 'unintended consequences' of action, sociology deals with meaning structures that correspond to those of no one individual or group of actors. It follows that first-order meanings simply do not circumscribe the concerns of sociological discourse. One course of action open to measurement is thus to begin by reaffirming sociology's traditional objectives as the explanation of social structures, cultural reproduction, emergent processes and so forth. The precise nature of societal constitution is, of course, permanently open to debate, but I think that it is fair to say that all major social ontologists are moving to a position that rejects the primacy of human agency for one that assumes the duality of agency and structure. It is not for me (thank goodness) to say whether societal constitution is best expressed by a discourse that speaks of figuration (Elias, 1978), transformation (Bhaskar, 1979), or structuration (Giddens, 1984). Indeed I only need to adopt a minimalist position which is that empirical sociology needs to address forces and process which go well beyond individuals' interpretations and meanings. This accepted, it follows that measurement can abandon its implicit (indicator selection) or explicit (scaling) base in ordinary language and instead be subordinated to the theoretical language used in mainstream explanation.

More surprisingly, such a conclusion can find support on good linguistic grounds. In insisting on term-by-term correspondence between sociological and everyday discourse, the postulate of adequacy (as well as scaling) is flying in the face of what has been called the *locus classicus* of linguistics, namely Frege's principle, 'never ask the meaning of a word in isolation, but only in the context of a proposition'. This idea that utterances, and not terms or concepts, are the bearers of meaning has consequences in every corner of the philosophy of language. Thus the understanding of linguistic issues such as sense, reference, truth, translation and so forth are all treated holistically rather than at the level of component elements (Harrison, 1979). For instance, if we consider the issue of translation, it turns out that no two languages can be successfully translated on a word-by-word basis. In using a word appropriately in a given context a native speaker calls upon an enormous amount of general information about the world. To translate a term adequately thus requires the necessity of sharing some of this body of information (Quine, 1960). Such a holistic strategy thus has to be at the heart of any process of translation, be it from French to English, machine-code to Fortran, everyday discourse to sociology. This confirms the thesis here that sociological measurement cannot be based on the inspection and importation of singular terms from ordinary talk, however minutely their usage is dissected.

The real response to the phenomenological critique lies in a much more indirect and holistic understanding of the role of measurement in sociological inquiry. Without, at this stage, working out any precise model of the linkages between language–meaning–action–society, one can foresee some broad consequences for a measurement strategy. Indeed, there remains a need for every sociological theory to incorporate the idea that human action and meaning plays a part in the constitution of all societal processes and institutions. Thereafter, any specific claims about everyday meanings can be substantiated by evidence which relates to the consequences of collective reasoning (rather than address first-order meanings directly). The form that this evidence will take, including our knowledge of measurement properties, will be derived from the theory as a whole (rather than imitating first-order talk directly). The validity of the data in general, and measurements in particular, will be part and parcel of the examination of the theory as a whole (rather than the matter of how faithfully they correspond with first-order meanings).

By operating in this more roundabout fashion, measurement can come to peace with the three arms of the phenomenological critique, and it is on this note of harmony I should like to conclude. In terms of the first and broad objection concerning variation of meaning across different and cultural linguistic settings, we already possess a tolerable measure of agreement that common meanings must and do exist if only on a limited basis. Such agreed-upon meanings never announce themselves, of course, and indeed it would be part of the theorist's job, in explaining the consequences of action in the structuration of society, to designate the social and cultural boundaries wherein consensus can be said to operate.

The second critique, concerning the arbitrary assignment of numerical scales, changes markedly when it is understood that measurement is to be subordinated to theoretical rather than natural discourse. The latter cannot be formalized, the former may be. Such a claim, naturally, needs to be subjected to further investigation, which you will find in Chapter 8. I am not claiming here that the whole system of mathematical reasoning can be purloined for sociological discourse, merely that sociological discourse, unlike ordinary talk, can pay attention to the basic presupposition of all formal language mentioned earlier. So when sociologists use classes and categories and sets in the description of some social issue, they can be rigorous in the identification of the basic units of analysis. They can be clear in distinguishing objects from the relationships they enter into and so forth.

The third critique, about the imposition of meaning in the course of the research act, also changes markedly under these revisions. If, like scaling, the inquiry is seeking to discover the perceptual structures of the respondent, then meaning imposition traps the research in a vicious circularity. To employ a particular conceptual structure is to forgo knowledge of its salience for the respondent. If one attempts to prevent research from providing frames of reference, all we would do is to prevent any exchange of meaning. If, however, research priorities are set in sociological theory the data construction becomes a task of trying to encourage respondents to use particular conceptual structures required by virtue of the theory at issue. In this case one faces the difficult technical problem of how to draw the line between making absolutely clear what information is required and revealing the actual hypotheses under investigation. No one is suggesting that this is ever simple, as Chapter 10 will show. At this point I simply claim that it is better to attack a problem which is technically complex rather than logically and linguistically impossible.

Part Two

A MEASURE OF REALISM

To this point I have argued that measurement has been needlessly embroiled in debates about the instability of ordinary language because of the failure to appreciate that empirical data should be constructed from a grounding within the language of sociological theory. I face an obvious flaw in my argument in that it could be said against me, that it is all very well placing ones faith in the need for theory-guided measures, had not this already been deemed one of the pillars of anti-empirical methodology. If I recognise those arguments which equate theory-laden observation with the selective rather than objective use of evidence, how can I call for an avowedly theoretical approach in the construction of measurement? It is all very well for relativist and anarchist philosophers and structuralist and critical sociologists to be extolling the virtues of theory but for a supposed keeper of the faith of empirical sociology, isn't this rather like proclaiming 'contrived measurement is dead, long live contrived measurement'?

The proposition that all observation is theory-laden is as true in the most exact science as it is in sociology. Part 2 is thus devoted to discerning why the phenomenon of evidence being theorized to the core apparently presents such different problems in natural and social science. I will show that every phase of standard measurement practice in the physical sciences trades on whole families of laws and theories, and indeed the improvement of measurement systems is deemed to follow from the continuing incorporation of ever more detailed theory. In sociology, by contrast, the moment evidence is harnessed in support of a particular body of theory, opponents from a rival

101

school are ready with charges of selectivity and circularity. The lesson to be learnt from all this is that natural science has still much to teach us about the use of empirical evidence, but this has precious little to do with the empiricism that has been carried in sociology in the name of science. This central section of the book thus attempts to develop a new model of measurement which still assumes the centrality of empirical evidence in theory-testing but which abandons any notion of direct observation into the real world of facts.

Chapter Four

THEORY AND OBSERVATION: SQUARING THE CIRCULARITY PROBLEM

Writing in 1970, on the relationship between theory and observation, Hesse felt obliged to see the problem in the following manner:

> Rapidity of progress, or at least change, in the analysis of scientific theory structure is indicated by the fact that only a few years ago the natural question to ask would have been 'Is there an independent theoretical language?' . . . Now however, several radical and fashionable views place the onus on believers in an observational language to show that such a concept has any sense in the absence of a theory (Hesse, 1974 (1970) p. 9).

Nowadays, one would have to say that though such views are hardly fashionable, they remain radical in their impact amongst those unfortunate souls whose lot it is to ponder upon the nature of scientific investigation. However one looks at it, to accept the notion that all observation is theory-laden is to accept the total failure of all those models of science which suppose that observation, in and of itself, provides the bedrock of objective evidence upon which scientific theories stand or fall. The matter of how one conducts empirical inquiry after one has accepted there are no 'facts' out there waiting to be discovered is the subject of this chapter. The first section discusses the problems that ensue from the interdependence of theory and observation, as viewed from the standpoint of philosophy of science, engineering and sociology. Curiously enough, it is that group most closely involved in the production of empirical evidence (the measurement engineers) who are least awestricken by the phenomenon of theory-laden observation. The second and third sections of the chapter go on to consider the nature of the crisis in methodology that has developed as a result of the 'discovery' of the impregnation of evidence by theoretical concerns. The so-called 'circularity objection' and the 'incommensurability problem' are selected as the key issues. I am thus prompted to ask whether there is something that instrument engineers know about theory-laden observation which sociologists and philosophers have failed to discover. The answer, as we shall see, is yes!

4.1 ON TESTING 'THEORY' WITH 'THEORY'

To my mind the most remarkable thing about the debates on the theory–observation nexus is the extreme difference in reaction it has provoked in different academic circles. Particularly relevant to this discussion are three scholarly contexts within which one can describe the reception to the changing view of observational statements, very briefly, as follows: in the *philosophy of science* the impact was truly revolutionary – without resorting to hyperbole one can say that it changed the face of the discipline; in *sociology* it simply added another crisis (albeit a major one) to a subject which is and was rather fond of wallowing in 'coming crises'; in *natural science* (in other words, where measurement is both crucial and routine) the issue did not cause an eyebrow to be raised. The explanation for these discrepancies is far more than a tale of disciplinary narrow-mindedness, but rests crucially on important differences in expectations of the role of evidence and measurement in science.

It is worth enlarging on the problem (or lack of one) as perceived by these different schools of thought because sociology has undoubtedly been led astray in its understanding of the theory–observation linkage. Basically it has preferred to follow a view of the ramifications of the issue as perceived in the reconstructed logic of the philosophy of science and rather ignored the reasoning of those who design and use measuring instruments.

To begin with the philosophy of science, one must allow that there certainly is a problem caused by theory-observation interdependence. Indeed it is fair to say that understanding the

104

sense in which scientific method can be objective whilst relying on pre-interpreted evidence is *the* problem facing this area of philosophy. I think that virtually all contemporary philosophers of science would agree that it was the 'discovery' of the problem of theory-laden observation (alongside perhaps the 'problem of induction') that led to the abandonment of the long-time standard view of science – 'logical positivism'. This accord, however, marks the end of the consensus in modern philosophy of science, with different camps laying claim to have led the revolution and, of course, creating markedly different positions in response to the overthrow of the received view.

We need not worry here whether it was Duhem (1906), Popper (1934), Quine (1951), Kuhn (1961), or Feyerabend (1975) who gave the first authentic interpretation of the upshot for scientific inquiry of the lack of an independent observation language. What is important is the level at which the issue is addressed and the manner in which it is transformed. Most of these philosophers begin their deliberations at the level of the individual datum, often using illustrations of how the meaning of a particular observation is dependent upon the frame of reference of the observer (think of Hanson's perceptual illusions, or the much-used imagery of the twilight observations of the modern and medieval astronomers, one of whom 'sees' the sun setting, whilst the other 'sees' the upward rotation of the earth's surface). Such cases, alongside genuine examples of dispute over observational records from the history of science, are used by all concerned to make the basic point that scientific theories cannot and do not stand or fall at the level of concrete observations. Thereafter, bang goes interest in the construction of specific datum, as the vital question is perceived to shift in order to discover the real level of decision-making about the acceptability of scientific theories.

All the above-mentioned philosophers follow variations on such a course. If we take Popper as a representative of the rationalist wing of the argument, one finds him, as early as 1934, making assertions to the effect that the 'empirical base is not absolute' and that 'observational neutrality is impossible'. Thereafter we see him and his followers travelling via models of 'falsificationism', 'sophisticated falsificationism' and 'scientific research programmes' to the view that theories are structures which control what empirical work gets done, and permit only the most tentative parts of that structure to be modified by empirical evidence. Though they differ in their terminus, note that relativists travel down much the same road. Thus Kuhn's work on the *Copernican Revolution* begins with a technical discussion of the observational consequences of the difference between sun-centred and earth-centred cosmologies. These ideas are then woven into a theory of their cultural and historical context, ending up with the idea that the 'paradigm' controls not only how people interpret observation but more or less the entire range of activities within scientific investigation.

It would be extremely silly of me to deny that all this raises questions of the first importance; what I am saying is that trying to locate the precise nature of the ideas and interests which control the course of science can lead to the initial problem being lost. The argument has progressed by virtually discounting experimental and measurement design as the focal point of scientific activity, in an attempt to locate the true engine of scientific change. A vital question is obliterated in such a move, namely – how is it that the basic activities of experiment and measurement are carried on ever more routinely in natural science when their function is so problematic? An indication of the veracity of my assertion about the course of methodological interest in these disputes is that, apart from a coterie of publications in that branch of mathematical philosophy called the theory of scaling, there exist only a handful of texts devoted to the philosophy of measurement (Ellis, 1968; Berka, 1983; Kyburg, 1984), and two of these begin, quite identically, by expressing frustration at the lack of epistemological treatment of so fundamental an aspect of science and engineering.

If, after perusing this philosophical literature on the enormity of the issues generated by the theory/observation nexus, one turns to the writings of scientists and engineers on instrumentation and measurement, one receives as acute a sense of culture shock as it is possible to receive in the closed confines of the academic world. Not only is the language different (measurement it seems is a matter of transducers, transmission paths and signal processing) but it is quite clear that the very objective of measurement is to incorporate and embody within an instrument, principles derived from theoretical science.

106

Instrumentation is thus seen as a branch of engineering, and engineering is nothing other than application of the laws, theories, hypotheses and principles of theoretical physics. One is rapidly forced to the conclusion that the incorporation of theory into the observational domain is seen not as the problem, but as the true justification of measurement.

Let me illustrate this key idea through one simple example. Note that any and every example of physical science measurement could be used, since all of them are light years away from these models assuming direct and untainted observation. For instance, if one is measuring electric current, the simplest instrument available is the moving-coil galvanometer. This rests on the idea that if a wire carrying current is placed in a magnetic field it experiences a force. The whole point of the instrument is to attempt to design a device which will marshal, in detail, this theory of electromagnetic forces. One way in which this is managed is to wind the wire in a coil so that it will experience a torque when placed in the magnetic field. This torque is balanced by a return spring and current is measured by the resultant angular deflection. So, though we are able to observe 'directly' that the galvanometer needle moves, the interpretation of that movement relies on this theory of motion in electromagnetic fields. What is more, the complete construction of the instrument calls on a host of secondary theories - the galvanometer needle is set on jewelled bearings so as to minimize friction, it is as light as possible to deal with the effects of inertia, the whole instrument is encased to minimize the influence of extraneous magnetic forces and so forth. In a full analysis, one ends up by understanding that every nut, bolt, and washer in the instrument is the carrier of some physical principle or the other.

I will return to a fuller analysis of the language and understanding of measurement according to the 'practising engineer' in a moment. However it is worth noting here one of Sydenham's conclusions to a major study of the history of measuring instruments.

There is very little evidence before this century, of any measurement practitioner giving serious, prolonged, thought to the philosophy of measurement. Measurements were simply allowed to happen as an extension of what had

already been achieved. Development . . . occurred
nevertheless and has been able to advance enormously
without practitioners needing to be concerned with what
happens in the process by which knowledge is gained.
(Sydenham, 1979, p. 452).

The reason why there has been such progress without falling into
the fearsome traps and conundrums set by theory-observation
interdependence stems from a quite routine and unspoken
assumption about measurement, namely that it is carried out
using instruments. In other words, one uses machines, and
machines, to quote a simple dictionary definition, are 'devices
capable of advantageously utilizing a given form of energy or
converting it to another form of energy'. This taken-for-granted
step is the essential solution to any potential theory–observation
circularity. To put it simply, scientific theories concern the
properties within one energy system which are tested by
converting these properties into other systems.

Finally, let us consider the sociological viewpoint on whether
there is a problem due to the fact that observation is
theory-laden. Undoubtedly this issue leads to a great deal of
distrust at the level of the individual datum, simply because
opportunities for the preselection and reinterpretation of
evidence are so rife. Consider that most basic of all statistics,
information on the distribution of wealth. If I was a believer in
the trend towards 'equalization', I would simply go to the *Inland
Revenue Statistics* to find records showing high but dwindling
levels of ownership for the top percentages of wealth holders. If,
however, I was of the 'polarization' persuasion, I would discount
this information on the grounds that wealth holders are able to
disguise exact levels of ownership from such data-gathering
bodies, one such tactic being to spread wealth holdings amongst
their immediate family, thus creating the erroneous impression
of more equity in distribution. By contrast, I would select specific
material on share-holdings, perhaps at the multi-national level,
to demonstrate the increasing stranglehold of the wealth-holding
classes.

Even such a simple example of picking and choosing one's
evidence shows that there is indeed a problem for sociological
research and, as we have seen, reactions to it are diverse. On the

one hand we have the modified empiricist position, that however suspect the individual datum, one can move towards objectivity by increasing care in the selection, construction and combination of indicators. Others have followed the lead of the philosophy of science and perceive that the theoretical impregnation of observation forces us to rely not on data but discourse (the most extreme variations on this position having already been described in the introduction). Strangely enough, there is not a coherent position taking up the interventionalist, system-minded model of evidence assumed by natural science instrument makers. One might argue that this is only to be expected since, being realistic, one must be loath to refer to social science data collection under the term 'instrumentation', let alone 'machinery'. What is worthwhile, however, is to pursue the logic if not the technology of the instrument makers, for it points the way to a central position between theoretical and observational absolutism.

4.2   THE CIRCULARITY OBJECTION

Our little trip around the corners of the university campus has provided us with the full set of answers (namely yes, no and maybe) to the question of whether theory-laden observation can provide objective empirical evidence. It is now time to examine in detail the exact nature of this dilemma, by getting to grips with the problem in its simplest guise, namely in the construction and use of a single datum. The objection that arises in this most immediate and basic scientific act is usually referred to as the *circularity objection*. Hesse (1974, p. 33) describes it as follows: 'if the use of all observation predicates carries theoretical implications, how can they be used in descriptions which are claimed to be evidence for those same theories?' To put this another way – if, in constructing evidence with which to test a theory, we cannot avoid being guided by the same body of theoretical presumptions, in what sense can the exercise be objective? Someone advocating measurement as the test-bed for theories and yet accepting that all observations carry theoretical preconceptions would appear to be making a plea that we test theories with theories.

Such objections are, in fact, simple enough to crush, being in part semantic trickery and in part an oversimplification of the theory-testing process. The word-play involved in making the circularity objection seem so plausible is the imagery of present-ing 'theory' as a kind of all-embracing world-view, a kind of thought-control responsible for labelling everything in its path. One has a single theory at work whose task is to fit everything into the pattern. Explanation takes the form – 'the world looks like this and this is how property X fits in'. Evidence about the nature of X gets pummelled into shape along with everything else. Sociologists may in fact be excused for thinking of theory in this way because much structuralist/functionalist theory takes on a similar form. This is how capitalism works; this is how the family, class, education must fit in and this dictates how we 'look' at family, class, education, etc. If, by contrast, one looks at the role of theory in the construction of natural science instruments, one finds literally dozens of separate, partial theories at work. The circularity problem looks much less vicious as soon as one grasps that theory can have this much more open-ended structure.

In fact one can find a working solution to the so-called problem in the routine practice of instrument makers, in their use of a strategy that I will call the *transformational model of measurement*. Their purpose, to modify a phrase, is not so much to define properties as to change them. The guiding imagery is thus not *conceptual closure* but something more akin to *information transfer*. The basic strategy in the measurement of a physical property is to harness an output of energy from a physical system, transforming that output into some kind of 'signal' and transmitting that information to some kind of recording device. In short, what happens is that the scientist/engineer measures a property by constructing a system which creates interlinkages between that property and a whole series of further properties. Rather than the all-pervading, self-confirming theory guiding observation, what one finds in practice is a whole family of theories being called up to forge the connections involved in processing a datum.

We can begin to examine this 'information-transfer' notion of measurement in a little bit more detail by inspecting some of the components in an elementary model used to teach the idea of instrumentation system engineering (see Fig. 4.1).

110

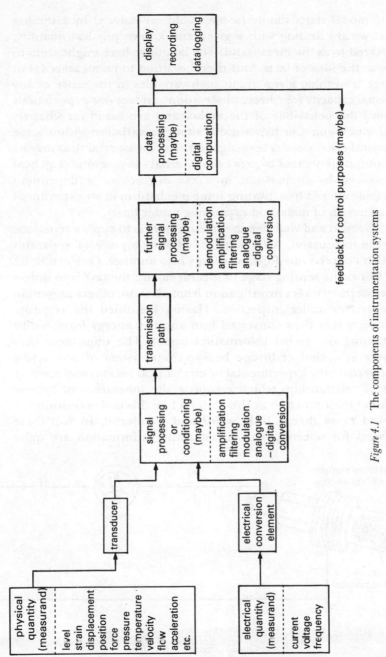

Figure 4.1 The components of instrumentation systems

Source: Open University T291, unit 1

The model starts simply (some would say naively) by assuming that we are dealing with a given and known physical quantity, referred to as the measurand. The language here might seem to evoke the idea of facts, 'out there', waiting to be measured, but there is nothing given about such variables in the sense of any special capacity for 'direct observation'. In fact our expectations about the behaviour of the measurand are based on what we know or assume or hypothesize about its variation within some physical system under investigation. The measurand thus may be an output generated by processes internal to a machine (e.g. heat produced by combustion in a car engine) or a dependent variable altered by activating some mechanism in an experiment (e.g. length of metal rod expanding under heat).

The next and vital step in measurement is to apply a *transducer* to the measurand. A transducer is simply a piece of apparatus which converts one form of energy into another. One can think of this as the sensing stage of measurement; the task is to isolate the property under investigation from all those others present in the system under inspection. Having identified the requisite property it is then converted into another energy form, whilst retaining the coded information signal. The transducer thus works as a kind of bridge between one system of interacting properties (the experimental or mechanical system) and another set of relationships which comprise the measurement system. Stating their function in the abstract like this makes transducers sound more than a little weird and wonderful. In fact these devices for selecting and transforming information are quite

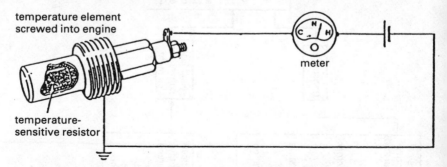

Figure 4.2 Electric resistance temperature gauge (motor-vehicle type)

(Source: Open University T291, unit 1

commonplace – a familiar example would be the temperature-sensitive resistor used to measure engine temperature in a motor vehicle (see Fig. 4.2). Heat is conducted into the resistor which is screwed directly into the engine. A voltage is applied to the resistor and the current in the circuit is regulated by the temperature of the resistor. Thus we measure one property via its relationships with another.

It is no exaggeration to say that experimental science became established with the ability to control and incorporate transduction processes into measurement apparatus. Sydenham, in the aforementioned history of instrumentation, lists some forty energy-conversion effects which were regularly implemented as measuring and controlling devices prior to 1800. Some of these are most familiar – e.g. pendular motion to measure gravitational force, liquid displacement to measure temperature and atmospheric pressure. Certain other pathbreaking devices may have escaped your attention – e.g. the saccarometer which measures sugar solution strength by the polarized light effect, and the actinometer which measures the sun's radiation by its chemical effect. Nowadays, of course, we buy transducers off the shelf and the energy-conversion principles they embody are so familiar as to become forgotten.

Apart from this idea of transduction, other aspects of the instrumentation system approach will repay examination by the social scientist. Initially here I want to make only the briefest inspection of the further stages in the process since direct analogies with social measurement rather come and go. What is of immediate significance is to confirm how every stage in the processes performs this function of the transfer and transformation of information. Referring back to Fig. 4.1, one notes that, after the transduction process, measurement utilizes some sort of *transmission path* for relaying the signal to its destination point in the system. Typical examples of such paths in natural science are electrical cables, pneumatic pipes and radio links. Once again this illustrates the inadequacy of that imagery which sees measurement as direct observation. In real measurement one always has to devise some sort of context to elicit the information. Properties do not reveal themselves – one has always to find some situation which coaxes the beast to perform.

The final, *data processing* stage of instrumentation embodies exactly the same idea of conserving, yet converting, information signals. The aim here is to render up the information in some way which suits the needs of the user/researcher. This is the stage where people typically become part of the information chain. Given our rather modest capacities for information handling, the processing, display and recording stages often consist primarily of devices which simplify the 'reading-off' process. A common example would be the analogue to digital conversion of an electrical signal. Once again a transducer is used for this purpose, in the form of an electrical device which produces electrical impulses at a rate directly proportional to the input signal.

To complete the picture according to Fig. 4.1, there is often a stage of *feedback* involved. Again this emphasizes the 'measurement as manipulation' philosophy of this school by considering other processes to which an instrumentation system might be conjoined. The most common objective of transformational measurement is to make measurements of a property in order to use the information to control that property. For instance, in the circuit involved in temperature measurement by electrical resistance (Fig. 4.2) one could include a feedback loop from the electrical gauge which would bring a cooling system into operation at certain prescribed temperature levels. A natural corollary of the idea that in order to measure a property one has to transform it, is that the transformational capacity can be put to use in the control of that property.

There are two absolutely basic points for social researchers to learn from the measurement strategies of instrument engineers. On a more general plane, we have to accept the total failure of the direct observation model of measurement to account for what is going on in these quite routine instances of measurement. The obvious implication here is that if we are going to be foolhardy enough to aspire to manufacture empirical evidence that plays as decisive a role as it does in natural science, then, at the very least, we must take care to imitate the authentic model. Rather than assuming an object representation model, and beginning at the level of so-called direct indicators, we need to duplicate that much more active process which relies upon the manipulation and control of situations to render up data. To summarize, social researchers could do no better than to follow the advice of Kuhn in a passage which grasps precisely the function of measurement in scientific discovery.

[It is possible] to indicate why new laws of nature are so very seldom discovered simply by inspecting the results of measurements made without advance knowledge of these laws. Because most scientific laws have so few quantitative points of contact with nature, because investigations of these contact points usually demand such laborious instrumentation and approximation, and because nature itself needs to be forced to yield the appropriate results the route from theory or law to measurement can almost never be travelled backwards. Numbers gathered without some knowledge of the regularity to be expected almost never speak for themselves. Almost certainly they remain just numbers (Kuhn, 1961, p. 174).

The second exemplary feature of the transformational model of measurement comes back to our immediate point of concern, namely that it provides a direct rebuttal to the circularity objection. One could not, for instance, suggest seriously to an instrument engineer that there is a vicious circularity involved in any attempt to measure engine temperature. I do not think one would get very far with the charge that theories and assumptions about engine temperature are simply reproduced in the measurement apparatus. Supposing for a moment that one could expect an answer when posing such a silly problem, then that answer could be made in the single word 'transducers' (perhaps you were thinking of another one!). To spell this out at its simplest, circularity is avoided since theories or expectations which lead us to inquire about the measured are not the theories and principles used in its measurement. In relation to the given example, the processes which cause the engine to heat (combustion, conduction, friction etc.), are not the mechanisms used to measure that heat (electrical resistance, electro-magnetism etc.), which in turn are not the principles used to display the data (signal amplification, modulation, conversion etc.) and which finally are not the methods used to regulate engine temperature (thermostatic expansion etc.). Unlike most sociological measurement, theoretical assumptions are not carried straight into measures and the process of transforming the measured into a different property (at least once) safeguards against directly self-confirming measurement.

4.3 THE INCOMMENSURABILITY PROBLEM

Next I want to see if this transformational model of measurement can be extended to provide an understanding of how empirical evidence can be said to adjudicate between rival theories. The phenomenon of theory-laden observation leads to a slightly different version of the circularity problem, if we suppose that there are two or more theories competing to explain certain events or phenomena. Utilizing the standard philosophical terminology we can refer to this as the *incommensurability problem.* It works like this – accepting the inevitability of the theoretical impregnation of observation would seem to allow that different bodies of theory will generate their own specific frames of reference as to what constitutes genuine supporting (or refuting) evidence for that theory. Theory A will lead us to believe evidence A is significant, theory B prefers evidence B and so forth.

The philosophical literature is full of (fictitious and semi-fictitious) examples of this dilemma, often in the form of dialogues between advocates of different scientific paradigms. The point is to show how the different schools talk past each other even when discussing the same observational report. The idea is that the theoretically informed selection and preference for a body of evidence leads to a position where it is impossible to perform any crucial experiments to adjudicate between theories, since they possess no common vocabulary. Every basic term takes its definition internally. Kuhn's basic example of incommensurability is that between the observational reports of Aristotelians and Galileans concerning the motion of a heavy body swinging back and forth on a string or chain.

> To the Aristotelians, who believed that a heavy body is moved by its own nature from a higher position to a state of natural rest at a lower one, the swinging body was simply falling with difficulty. Constrained by the chain, it could achieve rest at its low point only after a tortuous motion and a considerable time. Galileo, on the other hand, looking at the swinging body, saw a pendulum, a body that almost

succeeded in repeating the same motion over and over again ad infinitum. And having seen that much, Galileo observed other properties of the pendulum as well and constructed many of the most significant and original parts of his new dynamics around them. From the properties of the pendulum, for example, Galileo derived his only full and sound arguments for the independence of weight and rate of fall, as well as for the relationship between vertical height and terminal velocity of motions down inclined planes. All these natural phenomena he saw differently from the way they had been seen before (Kuhn, 1970, p. 119).

In short, the argument goes that theory choice involves us, quite literally, in a change of vision, leaving us without a neutral language of observational terms. The reason why philosophers of science can get away with such bunkum stems from the use of such broadly-based, contrived and theoretic examples. Theories are presented very much as singular world-views; it is the same story of that all-embracing, all-encompassing medium which defines the totality of scientific activities. I have already argued that the basic circularity thesis depends on this bogus assumption about a single theory directly informing every step in measurement practice. In a similar way the incommensurability problem looks quite different if one looks at genuine examples of theory competition. If we start with the more realistic image that evidence is culled via these series of information transformations then it is much easier to understand how there can be common ground between rival theories somewhere along the chains of reasoning. Scientists never perform measurement and experiments starting from scratch with the arrival of every new hypothesis (note, however, that sociologists come pretty close to just that). Even the simplest evidence, as we have seen, will call upon a host of primary and secondary theories during its construction. It is highly likely therefore that rival theories will employ common procedures and assumptions somewhere in their attempts to verify their own position. It is these *points of intersection* of theory packages, rather than the supposedly neutral language of direct observation, that become vital in theory-choice and prevent the lapse into complete relativism.

To show how this works one can look at a genuine example of theory competition in the science of pendular motion and forget for a moment those over-generalized fairy tales concerning schools of thought who 'see' a body coming to rest versus those who 'see' everlasting repetition. A good deal of the historical record on these matters has been set down in Koyré's (1968) renowned study of early experiments in the measurement of time using pendular motion. This particular study is of interest because it is often taken to lend support to the relativist's position since Koyré is writing about the potential circularities involved in the measurement of the gravitational constant (acceleration due to gravity) using an instrument (pendular oscillation) whose motion depends on the effect of gravitational force. Koyré's tale is basically one of the experimentalist's flagging and sometimes fraudulent attempts to produce results expected by Galileo's theory of the action of gravity.

In the early seventeenth century it was virtually impossible to measure acceleration due to gravity accurately, given the 'pitiful poverty' of the experimental means available. Galileo's famous inclined plane experiment used a 'hard, smooth and very round bronze ball' moving in a 'smooth and polished' wooden groove and measured time elapsed by weighing the throughput of liquid from a water clock. Koyré shows convincingly that the results obtained – 'spaces traversed were to each other as the squares of the times', simply could not have been obtained with the accuracy claimed. Indeed it took certain followers of Galileo to hit upon the idea of using a different and superior transducer, the pendulum, for the purposes of making more exact measurement of the time intervals lapsed by freely falling bodies.

Lacking exact knowledge of the properties of pendular motion the early experimentalists' work with such instruments was essentially a matter of trial and error. The beats of a pendulum appear regular and this led them to a range of investigations attempting to discover the properties which are significant in determining the periods of pendula of different construction, the aim being to devise a pendulum with a period of exactly one second. The most famous of these trials are those of Riccioli who used a 'human' clock, that is a team of Jesuit fathers trained to counteract the normal retardation of a pendulum by giving it a precise push after a given number of

118

beats and furthermore to count these beats on the basis of being selected for their 'gift for music' which allowed them to keep in time to the precise movement of the pendulum. (Note, even in the phase of crude operationalism, the use of secondary hypotheses.) Basically the problem that beset this entire school of measurement is that the experimentalists are all faithful to an (erroneous) assumption of Galileo's that motion along the arc of a circular pendulum is regular and follows the fastest line of descent. The consequence is that despite all Riccioli's ingenuity, and the lesser attempts of those such as Mersenne, a reliable instrument was never constructed. Once again, however, what is interesting to Koyré is that the experimental results produced with this defective apparatus 'confirm the Galilean law in so rigorous a manner that it is quite obvious that the experimenters have been convinced of its truth before starting' (1968, p. 107). All this of course invites the strongest interpretation of the theory-determines-evidence thesis, namely that results are carefully laundered to meet prior expectations.

Koyré's study ends by noting that the revolution in clock design does not occur until after this Galilean phase, instigated in 1659 by Huygens when he produced a formal demonstration that motion along the arc of a circle (as in the standard pendulum) was not regular; rather the quickest and most uniform line of descent followed a different geometrical pattern (the cycloid). In other words, the original trial and error approaches to pendular design are replaced by one based on a theory of how periodic time varies with distance of the axis from the centre of gravity (for details, see Feather, 1961, p. 187). The practical (engineering) problems of finding the means of constraining the motion of a pendulum to fit the cycloidal pattern remained before the Huygensian clock became established, but once this was achieved a basis for timekeeping was set which stood for several centuries.

Koyré concludes that the moral of this history is as follows:

We have seen Galileo, Mersenne, Riccioli endeavouring to construct a timekeeper in order to be able to make an experimental measure of the speed of the fall (the acceleration due to gravity). We have seen Huygens succeed, where his predecessors had failed, and by his very success, dispense with the actual measurement. This is because his

119

timekeeper is, so to say, a measurement in itself; the determination is already a much more precise and refined experiment than all those that Mersenne and Riccioli have ever thought of. The meaning and value of the Huygensian circuit is therefore clear; not only are good experiments based on theory, but even the means to perform them are nothing else but theory incarnate (pp. 112, 113).

This tale of two theories has been remarkably overstretched in the methodological literature, being used as ammunition for both the circulatory and incommensurability theses. Koyré can be read, in the final quotation, as suggesting that Huygens had no need to bother using his clock to determine constant acceleration because the principle of uniform acceleration is already embodied in the clock. Hindess (1973, p. 58) has in fact used the above quotation directly to support such a hard-line conclusion as being true in all instances. So for Hindess this episode simply confirms a general point that empirical evidence is always tautological and self-confirming. Such thoughts led him to become a founder-member of the structuralist school (described in Chapter 1) which goes on to conclude that theory choice can only be a matter for conceptual rigour and cohesion.

All this is vastly to overstate the circularity problem. The interdependence of theory and evidence produces self-guaranteed findings only in the case of the complete symmetry of hypothesis and measurement theory. So, indeed, we cannot use a theory of gravitational constraint on pendular motion to measure gravitational constraint. But we can use gravitational clocks as a measurement base in the assessment of any *other* processes which are affected by the passage of time – a list of which would be almost endless. Furthermore it is perfectly sound practice to measure the gravitational constant using instruments constructed without knowledge of that constant. Many of the experiments described by Koyré fall into this category, using what we would today call transduction principles. So, whilst Galileo's early experiment using a water clock to measure times of descent along an inclined plane may be technically primitive, it commits no sins of circularity. The theory under test (distance moved is proportional to square of elapsed time) is not the one presumed in calculating the measurand (constant outflow of water).

Coming back to the incommensurability problem, there would seem to be a *prima facie* case that, within this historical episode, the precepts of a school define its observational horizons. One could say that Galileans use instruments derived from Galilean theory, that these instruments generate the desired results and even when they do not, the findings are deemed well within obtainable limits of accuracy. Huygensians, starting with a different theory of fall, accordingly build different instruments and obtain different, self-consistent results, which once again by further (modern-day) standards probably would not hold up. Descriptively engaging as such a picture might be, it does not imply that each theory generates a unique and separate body of evidence, and that choice between the two is simply made according to theoretical or ideological preference.

In fact, it is (and was) perfectly easy to use empirical evidence to assess the superiority of different gravitational clocks. Recall that the early pendulum clocks were constructed on the basis of Galileo's assumption that motion along the arc of a circle is the quickest and most uniform line of descent. Huygens, as we have noted, later developed the mathematics to demonstrate the cycloid was isochronous and built a clock on these principles. How do we know which theory is superior? Clearly one is in trouble if one conceives, with the incommensurability thesis, that the only test of the Galilean theory is with the Galilean clock and the Huygensian theory with the Huygensian clock. However an independent test is quite evident – namely to have pendula of the same length set in motion instantaneously, though travelling along different geometrical curves. One should complete its period (or several periods) notably faster. Certainly there are theoretical assumptions involved in such a test, namely the hard-core assumption that a faster body covers the same distance in less time, but this is so basic it offends neither rival theory. In fact, if one reads Koyré closely, he points out that Mersenne made this discovery that circular motion was not regular well in advance of Huygens' mathematical theory of isochronous motion. Indeed, Mersenne experiments, showing that small and large circular oscillations were not performed in the same time, was one of the spurs to Huygens' discovery.

The real lesson of Koyré's tale is thus not really about the relative priority of theory and evidence. One can always debate how the precise balance is struck; for instance one could argue that Mersenne's experimental evidence is simply a matter of trial and error and we still require Huygens' theory to interpret just why large and small oscillations are not coincident. The point, however, is that both theory and empirical evidence have a role, since it is, in fact, the area of overlap between theories that is used to devise empirical tests to adjudicate between them. If one presumes that theories are not single conjectures but involve the usage of whole chains of ideas and propositions, then one can see how it is the area of intersection between bodies of theory that can provide crucial empirical evidence (cf. Hesse, 1974, p. 35). Thus though the Galilean and Huygensian theories differ radically in certain implications, both share a whole range of predicates, concepts, and laws about the basic mechanics of space, time and motion. It is the application of these common assumptions that provided the means to support the superior theory. This, of course, is not at all the same thing as 'withdrawal to a neutral observation language' but it provides a crucial empirical test none the less.

Where we stand

Let me pause now to take stock of the argument. I have tried to show that natural science has evolved some practical, indeed routine, answers to this philosophical puzzle that makes up the fourth of our fundamental problems about measurement strategy. Despite the undoubted influence of theory on the construction and design of measurement instruments, it is possible to use empirical evidence in a manner that is neither self-corroborating nor circular, providing heed is paid to the form of explanatory structures. I have argued that scientific research involves chains of reasoning, and that the whole point of explanation is to understand the network of relationships which make up a particular property. The key point is to think of measurement not so much as representing a given concept, but a way of interceding in these chains of reasoning. *Measurement is not operationalization but transformation.*

The ability of this revised model of measurement to resist both the brickbats and the blandishments of relativism rests on two key strategies: [A] the *transformation* process in which the measurand is converted to another property in order to avoid the circularity problem, [B] the usage of the *intersection* of chains of reasoning in order to find what is common to theories, in order to devise empirical tests that will differentiate between them. In due course I want to see what happens if we try to place these notions at the heart of a sociological model of measurement as replacements for the defunct objectives of the empiricist account.

First, it is important to say a little more about my understanding of the nature of these strategies. I am certainly not proclaiming them as key strategems of a new prescriptive methodology. These are not the heirs to inductivism, falsificationism, sophisticated falsificationism, and so on as the ultimate demarcation criterion, which will weed out good theory from bad theory and true science from the also-rans. It is not at all difficult to see what would happen if one attempted to elevate basic logic-in-use into the domain of reconstructed logic. For instance we would have to begin by formalizing the transformational strategy a little, perhaps stating it as the idea that we test theory A by measuring its constituent properties such as 'x', according to how 'x' is understood by independent theories B, C, D, etc, Now the relativist could always turn round here and say – how do we know that the concept 'x' in theory A is the same as the concept 'x' in theory B, C, D unless they really do share some basis in the same theoretical discourse? (e.g. 'time' in a theory of gravitational fall must bear some relation to 'time' in a water clock or there would be no reason for Galileo to regard his measure as relevant). In short, just how 'related' should an 'unrelated' test be?

To protect the transformational strategy as a fundamental scientific protocol one would then have to come up with some formulation of the appropriate relative levels of independence/interdependence between theories under test and theories in the test. Clearly even to attempt such a prescription would be an absurdity; it would be continually prey to relativists' arguments that what constitutes the requisite levels of theory/evidence independence is an internal and thus a social matter, open to whatever interests prevail in the scientific community. So, in forwarding the ideas of transformational measurement and the usage of the intersection of theories as the

123

key resources of empirical science, I am attempting to capture something much nearer to the actual reasoning processes of scientists when it comes to providing data to test a theory. My claim is that when scientists argue about what is a good experiment, what constitutes valid empirical evidence and so forth, they will conduct the debate in terms of how strongly observational reports are influenced by the theory under test, whether observations could support rival hypotheses and so on.

In this respect it is worth examining some of the literature from the strong programme in the sociology of science. Collins (1975, 1981), in particular has produced some influential work which relates to how science operates in the absence of a secure observational base. He shows that the physics of 'gravity waves' poses some particularly interesting problems of measurement since empirical work in the area is performed with the aim of detecting gravitational radiation caused by violent events in the distant universe such as exploding supernova, black holes, etc. Einstein's theory predicts that these waves should be detectable on the earth as a minuscule oscillation in the value of the gravitational constant. The problem is that the apparatus which has to be built to register such forces is so sensitive that precautions have to be taken to prevent someone sneezing in an adjoining laboratory producing a reading (well, almost!). The measurement antennae (or transducer as we professionals say) is in fact an aluminium alloy bar, of several tons, suspended in a vacuum chamber in an attempt to insulate it from other potential electrical, magnetic, thermal, acoustic and seismic disturbances. Interpreting the recorded signals from the apparatus is thus notoriously difficult and an argument has followed, full of personal and political overtones, about whether a genuine effect of gravity waves has been discovered, or whether results are artefacts of 'noise' generated by the action of these other forces.

Collins uses this tale as another example of the hackneyed old story that scientists masquerade as purveyors of objective knowledge whilst the necessary and inevitable process of the interpretation and re-interpretation of evidence really renders them slaves to social preferences and influences. He is able to get away with this only because his sociological audience still finds it news that hard science does not depend on hard facts. What is really interesting about the gravity wave experiments is how the arguments between the different schools of thought are conducted. They too discount the notion of 'hard facts' and concern the effectiveness of the transduction process, the elimination of noise in the transmission path, devising experimental variations at the intersection of theories which would allow researchers to distinguish between rival theories and so on. For instance, one way of distinguishing between 'local' noise and gravity waves was to have two widely separated antennae and examine them for coincidental excitations. The point, despite Collins's tittle-tattle about the dastardly motivations of the personnel involved in the rival camps, is that scientists bother to perform such experiments, they need to be seen to be performing them, and they use standard techniques of seeking empirical evidence at the intersection between rival theories.

In summary, I would claim that these ideas of transformational instrumentation and utilizing the intersection of theories as the source of empirical evidence are at the heart of measurement practice, from the most routine engineering application, to the most tentative frontiers on the boundary of theoretical and experimental physics. So whilst I would be first to agree that one cannot pre-specify which measurement transformation will be most useful, which theories will provide crucial areas of intersection and so forth, I would claim that such strategies are at the very core of empirical science. In sociological terms one would say that the *rules* of transformational measurement and intersectional evidence are best understood as both *medium* and *outcome* of research practice. Thus at one level (instrument engineering) they are simply matters of routine; one can choose between available transducers, one generally prefers to convert to an electrical signal because of display advantages and so forth. At another level (gravity wave detection), these are matters for negotiation; scientists attempt to use similar chains of reasoning, it is simply a question of some linkages being highly contentious. But then, as the pendula motion examples showed, the disputes of one generation become the transducers of the next.

Chapter Five

ON BEING 'EMPIRICAL' WITHOUT BEING 'EMPIRICIST'

I have established that the incorporation of theory within measuring implements is the objective rather than the problem of physical science measurement. The purpose of this chapter is to examine in much greater detail what it is about the structure of scientific theories which provides the platform for the construction of empirical evidence. These further explorations of natural science explanatory structures are vital for preparing the ground for comparisons back into sociological method. Valuable as they are, the lessons we have learned to this point about transformational measurement are tied closely to the physical manipulations involved in experimental production and instrument engineering. Accordingly one could argue that the strategy of measurement being advocated depends significantly on the fact that objects in the natural world are open to regulation in ways that the social world can never be.

Such a view omits cognizance of the whole range of other methodological considerations which provide the rationale for, and thus make sense of, these manipulations in the first place. Moreover, arguments for sociological naturalism are always going to be more plausible at the level of explanatory structure. Thus, rather than build bridges directly at the technical level (which is the very fault of variable analysis) it is necessary to draw some initial analogies between the structures of theoretical reasoning in science and sociology. Thereafter one is in a better position to see how these explanations can be supported by data, by rethinking the details of transformational measurement as appropriate to a social context.

In what follows I will show how the practical features of

126

measurement uncovered in Chapter 2 make sense in terms of the broader objectives of routine physical science investigation. In order to do this I will piece together some ideas from those 'post-empiricist' philosophies of science which have gone beyond an understanding of theory as singular propositions relating observable regularities. To gather these ideas is in fact no simple task, not the least because 'post-empiricist' philosophy is represented by no single school, nor any one guiding framework, save the most general aim of reasserting the notion that scientific theories can be adjudged in terms of their correspondence with the world, whilst at the same time granting that the internal linkages within scientific theories play the significant part in establishing the meaning of concepts. Given these rather abstract aims and some diversity in terms of philosophical method, it is certainly not the case that post-empiricist philosophy will deliver up any ready-made alternative to highly-developed strategies like 'variable analysis'. However, lest all this sounds rather too capricious a basis for a reconstruction of empirical research let me acknowledge that I am referring to certain of the *realist* models of science, associated with Harré (1972, 1978), Hesse (1974) and Bhaskar (1979) as well as other aspects of Lakatos' (1970) theory of scientific research *programmes*. What I want to try and do is to distil and develop the more descriptive elements on scientific practice from the works rather than to hanker after any ultimate defeat of relativism from which stems the philosophical interest in them.

Basic to the aforementioned philosophies are a range of related themes, namely the ideas of *generative causation, experimental closure* and the *network model of theories*, which I want to examine in detail. These were developed partly as correctives to the empiricist model of science, and it is interesting to see how well they adapt as criticisms of existing sociological research. However, I do not intend to rake over these old coals again, as the purpose of presenting these post-empirical ideas is to see if they foster a new way of thinking about empirical inquiry.

5.1   GENERATIVE MECHANISMS

Perhaps *the* distinguishing feature of realist philosophy of science is its view of causality. Throughout the history of philosophy a brawl has gone on between the proponents of competing accounts of the nature of causation. Best known is the rivalry between what Harré (1972) calls the *successionist* and the *generative* accounts. Both start from the supposition that scientific knowledge trades on the fact that certain sequences of events are linked by causal laws whereas others are regarded as coming together randomly or accidentally. Successionists, following Hume, argue that we cannot observe causality but only the sequence of events themselves, and we decide upon causality on the basis of the regularity of the joint occurrence of the events in question. These ideas live on in certain statistical and quasi-experimental methods of 'inferring' causation from patterns of observed regularities (viz. causal modelling). Generative theory, by contrast, holds that there is a real connection between causes and their effects, in the form of some 'natural necessity' which links the two. In short it posits that there is a more basic level of reality than the event, namely the process or mechanism. It is the activation of this underlying mechanism which brings about particular sequences of events. This means that so-called 'events', properly understood, are not discrete items but really the parts of an object or the components of a system. Moreover the causal link between these events is a matter of the 'causal powers' or 'liabilities' or 'ways of acting' or 'tendencies' of the underlying objects or systems.

Each of these metaphysical theories comes supported with its own favourite examples which I will borrow here from Harré (1972) and Sayer (1984). If we think about one billiard ball causing another to move, all we observe, according to successionists, is one event being followed by another; the presence of a mysterious underlying mechanism not being required to explain our expectations about action and reaction. On a more specifically scientific plane, this school would argue that we know the laws of gravitation with great precision whilst having precious little idea of the mechanisms of gravitational action. By contrast the generative style would be more adept at explaining matters such as why it is that certain people can jump seven or more feet into the air. The answer would lie with the 'powers' of high jumpers associated with particular features of their anatomy and musculature. Similarly one would explain the ability of certain metals to pass electric current because of the 'power' of that metal to conduct which depends on the presence of free ions in their molecular structure. Even within a discipline one finds rivalry over the understanding of causality most appropriate to its problems. Thus in medicine, the epidemiologist works with a model much closer to the successionist one in trying to discover the social and physical correlates of disease; the research clinician prefers to understand causation in terms of the progress of the biochemical mechanisms which actually constitute the disease.

Debate between these paradigms has, by all accounts, rather waxed and waned, until recently realism (in the shape of Bhaskar (1979)) entered the fray with a simple but devastating critique of the successionist view. His objection is that the discovery of the regular sequences on which the successionist view relies, is in practice dependent on the experimental activities of the scientists. Experimentation, of course, is hardly the same as routine observation; there is no need to detail here the complex, contrived and artificial situations that are manufactured in the course of successful laboratory work. It is part of the folklore of experimentation that the 'desired' results need to be worked for, that experiments never work 'correctly' the first time, and indeed that in teaching laboratories novice experimenters manage to 'refute' the classic experiments as often they 'replicate' them. What is more, the very point of carrying out observation under experimental conditions is the assumption that the regularity observed would simply not 'happen' in everyday conditions. One would not expect to find any constant relation between the pressure and temperature of the air in this room but would only bother to seek such a law for a fixed mass of gas under specific controlled conditions.

For Bhaskar the crucial failure of the successionist school in their search for the relationships between *events* is the failure to take into account the *event* constituted by the scientists' activities —

> Notice that as human activity is in general necessary for
> constant conjunctions if one identifies causal laws with them
> then one is logically committed to the absurdity that men, in
> their experimental activity, cause and even change the laws
> of nature! (1979, p. 12).

Thus if one is not prepared to say that regularities happen universally and spontaneously, nor is one prepared to say that it is people who determine physical laws, one is left with the need to explain empirical associations at some more basic level of reality. According to realists this requires that we turn to an understanding of the nature of the things investigated, and it is the kind of things they are which gives them their tendencies, liabilities and powers. The purpose of experimentation is thus to activate these internal mechanisms, and it is only these artificial and controlled situations which we can rely upon to trigger off the regular and certain interaction between the component parts of the thing or system studied. More generally, it follows that real causal explanation depends on the ability to answer the question of why regularities exist in terms of the mechanisms that generate them. Mechanisms thus become the basic unit of both the world and of explanation.

One thing needs to be made perfectly clear about the precise understanding of mechanisms here, especially to sociological readers accustomed to standard path analytic representation of causation. A generative mechanism is not the same thing as a 'spurious' cause or an 'intervening variable'. Figure 5.1 is an attempt to represent the different objectives. When realists say that the constant conjunction view of one event producing a second event (model A) is inadequate, they are not claiming the problem is resolved by the introduction of further variables into the picture. So the idea is not that there might be an external cause bringing about a spurious relationship between the original variables (model B), nor that the original relationship is indirect and really works through an intervening variable (model C). The idea of a generative mechanism is that it is responsible for the relationship itself (model D). A mechanism is not thus a single *variable* but an *account* of the constitution and behaviour of those things that are responsible for the manifest regularity. For instance if X and Y are the temperature and pressure of a gas, the idea is that one can never find a satisfactory explanation for their interrelationships by examining associations with further variables (volume, colour, etc.), but that an explanation in terms of the action of the molecules that constitute that gas is more likely to be fruitful.

130

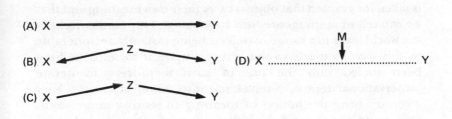

Figure 5.1 Models of causation

This notion of shifting the axis of inquiry to the discovery of the underlying features beneath the surface of appearance has proved an attractive one. In the social and biological sciences especially, the idea has intuitive appeal since it seems to describe a common denominator of all such inquiry, namely the investigation of the significant features of particular societies and organisms which give rise to particular behavioural possibilities. As we shall see, however, the methodological injunction to 'seek out underlying mechanism' is really just too generous. Everyone is able to recognize it as their very own *modus operandi*. To appreciate properly the importance of generative mechanisms it is necessary to examine some further detail of the realist analysis of natural science, namely the extension of the idea into a model of meaning and model of verification.

Meaning and models

It is to the understanding of the meaning of scientific terms according to post-empiricist philosophy to which I now turn. I have described in general terms how post-empiricism turfs out the notion of 'direct observation' in favour of a view which allows for the theory-ladenness of observation. Of course, it is not sufficient to gain the pyrrhic philosophical victory achieved by merely saying this, without providing some alternative theory of the meaning of scientific terms which does not leave us with the opposite dilemma of being left with an understanding of properties which is entirely relative to a body of pre-chosen theory.

Empiricism, for all its faults, operates with a very clear understanding of the meaning of terms. In its crudest versions it is taken for granted that objects carry their own meaning and that we can tell what things are 'just by looking'. Our familiarity with the world leads to a range of objects being instantly decipherable in this way, so much so that many empirical sociologists have been fooled into the use of such a process to define 'observational terms'. Natural scientists have, of course, long given up tying the notion of meaning to sensory impressions. One could just about defend the notion of observational terms through examples claiming that concepts like 'temperature' are synonymous with our rough-and-ready ability to sense 'hot' and 'cold'. However such direct perceptions are made on the basis of an understanding which does not even recognize fundamental scientific distinctions between 'heat' and 'temperature'. (Heat is the stuff that makes things hotter, whereas temperature only shows how hot the thing is.) We can thus be easily fooled in our estimates of temperature, by not taking into account the 'amount' of matter that has been heated. This is especially so if we are acting as the direct sensor and we are the matter being heated. The understanding of the notion of a temperature scale thus does not really get started in physics without an appreciation of the conceptual connections between temperature, heat, mass, specific heat and so forth.

We have seen that the most sophisticated empiricist approaches acknowledge the utility of such theoretical terms in scientific explanation and attempt to account for their usage in

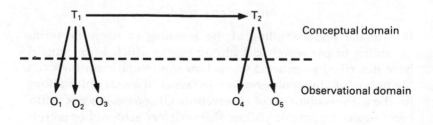

Figure 5.2 The two-language model

132

so-called *dual–language* models. The idea is that theoretical terms (T) like heat, virus, gene, elementary particle and so on describe ideas which are abstract and general, common to many different theories and not susceptible to observation. These contrast with the world which can be directly observed, manipulated and rendered up as observation terms (O) like temperature, pressure, mass, etc. The two languages are linked however through *rules of correspondence*; scientists work at both levels and check upon the veracity of theoretical ideas by slipping down the appropriate correspondence channel into the world of observables. In fact the multiple-indicator models of measurement described in Chapter 2 provide the clearest exemplification of the underlying logic (as well as neat diagrammatic representation of the idea – see Fig. 5.2).

On the double-language view, a kind of 'pyramidality' of scientific knowledge is assumed whereby the general laws will link abstract entities, whilst empirical tests will be performed with whatever local and specific indicators one can muster in specific observational circumstances. I will not repeat, chapter and verse, all the difficulties associated with this approach (see Chapter 2, verse 2). The basic problem is that although the two-language view quite properly recognizes these two different levels of activity, it does so in a manner which is totally ambiguous as a theory of meaning. If theoretical terms each have a number of correspondence rules, then as we have seen in both social and natural science examples, the possibility arises that the observational record will show these rules are incompatible. How then does one choose the appropriate correspondence rule? For instance, suppose T (in Fig. 5.2) is the concept temperature and the available indicators are O_1 –sensory observations (feeling hot and cold again), O_2 – liquid thermometers (several types), O_3 – thermopiles (not the painful type) and so on. These would undoubtedly give conflicting results in any particular experimental setting. The selection of the appropriate correspondence rule would have to be made either by some arbitrary operational preference or by reference to the theoretical postulates which led to the development of a particular indicator. Any notion of correspondence as the meeting of two realms is thus lost to a model entirely defined and determined at one or other pole.

Post-empiricists get to grips with this problem by regarding the distinction between theoretical and observational concepts as a practical rather than logical or metaphysical one. It is assumed that some of the concepts we use will be identified with empirical operations as a matter of routine, whilst others will play a part in the unseen, underlying mechanisms that order the regularities we can observe. Such distinctions are not a feature of the respective concepts (or objects) themselves but are merely a function of their overall place in explanation. Hesse provides a useful summary of this change of perspective.

> it need not be denied that there is sometimes a useful distinction to be made between comparatively theoretical and comparatively observational descriptions. . . . But this does not mean that the distinction is more than pragmatically convenient, nor that the correspondence rules form a logically distinct class of statements with unique status. Statements commonly regarded as correspondence rules may in different circumstances function as independent theoretical postulates, as theorems, as inductive inferences, as empirical laws, or . . . as analytic definitions. There is no one method of bridging a logical gap between theory and observation. There is no such logical gap (Hesse, 1974, pp. 39, 40).

Most post-empiricist theories use some version of a systemic or holist theory of meaning. The idea is to try and capture this idea that science is not the study of external relationships between

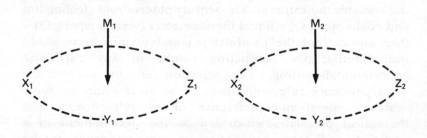

Figure 5.3 The systemic model of meaning

discrete objects or events, but an investigation of a system of internal relationships brought about by the occurrence of an underlying mechanism which connects the parts of the system. Regardless of whether they play a relatively theoretical or relatively observational role in the final version of a particular explanation, the meaning of all terms can be established internally via a *model* of the working of the internal mechanism. We can make a start in distinguishing this idea from the double-language model by contrasting Fig. 5.3 with the previous diagram.

On this view concepts derive their meaning by being viewed as components of a system. The idea is that one can only understand a particular property (X) as part of a series of interrelated properties (X,Y,Z etc.). These properties form a system and the variation in the component properties are caused by the changing action of the underlying mechanism (M). Figure 5.3 shows how the whole system varies as M passes from state to state. I have marked the interrelationships between the component properties by a dashed line to indicate they are initially to be thought of as analytic relationships, internal to the particular model. It is only later in the process that some of the properties are identified by observational instruments.

To say all this is not simply to say that the meaning of terms is learned discursively. One could undoubtedly argue that we learn to use any predicate in ordinary language via the way we speak of the relations it enters into (e.g. 1: *'balls'* are *round*, they *bounce*, we play *games* with them; e.g. 2: *'capitalism'* is the *mode of production* which depends on the *exploitation* of *labour* by *capital*). Science depends on a very specific version of this holist theory of meaning. The idea is not that we depend on an open-ended system of relations which can be used to define and redefine terms but that meaning is ascribable within a 'closed system' or 'model' in which all the terms in the discourse are derivable from an understanding of the underlying mechanism.

We can now pick up the example of temperature again as a prime example of this realist theory of meaning. The early use of the concept was marked by an empiricist phase wherein usage of the notion was tied either to specific indicators (length of liquid column) or general conceptualizations (degree of heat). Not surprisingly notions of appropriate scales and units were, at this stage, essentially arbitrary. We know now, of course, that many of the basic properties of solids, liquids and gases can be explained at the microscopic level. The great leap forward in the understanding of temperature came when the behaviour of gases in heating under compression inspired the thought that such a process might be explicable in terms of molecular action.

In kinetic theory, temperature is no longer considered as a given property of a mass of gas, but instead the guiding notion is to understand the gas as a closed system. It is by *trying to understand how this system passes from one state to another that we comprehend the nature of the variation of its component properties.* The model, proper, begins with an analogy comparing gases to a swarm of microscopic, perfectly elastic particles in motion in a confined space. Bernoulli is usually credited with the idea that the motion of the particles would produce *pressure* by bombarding the walls of the container, and suggesting furthermore that raising the *temperature* of the gas must make the particles move faster. More formally we might say that the mechanism of molecular action allows us to define pressure as the resultant force exerted on the wall and gas temperature as the overall level of molecular activity (the average kinetic energy). Creating a mathematical model of this mechanism allows us to derive exact expressions for those properties. So if M is the mass of molecule, V is velocity, L the length of the container and N number of molecules, it is possible to use the laws of classical mechanics to derive the expression for the force exerted on the walls ($F = NMV^2/3L$). Further if we derive an expression for the kinetic energy of the molecules ($E = NMV^2/2$), these equations can, with further substitution of terms, provide an entirely theoretical derivation of the gas laws (PV/T = constant). (For an elementary account of this derivation see Rogers, 1960.)

Whilst such an example hardly sets realistic standards for sociological theorizing, it is most instructive as a point of comparison for the derivation of the meaning of concepts. A mathematical model of the underlying causal liabilities of the system will give us advance notice of the parameters of its constituent properties. It tells us, to put it succinctly, how a variable varies. In other words, such models prespecify the internal composition of a concept, they tell us if it varies continuously or whether it is categorical, they tell us what might constitute a zero point and so on. In short, they answer some of the dilemmas raised in social science about the appropriate *level of measurement* of concepts. This strategy is quite unlike the derivation of measurement scales in social research which, as we have seen, depends on either *a priori* speculation about individual terms or the ordinary language formulations implicit in so-called direct indicators (see section 2.1).

Coming back to our example, if we produce a model in which temperature is conceived as the average kinetic energy of the gas molecules, then we have a ready-made conception of why temperature should be considered a continuous variable, as well as a precise understanding of zero temperature corresponding to a lack of molecular activity. Its value can be calculated by extrapolating back a relationship between pressure and temperature as observed on a gas thermometer to the point of zero pressure. Such a decision on measurement properties is of course derived neither from observation nor *a priori* introspection. Gases liquefy and solidify long before they reach zero temperature, and our common-sense perceptions of hot and cold carry no means of contemplating just how cold, cold can be. The absolute temperature scale, of course, refers to an 'ideal gas' and has no exact empirical equivalent. One could add a concluding note here to the effect that ratio measurement is virtually universal in natural science because the underlying explanatory mechanism so often consists of a model of 'matter in motion' which leads quite naturally to perceiving a whole range of properties as varying continuously.

5.2 CLOSURE

To this point we have a theory of causation and meaning that opposes the traditional empiricist account without at the same time abandoning the notion of an empirical component in science. However, I have said little in detail about the production of evidence itself, other than to note that the properties referred to in generative models can be relatively theoretical or observational, according to the circumstances that prevail in a particular investigation. Now whilst this allows us to escape the logical pitfalls associated with the idea of 'rules of correspondence', it does not get to the heart of the problem of showing how empirical evidence can be used to test out theories.

To grasp the nettle, we need to move first to Bhaskar's claim that transcendental realism alone can explain why scientists regard experimental evidence as vital for the production of knowledge. The reasoning here takes us back to the confusion between regularities and causal laws that was mentioned earlier in the chapter. Bhaskar, you will recall, identified causal laws with the action of an underlying mechanism rather than with our attempts to observe the constant conjunction of events. To this he adds the further step, arguing that experimentation provides the unique window through which we can confirm our understanding of the action of mechanisms.

> mechanisms endure even when not acting, and act in their normal way even when the consequents of the law-like statements they ground are, owing to the operation of intervening mechanisms or countervailing causes, unrealized. It is the role of the experimental scientist to exclude such interventions, which are usual; and to trigger the mechanism so that it is active. The activity of the mechanism may then be studied without interference ... It is only under closed conditions that there will be a one-to-one relationship between the causal law and the sequence of events. And it is normally only in the laboratory that these enduring mechanisms of nature, whose operations are described in the statements of causal laws, become actually manifest (Bhaskar, 1979, p. 46).

For the Bhaskarian school then, there is a world external to us which we experience as a flux of events. Certain of these events can be explained because they are tied together with other events and their joint occurrence is to be understood as a consequence of some underlying mechanism that connects them. However, these two levels of reality (event and mechanism) are not naturally or normally 'in phase'; sometimes mechanisms can persist without being activated, sometimes their effects can be marked by the counter-action of other mechanisms. Bhaskar's example of the first situation is to consider the mechanism of the chemical composition of gelignite which is what gives it its causal powers to explode. Whether this liability is actually brought about on any occasion depends on it being in the right conditions. As an example of the second situation, consider the relationship between pressure and temperature in a gas which we know depends on the internal action of its constituent molecules. However, if our sample of gas is, say, the air in this room, the said molecules are constantly changing under a barrage of external and internal physical forces, leaving no possibility of observing the empirical regularity.

For this school, then, scientific research simply cannot dwell at the level of events and if we were to confine observations solely to the business of monitoring events, we will end up with endless descriptions of more or less random sequences. Consequently, a much more active process of the marshalling of evidence is proposed which portrays the observational phase of inquiry as being a matter of duplicating empirically what goes on in mathematical models of the workings of causal mechanisms. As we have seen, these models consist of an image of an 'ideal world' in which a system of properties is linked to the action of a unique and singular generative mechanism. This *conceptually-closed system* is the target for empirical research and the means of testing the hypothesized model is through the production of the corresponding *empirically-closed system*. This, for Bhaskar, explains the unique function of experimentation in empirical enquiry:

> The experimental scientist must perform two essential functions in an experiment. First, he must trigger the mechanism under study to ensure that it is active; and secondly, he must prevent any interference with the operation of the mechanism. These activities could be designated 'experimental production' and 'experimental control'. The former is necessary to ensure the satisfaction of the antecedent (or stimulus) conditions, the latter to ensure the realization of the consequent, i.e. that closure has been obtained.

And (for once) he provides a neat example:

> In a simple electrical experiment designed to illustrate say Ohm's Law, the wiring of an electric circuit and the generation of an electric current would constitute 'experimental production'; maintaining the appropriate

resistance levels, ensuring that no new magnetic field is suddenly placed in the neighbourhood of the circuit, etc. would then constitute 'experimental control' (Bhaskar, 1979, p. 53).

For completeness' sake we can present these ideas diagrammatically as in Fig. 5.4. This, of course, simply transposes the conceptual model Fig. 5.3 into the empirical realm. M thus represents the physical, rather than the mathematical, manipulation of the mechanism. X and Y are two components of the system that are relatively observational and investigation of the relationship between them should reveal the expected empirical correlation. All this of course takes place under conditions of experimental control, as signified by the oval boundary.

Several interesting features flow from this model of empirical evidence. Notice (only in passing, unfortunately) that this is not the model of experimentation as prescribed in the classic empiricist account, and certainly not the one portrayed in the social science spin-offs. In the standard account the task is to produce and isolate a single stimulus and then observe its effects. Once this stimulus is marshalled, experimental manipulations end, nature unfolds and the experimentalist becomes the passive observer of the outcome. In social science applications this has come to mean using control groups so that experimental and control conditions are identical save for the stimulus condition. Any difference in the behavioural outcomes between the two

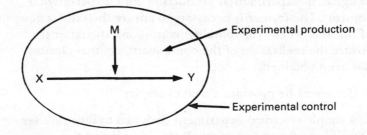

Figure 5.4 Experimental closure

situations is thus accounted for in terms of the action of the stimulus.

This contrasts sharply with Bhaskar's account in which experimentalists are supervisors of all they survey. Instead of firing off the independent variable and watching for its effects on a dependent variable, the task is to manipulate a physical system so as to achieve the desired interrelationships between two component variables in that system. Experimental control is far more than the action of setting up certain initial conditions. The experimentalist is a *system-builder* and experimental evidence is produced, not by observation, but *work*. In describing the production of evidence in this way, the aim is to get away from certain features of the two-language interpretation of science, namely that empirical data are won on a variable by variable basis, and that the validity of a datum is a matter of how well a measure or indicator represents a particular item in the conceptual universe. Under realism, evidence and, therefore, matters of validity are treated holistically; data are created and evaluated through the process of attempting to build an experimental system which duplicates the blueprint set down in the mathematical model. The guiding metaphor is much more nearly one of experimentation as a piece of precision engineering than as a sequence of controlled observation.

This change in emphasis can be best appreciated by re-examining a few of the illustrations we have met already. Recall that Huygens' theory of pendular motion was based on the notion that motion along the arc of a circle was not regular.

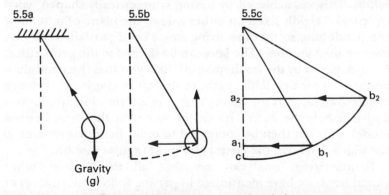

Figure 5.5 Forces on a pendulum bob

To show this he went right back to the mathematics of the process. Without going into this fully one can illustrate the first steps in reasoning as follows (see Fig. 5.5). Basically there are two forces acting on a simple pendulum: the downward force of gravity and the retaining tension in the string (Fig. 5.5a).

We can think of the force in the string as having two components, one counteracting the downward force of gravity (i.e. holding the whole thing up) and one providing an inward force on the bob (i.e. causing it to oscillate (Fig. 5.5b)). At any particular moment this inward force on the pendulum is proportional to the horizontal displacement of the bob (a_1 b_1, a_2 b_2 in Fig. 5.5c). For small amplitudes this force is more or less equal to the displacement along the arc (a_1 b_1 = b_1 c approx). However for large swings this approximation is a bad one (a_2 b_2 ≠ b_2 c). Thus the inward force on the pendulum does not vary constantly with displacement along the arc and the simple pendulum is not isochronous. This model of forces can be further developed to show that the cycloid is the most regular line of descent (Bos *et al.*, 1980).

Being a perfectly regular guy within the scientific community, Huygens found the need to demonstrate the model empirically, basically by adapting a simple pendulum to follow the theoretically defined isochronous path. Further derivations from the above model tell us that for a given pendulum there will be a slight increase in period for larger amplitudes. If some way could be found to shorten the effective length of the pendulum as its angular displacement increased, regular oscillation should follow. This was achieved by having symmetrically shaped 'jaws' or 'cheeks' rigidly fixed on either side of the plane of motion of the pendulum, so that the string wraps itself partially onto one jaw and then another. The jaws can be shaped to the geometrical form required by the mathematical theory so that the pendulum bob will follow a cycloidal path. In short, the empirical evidence required to support the theory comes in a form which duplicates and marshals the entire system of forces in the hypothesized model. This can then be compared to other pendular systems to see which produces the fastest and most regular motion.

Summarizing, one can say that all the various other experiments we have mentioned in passing follow this strategy of activating and isolating a mechanism to produce a physical system that accords with a theoretical model of that system. Nowhere will you find in practice the test–retest, control-group designs that are prescribed in the empiricist methodological literature. To confirm this impression it is worth consulting any standard physics test. Rogers (1960) is a good example, since it goes in for rather vivid illustrations of 'matchstick' scientists in the process of actually building and operating the systems required to produce empirical evidence.

We now come, however, to a note of qualification. Important as Bhaskar's analysis is for 'bringing experimentation back in' to the philosophical analysis of scientific discovery, and important as is the lesson for social scientists that evidence is holistic and manufactured, this particular realist model is incomplete in certain vital respects. Bhaskar's transcendental realism has no conception of *measurement* as a significant and separate stage in empirical inquiry (the term does not even appear in the index of his *Realist Theory of Science*). So though he stresses the importance of activating a system and controlling that system, he omits to mention how one obtains results from that system. Vital as it is to show that events in the world happen in entirely the way prescribed by theory, Bhaskar's experiments remain 'happenings' rather than occasions for sifting and recording evidence.

This is a more significant matter than the old story of not being able to cover everything in one account, because it leaves us with an analysis of evidence as an entirely confirmatory device. There seems no room for falsification of theories or even adjudication between theories in a model which describes the job of producing evidence as the business of manipulating a physical system to imitate the behaviour of a mathematical system. Since researchers are called upon to generate evidence in closed and artificial situations, the realist model would seem to allow them to bash the system into the requisite shape, however relentlessly, all in the name of 'experimental control'. In the last analysis, one is driven rather a long way from the notice of the experiment as an *independent* test of a theoretical system

However one feels about the descriptive advantages of Bhaskar's account of holistic and manufactured evidence, it remains entirely driven by theoretical assumptions about the underlying mechanism. What counts as empirical evidence, where to look for evidence, what devices need to be constructed, what are the margins of experimental error and so forth, would all seem to be questions answered with reference to the theoretical model. So whilst there is plenty of empirical evidence floating around in this account, none of it seems to act as an external and, dare we say it, objective check upon theory.

5.3 NETWORKS

We now have a theory of causation, measurement and experimental closure that seems to do a fair job in describing the nature and the usage of empirical evidence in natural science. However, we have largely failed to give an account of the road to the production of evidence as an independent test of theory. Is there in fact no viable alternative route to the cul-de-sac of the empiricist's independent observation language and the roundabout of the relativist's theory-impregnated observation language? Post-empiricism has toiled away at this problem for many a year and the most refined strategy constructed to deal with it is probably Hesse's (1974, Ch 1 and 2) *Network model of theories.*

This begins, as we have seen, by recognizing that some terms of scientific discourse are relatively theoretical and some are relatively empirical. However, all terms take their meaning internally, regardless of whether the relationships which define them are derived from abstract mathematical models or concrete experimental settings. In short, meaning is relational. The important point, however, is that science does not just consist of a series of separate little mathematical models and one-off experimental arrangements. Thus a term never takes its meaning by way of a singular relationship. Instead there is a great deal of borrowing of concepts, metaphorical extensions of mechanisms, adaptation of experiments and so forth as scientists move from problem to problem.

Science, then, grows as an open-ended *network* of systematic interrelationships. A range of different theories and explanations will keep returning to the conceptual and empirical resources found useful in solving earlier problems and thus, in effect, lay down a hard core of concepts with universal meaning. Pursuing this network metaphor (as Duhem, Quine, Lakatos and

Hempel did long before present-day realists got their hands on it) leads to the idea that certain properties will figure prominently in scientific discourse, simply because they have so many threads converging upon them. It is such properties which have a key systematizing role in science since they are identified in many theories, in many experiments and by many instruments. Such a development, of course, takes place over a long time span and the interesting consequence is that usage of certain of these 'knot concepts' becomes taken for granted in the course of the history of science. The parameters of certain concepts are fixed over and over again in different models and experiments, so much so that this ancestry gets forgotten and they become regarded as fundamental measures, the great yardsticks of nature.

To see this it is worth picking up again the example of the measurement of length from section 2.1. Our familiarity with the family of rulers, yardsticks, tape measures etc. has led to a situation in which our notion of the property becomes almost synonymous with the instrument used to measure it. In ordinary language if we are thinking about length, the problem at hand would be likely to be something of the order of 'how many rows of knitting to the armhole', or 'how many yards of carpet to buy', and so indeed the conceptual universe is just about wrapped up by these instruments. In the methodological literature the fact that the usage of the yardstick obeys all the rules of cardinal measurement (transitivity, commutability, association etc.) has led to the supreme empiricist accolade – 'here is a concept capable of fundamental measurement'. I would argue however that these operational definitions cover only a small part of our understanding of matters of length and distance, and that it is illusory to imagine that it is these simple instruments which give the concept such a ready and universal meaning.

In fact we use an enormous range of instruments for measuring length and we can pass from one to another because we know the network of relationships which enclose the concept. Two simple alternative instruments for measuring length will illustrate the idea: one uses a wheel of known circumference (hodometer) to measure irregular lines, the instrument embodying simple principles of geometry to relate number of rotations to length; similarly principles of trigonometry are assumed in the many triangulation devices used in navigating and surveying for the measurement of great distances. The network of experimental and mathematical linkages becomes even more complex when one considers some of the more esoteric devices for measuring distances. For instance, we use the lawful decrease in barometric pressure with height as the underlying principle of the aeroplane altimeter; underwater distances are determined via the travel time of sound signals; astronomical instruments measure great distances via the apparent brightness of stars, and so on (Hempel, 1966, p. 94). Finally and conversely, the concept of length finds its way into the construction of both the mathematical and empirical models used in the investigation of other properties. We have seen at least two in this chapter: temperature measured by length of mercury column, and pendulum time depending on its length. One concludes that the concept of length carries universal meaning and comprises part of the basic unit system of science, not because it is capable of so-called fundamental measurement but because it acts as a 'knot concept', a point of access from one physical system to another.

This image of networks, knots, and relationships allows a rather different consideration of the nature of the independence of theory and evidence. Lakatos, who uses the term 'pluralistic model' to describe the idea, puts it as follows:

> In the pluralistic model the clash is not 'between theories and facts' but between two high level theories: between an *interpretative theory* to provide the facts and an *explanatory* theory to explain them; and the interpretative theory may be on quite as high a level as the explanatory theory.

Accordingly,

> It is not that we propose a theory and Nature may shout NO; rather we propose an image of theories and Nature may shout INCONSISTENT (Lakatos, 1970, pp. 129-30).

Once again it is useful to attempt to represent these ideas diagrammatically. In Fig. 5.6, X, Y and M represent the various ingredients of a model under development which could either be relatively theoretical or empirical. The idea is that the test of the model is not simply to produce the internal correspondence

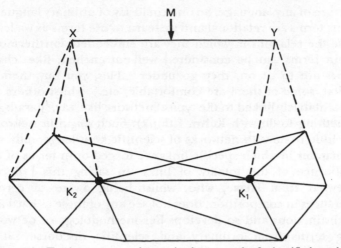

Figure 5.6 Testing as entrenchment in the network of scientific knowledge

between mathematical and physical versions of the hypothesized closed system, but to explore linkages to other systems (marked by dashed lines). However deductively tight a mathematical model, or however reproducible an experiment, a new 'theory' or 'finding' does not gain its spurs without some form of interpretation in terms of the existing network, especially the strategic 'knot-concepts' (K_1, K_2).

On the network model, then, the process of empirical testing is basically one of seeking the entrenchment of new models into the existing system. The researcher will indeed try to imitate theoretical models with experimental systems but incorporated into the experimental design will be measurement apparatus which already carries in its construction many core laws and regularities from the existing network. It is this incorporation of existing knowledge within the standard instruments which provides for a measure of independence of theory and evidence, whilst at the same time acting as a safeguard against the wildest excess of imagination in experimental manipulation.

One must interpret the meaning of the linkages that comprise the network of scientific knowledge with some care. One could argue that there is no special significance in the notion that scientific terms take their meaning according to location in a network of discourse, since such a format is the essential structure of any language. So one could say of ordinary language, that its terms are relational and we learn to use terms as we learn to use the relations in which they are embedded. Furthermore, certain terms can be considered well-entrenched, like 'chair' (chairs are to sit on, they go under tables, you buy them at Habitat, some of them are comfortable, etc.), whilst others are only tentatively linked to the typical network like, say, 'paradigm' (something to do with Kuhn, I think). Such *linguistic* networks have little to do with networks of scientific knowledge, either in the manner in which specific links are forged or in terms of the significance of the totality of links. In saying this I depart somewhat from Hesse, who, whilst being aware of certain differences in composition, does not see any of these as hard and fast distinctions and so develops her methodology of networks using terms from ordinary and scientific discourse rather interchangeably (1974, p. 27).

The idea of the networks of scientific discourse, advocated here, is that researchers utilize them to establish a sense of objectivity about their ideas. Objectivity flows, not from empirical corroboration, but from seeking entrenchment within a pre-established system of theoretical models and empirical regularities. Superficially this sounds like the process of establishing the meaning of a word in ordinary language by tracing its linkage back to predicates which are commonplace and well understood. There are, however, important differences between the two processes. Ethnomethodology and ordinary language philosophy have provided us with a range of terms to describe the structure of everyday discourse: it is 'open-textured', all usage carries a 'fringe of incompleteness', all of its terms are 'indexical', accomplishing talk always requires 'filling in' unspoken meaning and so forth. The resultant picture is that the meaning of any term is ever open to revision because terms can be linked in a virtually infinite number of relationships to a virtually infinite number of other terms. The upshot of this, of course, is that linguistic networks can be as much a source of ambiguity of meaning as consistency of meaning. A prime and ironic example of this is the term 'paradigm' itself; even within the close cultural confines of philosophical discourse, Kuhn managed to produce a treatise on paradigms which, according to another philosopher, covered twenty-one different usages

(Masterman, 1970). The argument continues on just how many of these are consistent.

One gathers that it is certainly not this linguistic understanding of networks to which I, and most realists with the exception of Hesse, consider as a potential source of objectification of theories. If one allows that scientific knowledge takes on exactly the same form as ordinary discourse, then one has to confront Quine's famous thesis that any statement can be maintained true in the face of any evidence.

> Any statement can be held true come what may, if we make drastic enough adjustments elsewhere in the system . . . Conversely, by the same token no statement is immune to revision (Quine, 1951).

A close parallel can be drawn between this thesis about the revisability of propositions and Bhaskar's thesis about the chance and haphazard occurrence of regularities in open systems. Recall that Bhaskar supposed that causal regularities would only be found in systems that were conceptually or experimentally closed. The arguments are virtually interchangeable; one could have Bhaskar saying.

> Any regularity can be manufactured come what may, if we make drastic enough adjustments elsewhere in the experimental system . . . . Conversely, by the same token no regularity is immune to experimental falsification.

We are left with the dilemma of saving the insight that we can validate one part of the scientific network against another, from those connotations stressing the completely open texture of linguistic networks.

Networks and the significance of measurement

At this point we reach the stage where an important connection can be made. Bhaskar's realism (if we can term it thus) was deficient since whilst it recognizes that the causal mechanisms which lie at the base of scientific knowledge can only be discovered in a closed system, it poses no strategy for validating knowledge of that system, which is independent of the system. Hesse's realism (if we can term it thus) is deficient, in that whilst it shows how we can provide a relatively independent check upon a new chain of scientific reasoning by showing how the elements in the chain fit in with a pre-established network of existing relations, it fails to deliver any model of the process of interceding in the existing network which is not open-ended and thus virtually random.

Since each model seems aimed at the deficiency in the other, these two realisms, it would seem, were destined for each other. The matchmaking would involve a balancing act which I think is at the heart of most post-empiricist philosophy, namely that between the needs of the context of discovery (which requires the harnessing of a closed system) and the requirements of the context of justification (which requires the traversing of open systems). We can develop a model which satisfies both demands by carrying over the rules which apply to the development of the closed experimental system to govern the processes of making links to the established network. In other words the key idea is that the networks of laws, theories, relationships and instruments which comprise the major research programmes in science are in fact composed of an interlacement of closed systems. So, rather than firing off in diverse and possibly contradictory paths as in a linguistic network, each linkage in the scientific network has withstood demonstration in a closed system.

One can represent this diagrammatically by simply superimposing the requirement of closure on to every linkage in

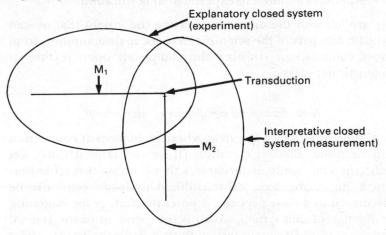

Figure 5.7   Realist empirical inquiry

the previous diagram. One ends up with a model of investigation as in Figure 5.7. Basically this simplifies Figure 5.6 by reducing the network to the production of just one interlinkage (in practice dozens of relationships would be established, even in the single investigation). Within this idealized form, the sequence of research becomes the process of creating an *explanatory closed system* which one tests through the application of an *interpretative closed system*. The most routine instance of such a strategy in natural science is to reproduce the explanatory closed system in the form of an *experiment* with the insertion of the interpretative closed system as the application of *measurement* apparatus to a given property in the experiment. This is the situation portrayed in Figure 5.7.

Note that the two systems are entirely equivalent in form; it is merely their function that differs. We can think of the first stage according to a Bhaskarian model whereby a mathematical model of the underlying mechanism responsible for a regularity is duplicated in experimental conditions. However, this closed system has to generate data and to ensure that these data are not simply determined according to the internal logic of the explanatory system, certain elements of that system are transformed via a measurement system. The measurement system, however, operates under precisely the same constraints as the initial explanatory system; indeed it is usually a modified form of some erstwhile experimental system which in turn has its roots in a mathematical system.

Examples of a mathematical-system-becoming-an-experiment-al-system-becoming-a-measurement-system have been mentioned already. Huygens' mathematical theory of the motion of a cycloidal pendulum was transformed into a range of experimental devices which underwent testing via a range of other interpretative systems. Once the experimental apparatus was devised which more nearly duplicated isochronous motion, then this apparatus itself became a measuring instrument. New explanatory systems could be tested by conjoining them to an interpretative system comprising the Huygens' clock. For instance the explanatory system used in navigation to locate a ship's longitude uses the principle of measuring 'position' on earth through 'time'. We know that the earth rotates once in 24 hours, so we can work out how many degrees it will rotate in any given time. If we reckon that it is noon at any place in the world when the sun is at its highest we can calculate this position by comparing this particular 'noon' to the time of a clock set at Greenwich Mean Time. Hence if a ship carries a very accurate clock set at GMT it can locate its position through sextant readings of the sun and a bit of clock-watching. Thus the cycle continues, the mathematical model becomes an experiment, which becomes a measure, which when conjoined with further systems becomes a measure of still further properties and so on.

Conclusions

This account (I trust) allows us to see clearly for the first time the importance of measurement within a model of science which is broadly in line with the tenets of realist philosophy. Previous accounts which have acknowledged the theory-dependence of observation, even avowedly post-empiricist ones, have allowed the role of measurement to become rather obscure. This is especially so when one compares them to the power of measurement as indicated by the time and effort spent on this function in real research. The true significance of measurement, then, has nothing to do with rooting scientific theory in an objective empirical base; what is vital is that the measurement process is unique in its ability to weave together the network of scientific knowledge. Measurement identifies and isolates a single element within one closed system which is varying under the influence of an underlying mechanism; it then uses that variation to stimulate a further mechanism, so triggering off a controlled relationship in another closed system. This second controlled relationship takes the form of a signal production in a piece of physical apparatus, and it is such readings which are sometimes mistaken (incredibly enough) for direct observation.

Remember that this description is itself simplified and idealized, and that in a complex measuring instrument literally dozens of different theories and mechanisms will be assumed and activated. The result is that there is a virtually instantaneous manufacture of scores of linkages back into the scientific network in any successful empirical test. Moreover, since it is the case that a measurement system will encapsulate the historical development of lines of theory (e.g. the time–pendular motion–clocks–navigational instruments example), the act of measurement has the effect of attaching provisional theories, at a stroke, right back to those 'knot concepts' or 'hard-core' theories which enjoy the most secure place at the heart of scientific discourse. There are of course many other ways of traversing and thus securing the network of scientific knowledge using strategies that could be described as 'relatively theoretical'. The important point, however, is that not one step in this model of measurement denies the importance of theories in the network of scientific discourse; on the contrary *the reason why the measurement process is so strategic is that it encapsulates and concentrates centuries of theoretical development into single observations.*

As a final point of conclusion one should note that this description of the functions of measurement, which has been derived from a consideration of the character of explanation in natural science, is exactly the same as that discovered in an examination of the engineering principles of measurement in the previous chapter. As we have just seen, the vital explanatory power of measurement stems from its function of being able to transform the properties of one closed system to those of another. This is, of course, none other than the principle of *transduction.* Transducers are a type of relay which transfers information signals from one physical system to another and form the taken-for-granted point of departure in the construction of any measurement device. Furthermore the next stage of instrument construction, which is to achieve control of the *transmission path*, is simply another way of saying that the measurement process itself must act as a closed system. The attempts to suppress and filter 'noise' from transmission paths are endeavours designed to meet the very definition of a closed system, namely that a single well-understood mechanism alone should control the flow from input to output signal.

One has to acknowledge that the pedigree of these ideas as part of the logic-in-use of instrument engineering represents a somewhat more secure lineage than as offsprings of the mongrel stock of realist philosophical principles. Nevertheless between the two we have a picture of the significance of measurement that stands second to none as a point of comparison for any discipline evaluating its own potentiality and fitness in the field of measurement. The assault course to be survived can be summarized as follows, starting with the broadest ontological and epistemological assumptions and working towards the technical:

> The basic constituent of the world is the *generative mechanism*. It is these underlying forces which bind events together and allow us to experience the world as a series of regularities. However, such regularities are merely contingent and depend for their law-like occurrence on the production of *closed systems* in which only the single mechanism acts. We have to shape inquiry to investigate a world so constituted. Concept *formation* is thus *systemic*, that is to say concepts take their meaning according to how we perceive their location within such closed systems. The basic act of investigation is thus to isolate closed systems experimentally to see if they correspond to the conceptual systems we have modelled theoretically (often mathematically). Scientific understanding grows as a *network* connecting concepts according to how they are shaped by different laws and mechanisms. Scientific discovery is the process of adding linkages to the network so that certain *knot concepts* become *entrenched* by many linkages. Securing the linkages is a matter for traversing from one closed system to another and this is the function of *measurement*. Measurement is thus the process of testing our theories of one system against those of another. The *empirical evidence* produced is thus neither circular nor incommensurable since testing single theories always involves a *transduction* process and testing rival theories uses measures which lie at the *intersection* of the theories.

All of this has of course travelled rather a long way from the view of investigation and measurement assumed in sociological research techniques like variable analysis and scaling. Nevertheless, the above model constitutes the real agenda for naturalistic, quantitative, empirical research. With these thoughts it is back to sociological research that we thankfully but timidly retreat.

Part Three

PRACTICAL MEASURES

With this section I begin in earnest the task of rethinking the fundamentals of empirical sociology. In Part 2 I developed a model of scientific investigation which reinstated empirical evidence in general and the measurement process in particular to the centre-stage of inquiry. The primary task of this third section of the book is thus to evaluate some of these strategies and tactics in terms of their applicability to the practice of social investigation. Broadly speaking, I have argued that progress in measurement depends on matters which, superficially at least, seem quite remote from measurement practice. Thus the apparatus used to construct data in natural science is like it is because it embodies the transduction process, the search for evidence at the intersection of theories and the use of explanatory strategies which utilise generative mechanisms, closed systems, networks of theories and a whole lot more besides. The fact that certain parts of this model (viz. those dealing with energy transfer, physical manipulation of apparatus, etc.) cannot be remotely useful in social research does not disqualify sociology from attempting to share some of the broader logic and method involved. Recall that realist methodology is not prescriptive and the realist measurement model is not intended to define a set of absolute prerequisites for empirical inquiry. Measurement practices undoubtedly reflect certain functions prescribed in accounts of the so-called logic of scientific discovery, but it is the fact that scientists are forever refining their method to meet practical research problems that actually establishes and regenerates these broader principles of inquiry. In attempting to borrow this measurement strategy for

155

sociology, I am simply broadening the range of this mutual inspection of principle and practice.

A further, but by no means minor, objective of this final section lies with the substantive focus brought to the discussion. By contrast to the precision of physical science measurements it is rather revealing to examine the parlous state of quantification in even one of the stock-in-trade aspects of social investigation like the measurement of social class affiliation, socio-economic status, social standing, occupational position and so on. The fact that I am able to use these diverse expressions as rough synonyms to describe a target for measurement goes half way to confirming the thesis under proposal here, namely that the ambiguity of sociological measurement arises from the failure to locate it within the totality of theoretical discourse and an overall empirical strategy. Instead of demonstrating this lack of conceptual and methodological rigour by tracking the remarkable range of *measures* that have found use as social class indicators, I want to pursue the positive side of my thesis by comparing types of *investigations* in respect of the degree to which they are informed by each component of realist inquiry. In particular I will focus on those studies which have pressed furthest into such a strategy. In trying to produce a methodology which enables as well as constrains, and which is rooted in practice as well as principle, the aim is very much to learn from as well as evaluate these studies.

Chapter Six

FROM VARIABLES
TO MECHANISMS
(AND BACK AGAIN)

Sound measurement presupposes sound theory, and so the search for parallels between sociological and scientific measurement must start with an examination of some of the broader features of explanatory strategy. Let me begin with an instant recapitulation of the significance of *generative mechanisms* in scientific explanation. The basic claim is that it is only by understanding the action of underlying mechanisms that we can make sense of scientific explanation as the search for regularities in the joint-occurrence of events. The idea is that reliance on a completely open-ended observational record will have the result that no two events will turn out to be perpetually and universally fixed in a causal relationship. Rather, we can only identify these law-like interconnections in the rather extraordinary conditions typified by experimental observation. It follows that there is a basic atom of inquiry, more fundamental than both the event and the regularity, and this must take the form of an underlying mechanism that generates a process which links two events in a regular fashion. Knowledge of the underlying mechanism gives us knowledge of the conceptual form of the variables involved in inquiry. It is only in conditions where such a mechanism operates, and operates alone, that causal laws occur. The harsh conclusion is that the search for regularities in the sequence of events (happenings, properties, variables, etc.) will be futile without knowledge and control of the generative mechanisms that operate in a particular context.

We have already seen that a sensitivity to underlying processes and mechanisms leads to a re-writing of the rule-book of physical science. In this chapter I want to see what equivalent changes

157

would be engendered if empirical research was to become more mechanism-oriented in a non-experimental science like sociology. One immediate point of equivalence is apparent, even in terms of the brief resumé of the significance of generative thinking above, namely that it is the lack of appreciation of underlying mechanisms in variable analysis that accounts for another of the woes of that misbegotten investigative style. Although I have examined the deficiencies of the mode of construction of variables in great detail in Chapter 2, I had little opportunity there to describe the outcome of arbitrary measurement practices, which, as one might suspect, is none other than arbitrary research findings.

A standard charge made against sociology in general, and its survey findings in particular, is that it has simply failed to deliver a body of reliable, replicable and cumulative knowledge. Any number of commentators (e.g. Brown, 1973, Chs 5-9; Sayer, 1984, Ch. 3) have pointed out that a roll-call of social laws, of which Berelson and Steiner's (1964) inventory is the most (in)famous attempt, will be filled only with quasi-laws and local tendencies, that are often not so much regularities as banalities. Moreover, if we consider an example of what must amount to the most secure of the regularities we do lay claim to, namely that of demon-strating class inequality in educational success, one finds that the strength of this association varies markedly from context to context, from investigation to investigation, and from measure to measure. Even here one can find trenchant analysis which vigorously protests that 'claims about educational inequality are certainly premature, probably overdrawn and possibly mistaken' (Murphy, 1981, p. 182).

The fact that genuine empirical generalizations are non-existent, and that the quasi-regularities we do attest are so conditional, finds a ready explanation in realist philosophy. If the search for empirical evidence is pitched primarily at the level of variables (events, properties, etc.) and without due regard for the underlying mechanism, then the relationships discovered will necessarily be contingent. In any real social situation the action of the underlying mechanisms that bring about a relationship may stop or change, and its effects may be further distorted, exaggerated or disguised by the action of other mechanisms. Given that the primary means of gathering information about potential social regularities is the one-shot survey, and given that the logic of variable analysis is still all-pervasive within this strategy, small wonder we are short on powerful empirical generalizations. This is no place to make another song and dance about variable analysis. I simply want to remind the reader that my lashes against the whipping-boy of sociology are directed against the 'analysis' rather than 'variables' *per se*. That is to say the majority of survey research is carried out within an explanatory style that asks no more of theory than to produce statements of the X-should-influence-Y type. Any survey worth its salt will attempt to deal with a handful of dependent issues and, perhaps, scores of potential explanatory factors. Compared with the time and effort and money involved in conducting a survey as a whole, the marginal cost of including a few more variables is small. The result is there is little need or inclination to conceive of variables in terms of their conceptual roots within bodies of generative theory. Hence researchers will (have to) take the liberty of producing data by using any indicator, any level of measurement, and measurement technique that they find convenient and reasonable.

I should add that generative theorizing is equally rare amongst the ranks of so-called theorists in mainstream sociology. Although the model of measurement I am pursuing here does not acknowledge a real division of labour between theorists and researchers, I have argued that it is the theoretical precision with which models of generative mechanisms are constructed in natural science which lends exactitude to the measurement process itself. By and large theorists in sociology would not recognize this as a description of their endeavours. In place of precise substantive theory we seem to have a much greater appetite for 'social ontology', 'meta-theory', 'conceptual historiography' and so forth. By way of a change, then, one can point the accusing finger at theorists for abandoning measurement to its own ends as a separate technical exercise.

The task of this chapter is therefore plain, namely to examine the potential for increasing the role played by generative reasoning in the production of sociological data languages. The current position is in fact not so stark as in the simple polarization presented above in which theorists specialize entirely in speculative theory and technicians alone are responsible for measurement. I will suggest that we have already witnessed some movement towards the harmonization of theory and data languages which I shall treat in two separate steps. Firstly we have a tradition of the *implicit* or *ad hoc* use of generative mechanisms to support measurement decisions. The qualifications used here will be sufficient to alert the reader to my belief that, though they are a step in the right direction, such strategies lack the power to shift measurement from its arbitrary base. The second and vital step brings us to the rather rarer examples of the *explicit* usage of generative reasoning to prespecify measurement parameters. Here I will consider the operation of a research strategy that you will not find in the textbooks (but whose characteristics are identifiable enough in certain key works) which I shall call 'generative modelling'. This will be followed by a final section of the chapter providing a closer examination of the nature of those mechanisms that come under consideration in sociological explanation. If one accepts, with realism, that mechanisms constitute a more fundamental level of existence than events, then it is through an examination of our understanding of the underlying generative processes of society, and not any contemplation of the supposed nature of social variables, that we can make the first genuine stipulations about the potentialities and limitations of quantitive sociology.

6.1 THE IMPLICIT USE OF MECHANISMS

Although I have shown that research and theory are, in the main, led by other priorities, it is quite possible to detect certain strategies, bordering on the generative style of reasoning, which play a more implicit and supportive role in researCh. These can be described under two sub-headings: (i) explanation in the form of *concomitants*, (ii) *post-hoc* generative reasoning. In the first the explanatory device takes the form of specifying certain concomitants, contextual features, precipitating conditions etc. which are conducive to a particular regularity. In the second case explanation takes the form of suggesting the underlying pro-cesses which might have been responsible for patterns and associations revealed in existing data. Both of these strategies take us to a level of explanatory sophistication beyond that of the

160

'X causes Y' propositions of variable analysis. I shall discuss each in turn.

In the first case there is an attempt, not only to postulate and establish a causal regularity, but also to actually interpret why the expected relationship should take on the form it does. As a good example of this we can consider the interpretative structures which have been used to support a proposition which must be one of the most widely held in social science, namely that assuming economic development and social mobility are positively associated. The crucial methodological point here concerns the nature of the theoretical interpretation produced to account for the presumed association. What one finds is that they typically fall somewhat short of producing a generative model of the underlying mechanisms which *constitute* a system of economic change and social movement; rather the aim is the more modest one of explaining why certain social conditions may be *conducive* to economic change and/or social mobility.

Goldthorpe (1985) has recently made a critical review of some of the literature on comparative social mobility, casting doubt on the veracity of its most taken-for-granted proposition under consideration here. What I want to do is follow his preoccupation with the tendentious language with which the basic development/mobility hypothesis is supported, but in this case I want to make a rather different point about its lack of justification. At a first glance, the arguments put in support of the basic thesis are made in something akin to the language of generative causation mentioned earlier (Ch. 5). So the talk is not of external constant conjunction but of potentialities, liabilities, underlying tendencies of a particular type of society. For instance Davis (1961) argues that occupational mobility is a *precondition* for the transformation of society into the industrial age. One needs new opportunities, new motivations before real development can take off. Lipset and Zetterberg (1959) figure out things the other way round; that is to say, high rates of social mobility are a *generic property* of industrial society. One can get a flavour of what passes for explanation here in Goldthorpe's paraphrase of their argument. '[High mobility rates] are a *concomitant* of the *inherent* dynamism of the economies of these [industrial] societies which continuously transform their occupational structures' (1985). Another argument of this ilk,

161

originating this time with Kerr *et al.* (1960), is that the association between development and mobility stems from the fact that both are *expressions* of the changing normative values; they embody, in short, the *tendency* to rationality in modern society.

What Goldthorpe has to say about all this is that one of the supposedly most reliable propositions of comparative sociology is thus supported in quite confused and contradictory bodies of theory. These explanations do not even agree on what is the causal direction of influence connecting development and mobility. They do not agree on the meaning of economic development, some theorists seemingly referring to stages of development (non-industrial/industrial), others to different degrees of industrial development. They do not come close to specifying what type of mobility is involved (is it change in occupational structure or individual opportunity?). Goldthorpe then delivers the *coup de grace* and attempts to show that it is all misguided speculation anyway – recent data reveal that there is no such relationship in the first place!

For myself I am rather less sanguine about the idea of new data being able to wrap up the issue in the absence of more reputable and refutable bodies of theory. The question really is not so much whether the basic proposition is right or wrong but whether it is testable in the first place. My point is that this form of theorizing, using the explanatory device of concomitance, contextual appropriateness etc., does not generate sufficient clues for measurement to provide for decisive test situations. I have shown that the language used evokes the generative style I have been advocating here but when these hypotheses are examined closely, they in fact stop well short of showing how a system of properties is controlled by an internal mechanism.

In general, if the weight of explanation is carried by the notion of concomitants, constraints, preconditions, tendencies etc., then only the weakest of empirical tests are possible. In the example in question, the hypotheses generated are of a type which implies that we should find increasing social fluidity between succeeding generations in a society experiencing sustained economic growth, or that mobility will be higher in economically developed nations than in underdeveloped nations. By sociological standards this sort of stuff sounds relatively rigorous. It is certainly a step up from the base line of variable analysis which demands only that one should expect to discover a positive or negative relationship in a given situation. However, we are still left with the standard situation in which anything goes in regard to the level of measurement or indicators chosen to adjudicate the mobility hypotheses. Researchers can and do attempt to verify the various propositions relating mobility and development by using four-fold tables, by using any number of ordered or non-ordered categories, or by assuming metric measurement. Similarly a variety of scales and categories, using any concept from 'work situation' to 'socio-economic status', to variations of a theme of 'manual/non-manual/farm' categories, can be utilized as the indicator of social position without greatly prejudicing these broad contextual explanations.

All of this leaves us far short of the goal here; that of obtaining a clear expression of measurement properties within substantive theory. If blame is to be apportioned, once again it might seem appropriate to prefer that rather perverse charge that it is ineptitude or laxity on the part of theorists that is the root cause of the empirical researchers' problem. However, this type of mud-slinging is not quite appropriate here, since we are now talking about genuine attempts to do substantive theory rather than the tendency, noted before, for theorists to prefer amateur philosophy. What we need to discover next is whether sociologists are simply unwilling or actually unable to produce the more rigorous generative models required to sustain valid measurement systems.

We can get some vital clues on this matter by examining what I consider to be the next level of sophistication on the way to the incorporation of generative models into sociological explanation. This is the phase of research in which researchers routinely get closest to the form of explanation in which underlying processes and mechanism are used to interpret the form of empirical regularities in considerable detail. Once again, however, the strategy is rarely recognized, let alone formalized, in the methodology texts. Certainly when compared to the well-established sequence of stages in survey work (hypothesis making, variable selection, questionnaire design, coding, processing, statistical analysis, etc.), these procedures are probably considered quite beyond standardization. I refer to the final stage of research, or what is called 'moving beyond the initial analysis' in one of the few methods texts in which it is acknowledged (de Vaus, 1986, Ch. 16). Its most familiar location is in these final chapters of research monographs with headings something like 'Conclusions and Prospects'. In terms of our interest in realist analysis here, one might best describe the strategy as the (*post-hoc*) use of explanatory mechanisms to interpret features previously uncovered in the primary data analysis.

The normal sequence of events is that after all of the standard procedures listed above have been been executed, certain results are deemed worthy of special commentary. Sociological research does not, after all, conform to the hypothesis-testing style of laboratory work in which the single, carefully formulated hypothesis is assessed in great detail. Social researchers are compelled to use *ex post facto* analysis, indeed one might say, prefer to use it, for a variety of reasons. Partly, this is due to the low-grade beginnings of the theories under test, given that they are often formulated in the guise of variable analysis and concomitant analysis. Partly it is due to the fact that surveys are overstuffed with data due to the low marginal costs of adding questionnaire items here and there. To be more charitable, one might say that such reasoning allows researchers to take account of the genuine complexities of social forces and the fact that not every single social influence can possibly be anticipated in the original hypothesis. All this of course is acknowledged and sustained in the process of review, criticism and counter-interpretation that one anticipates with the publication of any half-decent survey. It is probably true to say that, as a result of this, the reputation of the best-known studies depends more on the quality of the 'conclusions and prospects' than the care and attention given to the likes of measurement decisions.

All this scope for interpretative richness is, of course, not without its drawbacks. To illustrate the format and its difficulties one only needs to refer to any work from the latest wave of mobility researCh. The normal turn of events is to decide on a framework of social (class) categories, construct tables of inflow or outflow with respect to such positions, inspect the mobility tables for the most remarkable shifts and finally to provide some commentary on the contemporaneous social processes likely to have been responsible for these particular movements.

Explanations are thus couched much less in terms of broad concomitants of mobility and much more in the generative style. Hence particular features of the inflow and outflow are explained by specific mechanisms referring to such matters as group expectation about the likelihood of mobility and the institutional arrangements which meet or frustrate these ambitions. The key methodological point here is that the strategy provides an internal analysis of the various subsets of the mobility matrix and thus makes much closer reference to the classifications and categories within the data structure as compared to these versions of theory which stick to predicting overall mobility levels and their concomitants.

As an example of this consider some of Goldthorpe's interpretation of the relatively high rates of upward mobility into the 'service class' in mid-century Britain. It is impossible to summarize a book-length argument here, but basically this is put down to the mechanism of economic and technical change which has led to the creation of more professional and managerial jobs. This, argues Goldthorpe, has created a climate of opportunity and has meant that a substantial degree of 'recruitment from below' has been inevitable. Further explanations of the over-time changes in mobility patterns can be added by considering the action of other mechanisms associated with work organization and education. The expanding service class is essentially a bureaucratic one and a typical feature of such organizations is the recruitment of personnel on the basis of formal qualifications. However, Goldthorpe continues, the rate of expansion of the service class in modern Britain has outstripped that of institutions of higher education (at least, that is, until the late 1960s). All this explains particular features of the data such as the fact that widespread promotion into the service class has been largely accommodated by within-career advancement, and that only in the youngest cohort in the Nuffield data can one detect the growing importance of the more direct route via formal qualifications into class I.

What can be glimpsed in this little example is the way in which explanations using underlying mechanisms get right into the texture of the data. When theory gets beyond the business of telling us about contextual accompaniments to a particular relationship, and gets down to telling us how it is actually

165

constituted, we have a growing understanding of the nature of the properties involved. In showing why there is a particular level of mobility between classes, these explanations tell us something about how their boundaries are maintained, about the channels of recruitment into them, about the levels of aspiration to penetrate them; in short, they tell us about the very nature of the classes themselves. We approach for the first time the potentiality for finding a clear rationale for classification and measurement decisions within bodies of explanatory theory.

As usual in sociology, no strategy turns out to be free of imperfections, and so it must be noted that, powerful and astute as some of this after-the-fact theorizing is, it does have costs in terms of the development of a measurement model. The faults of a research style which gathers data first and then goes on to explain the findings are legion and too well known to require lengthy comment. I shall describe the general problem briefly before concentrating on the implication for measurement. The first difficulty of such inductive strategies is that any regularity will normally lend itself to any number of interpretations and without more specifically constructed data no further adjudic-ation between competing theories is possible. The best-known case of interpretative riches in sociology would, I suppose, be the mass of interpretations available to explain class inequality in educational achievement. This relationship has been argued for in terms of loaded school ethos, culturally biased curricula, covert teacher preferences, differential future expectations, different levels of parental support, residential segregation, linguistic and conceptual handicaps, to name but seven (or is it eight?). Too many surveys find themselves with evidence which will accommodate several such explanations and rely on *post hoc* analysis to achieve a preference.

Another fault of this explanatory strategy is that it commits the major sin, in the light of Popperian methodology at least, of being *ad hoc*. I am aware, of course, of the counter-philosophical position which argues that there is no analytic distinction between 'brilliant insight' and 'ad-hoc theory-saving evasiveness'. I am not, however, trying to uphold the idea as a demarcation criterion for protecting true science, but simply describing the greatest cost of sociology's preference for *ex post facto* theorizing, which is the exacerbation of the arbitrariness of measurement practice. If the explanatory theory only addresses the patterns, movements and relationships revealed in a particular data set then clearly we have to face the possibility that an alternative measurement framework might reveal quite different patterns of activity, which might, in turn, require a complete reformulation of theory to explain them.

This is the most oft-repeated charge against mobility research, and boils down to the claim that different classifications of social position will highlight quite different routes and flow-rates of individual mobility. I suppose the most famous example of this is the debate over Goldthorpe and Llewellyn's (1977) attempt to refute the Marxist 'closure' thesis using a Weberian-inspired measure of social position. Their findings, showing considerable long-range mobility into class I of their schema, succeeded only in raising Marxist hackles rather than settling the issue. They are of course aware that the diverse inflow into their 'service class' is conditioned by the fact that such a group represents 10–15 per cent of the male working population, and acknowledge that the closure thesis might well be less broadly conceived. However, they simply go on to bemoan the imprecision of the concept-ualization on the part of proponents of the closure thesis without acknowledging the other side of the coin, that any measurement system (including their own) is conditioned by, and thus will favour, a particular view of the world.

Social research faces an obvious tension here. I have tried to show how *post-hoc* theorizing of this kind represents the phase of research where the mutual support of theory and data become best realized. However, it is pretty clear that, given the interpretative richness of sociology, it is not difficult to imagine that any pattern of data can be swiftly accounted for in considerable detail. Regardless of whether mobility channels into a particular elite group were shown to be open or blocked, a plausible set of mechanisms could pretty soon be evoked to explain the situation. *Post-hoc* theorizing, by definition, can never pre-specify measurement parameters and, however sociologically astute, can never use evidence other than that which is arbitrarily given. Clearly the next task is to see what steps can be taken to restore evidence to its role as a check upon theories, whilst retaining the coherence of theory and data displayed in the *post-hoc* use of generative mechanisms.

6.2 THE EXPLICIT USE OF MECHANISMS

Let us turn, then, to those research strategies which utilize generative mechanisms on the basis of forethought rather than hindsight. This book is by no means the first to make the suggestion that social research should begin with the search for mechanisms underlying social regularities. Realism is enjoying something of a vogue in sociology; it has been quite broadly canvassed as the philosophical vindication of a research strategy that will avoid the slide into empiricism or relativism (Keat and Urry, 1975; Harré,1978; Bhaskar, 1979; Sayer, 1984; Outhwaite, 1988). Diverse as some of the methodological ideas of its authors are, all would undoubtedly follow the first principle of realism – that science is the business of understanding the unobservable structures and mechanisms that stand behind and produce concrete features of social reality. As you might expect, however, this rallying cry has not quite meant the same thing to all persons, and so it is important to identify those examples of generative thinking which seem to me to be the most productive.

The crudest interpretation of the injunction to seek for generative mechanisms is for analysts to proclaim the importance of their own work in terms of their ability to grasp the essence of a phenomenon whilst others are labouring away inappropriately at the level of outward appearance. Personally I feel there is much more to realist analysis than this *appearance/reality* distinction. Nonetheless one cannot get away from the feeling that even in the hands of its most sophisticated exponents realism represents little more than the justification for asserting that certain analytical priorities should apply in social analysis.

For instance Harré's interpretation of realism allows him to assert that the vital generative causal mechanism is the human individual's self-direction. The empirical analysis which is recommended on this basis thus concentrates on the everyday reasoning which underpins action. For instance, Marsh *et al*'s (1978) research on football 'aggro', which is in this tradition, is concerned with 'teasing out' the rules which direct aggression on the terraces and, underlying this, the further set of rules which exist to govern how such actions should be spoken of. The only significant change from the traditional 'hermeneutic' orientations of this 'new' perspective lies in the metatheory

168

telling us why reasons and motivations should be the focus of concern, namely that they are now labelled 'unobservables' because of their explanatory function as 'generative mechanisms'. In short, for 'realism' here, read 'ethnography/ethnomethodology'.

The same sleight of hand is applied, albeit on a completely different plane, in Keat and Urry's version of realism. In this case they claim, on behalf of Marx, that his method was basically realist. Thus,

> The term 'class' is used by Marx in a realist manner. It refers to social entities which are not directly observable, yet which are historically present, and the members of which are potentially aware of their common interests and consciousness. The existence of class is not to be identified with the existence of inequalities of income, wealth, status or educational opportunity. For Marx, and generally for realists, class structures are taken to cause such inequalities. The meaning of the term, 'class', is not given by these inequalities. Rather it is the structure of class relationships which determines the patterns of inequality. The positivisation of class involves treating these more or less observable inequalities as providing us with the meaning of 'class' (1975, p. 94).

Whilst we obviously welcome any protection from the perils of 'positivisation', applaud the insight that class is a 'relational' concept whose meaning supposes a whole system of further concepts, and appreciate that inequalities of social position may have deeper roots, none of this will necessarily lead to significantly new research strategies. Keat and Urry, for instance, go on to identify a generative mechanism with the concept of 'mode of production'. What happens, however, is that 'mode of production' is not in fact analysed as if it were a single underlying causal mechanism whose action brings about changes in various properties of an overall system: rather it is a label for the totality of properties within that system. Keat and Urry go on to outline passages from Marx which seem to exonerate the view that:

> Any adequate analysis of classes must refer not only to their place and function within the relations of production but to

the complex configuration of related constituents of any given mode of production, including the ideological superstructure, the state machinery, patterns of political action and so on (1975, p. 109).

In short, for 'realism' here read 'structuralism'.

Little wonder then that the first wave of critical reaction to the 'new realism' has been of the 'old wine in new bottles' type (Johnson et al., 1984; Layder, 1985). Generative thinking needs to do rather more than assert a ready-made ontological priority for a certain feature of the social world and then lapse back into traditional modes of analysis. If we think back to the natural science sources of inspiration for realist philosophy, there one sees a markedly different focus for generative thinking which Harré and Secord identify as follows: 'the key to understanding of the epistemology and logic of creative science is to be found in the notion of the model', (1972, p.72). Returning to the molecular theory of gases as the classic example of a generative model, it does indeed point to a more fundamental (atomic) level of reality, it does indeed show how outward features of gases are related by underlying processes, but neither of these features, of themselves, plays the crucial explanatory role. Generative thinking in kinetic theory takes the form of a mathematical model which provides us with an account of the determinate relations between properties in a closed system. All the properties of the gas are defined internally via equations describing the motion of gas molecules. This conceptually closed system is then subject to empirical investigation in which physical systems are transformed through experiment and measurement to see if the empirical regularities that emerge take the form of the relationship as predicted in the mathematical model (see Ch. 5).

No such steps are envisaged in 'ethnographic realism' or 'structuralist realism'. There is no generative model to act as template for empirical investigations. Both of these styles of generative thinking depend on explanatory narratives which are essentially descriptive and open-ended. Neither has developed rules for specifying conclusively what constitutes adequate descriptions of underlying mechanisms, be they meaning structures or modes of production. The relationship between the

170

supposed generative mechanism and the observable regularities is thus again reduced to the level of concomitance, of plausible story-telling. In terms of explanatory power one is left with a heavy reliance on the highly contestable and essentially metaphoric notion that generative explanation is somehow a matter of getting down to the 'deep', 'underlying' and 'basic' structures (cf. Keat and Urry, 1981, p. 237).

Generative (realist) thinking, then, in and of itself, need not displace sociology from any of its current bolt holes. What we are searching for here is that much more specialized and evolved creature, the *generative model*. It is only when one has a full-blown model of how the system under investigation is constituted that research hypotheses become explicit enough to have direct consequences for empirical research and measurement practice. Whilst it would be absurd to suggest sociology can operate with mathematical models carrying the exactitude of kinetic theory in physics, there are in fact several research programmes in existence which offer something close to the basic strategy. I want to examine some examples from the sociology of stratification which are concerned with the specification of the underlying mechanisms of class formation and which are stated with enough care and precision to generate forecasts which can be checked against empirical material on the activities and constituencies of the various classes.

Generative model I

As a first case we can consider a generative model produced from a source we have commented upon several times already, that is the Nuffield study of social mobility. Since, in the dozen or so years duration of this study, the objectives, methods and measurement techniques underwent a remarkable trans-formation, it is obvious that this instance will hardly count as the definitive example of the logic of generative modelling. Nevertheless, the reasons for the changes in emphasis during the course of the study are, of themselves, instructive with regard to the general strategy. In terms of publications associated with the study, one can trace three distinct phases of measurement practice. The first explanatory analysis relied on scaling techniques and led to the production of the Hope–Goldthorpe scale. However, when it came to the analysis of the main survey data, the measure was immediately abandoned in favour of a scale based on a theory of class position. The reasons for this are never made quite clear, and are in fact disguised by somewhat disingenuous remarks about the class schema being derived from collapsing and aggregating Hope–Goldthorpe classifications. Be that as it may, the change of emphasis is undoubtedly a sound one given the artificial results produced by scaling as described in Chapter 2.

The second phase of measurement in the Nuffield study was organized around the production of a seven-fold class schema in which the classes are designed to differentiate jobs in terms of both 'occupational function' and 'employment status'. The seven-class model was first introduced into the literature without an extended justification. The authors simply said:

> We combine occupational categories whose members would appear, in the light of available evidence, to be typically comparable, on the one hand, in terms of their sources and levels of income, their degree of economic security and chances of economic advancement; and on the other, in their location within the systems of authority and control governing the process of production in which they are engaged, and hence in their degree of autonomy in performing their work-tasks and roles (Goldthorpe *et al.*, 1980, p. 39).

Despite the fact that such a classification offers a clear line of descent from Weber through to Lockwood, I think it is fair to say that at its initial stages of development the schema is basically an operational one. There is much less justification concerning why the particular categories of 'work performed' and 'employment position' are critical, and much more concentration on producing an operational algorithm for combining the two properties into the seven-fold scheme.

Since operational definitions are always open to the criticism that they are arbitrary, that they implicitly favour certain hypotheses and disfavour others, it is no surprise that the seven-class model received just such attention (Crompton, 1980; Penn, 1981). At this stage I will avoid any attempt to assess these arguments about what is, and what is not, implicit in the schema,

172

save to make the general point that the solution lies in making the theoretical commitments quite explicit prior to analysis. Now, whilst Goldthorpe and colleagues are obviously in no position to go back to square one and pretend that the measurement parameters are in fact really developed on the base of a generative model, they do become involved in such an exercise, somewhat belatedly, in the third phase of measurement in the Nuffield project. As they put it themselves:

> We shall attempt to develop a model of the regime prevailing in modern British society . . . which does, at least, in some degree possess a *theoretical rationale,* that is one informed by *extensions* of the theoretical ideas *implicit* in the seven fold schema in terms of which we have made our observations of absolute mobility (Goldthorpe *et al.,* 1980, p. 95; *my emphasis*).

At the core of this analysis is a theory of social class formation which considers how each class is constituted in terms of the perceived *desirability* of obtaining that position, in terms of the *advantages* and resources afforded by that position, and in terms of the institutional *barriers* erected to limit or condition entry into that class position. The model is constructed by hypothesizing the different levels of mobility (relative mobility densities) that exist between each and every social class position on the basis of a detailed consideration of these mechanisms of class desirability and penetrability.

The particulars of this generative model are too complex to summarize here, but a couple of examples will illustrate the logic involved. Certain mechanisms are perceived to lead to high levels of self-recruitment to particular classes. Amongst the surest advantages and the most decisive barriers in regard to class mobility are economic resources and requirements. Goldthorpe and colleagues figure that direct transmission of economic resources (wealth, family business etc.) will result in the highest levels of self-recruitment at the two points in the class structure. At the highest level of ability to pass on resources, they consider large proprietors and independent professionals, which they group together as part of the 'service class'. A similar mechanism should account for the high (but not quite so high) level of self-recruitment of the 'small independent' or 'petit-bourgeois' class.

173

Table 6.1 Generative model of mobility densities

Father's class	Sons's class						
	I	*II*	*III*	*IV*	*V*	*VI*	*VII*
I	1	3	4	6	7	7	7
II	3	3	4	6	6	7	7
III	4	4	4	6	5	6	6
IV	5	5	5	2	6	6	6
V	5	5	5	6	4	5	5
VI	7	6	5	6	5	4	5
VII	7	6	5	6	5	5	4

Source: Goldthorpe *et al.* (1980, p. 100)

Reasoning of this ilk continues until each potential class move is assigned a predicted mobility density. Goldthorpe uses seven levels of mobility density as in table 6.1. Thus 'service class' self-recruitment (class I to class I) is granted the highest density (numbered 1), 'independent' to 'independent' recruitment class IV to class IV) the next highest (numbered 2) and so on.

The sensitivity with which the generative model can operate can be illustrated by considering the theories underlying movement out of the service class into the manual ranks (class I into V, VI, VII). In terms of the perceived desirability of manual jobs Goldthorpe supposes they will be an approximate ranking technical > skilled > unskilled (V >VI > VII). However he suggests there might be a counter-balancing tendency, namely the requirement of job experience/apprenticeships normally found in the technical and skilled grades. This will act as barriers for demoted service class sons, since even the 'academically undistinguished' amongst them tend to wallow in the educational system for some time and so be denied the requisite early entry into such trades. Hence the Nuffield team forecast a similar, and in fact the lowest, level of recruitment from the service class into all three manual groupings.

What we have here is more than a mere account of mobility patterns but a theory of class structuration. The mechanisms that prevent or allow intergenerational movement (economic resources, closure strategies, work expectations) are the very factors which constitute identifiable classes. Armed with this

174

comprehensive generative model, the Nuffield researchers are able to go back to the data and, using a method called log-linear analysis, examine the actual mobility densities between the defined classes. Basically they claim a thorough success in fitting these predictions to the data, save for the needs of a few minor amendments, none of which affects the basic tenor of the theory of underlying mechanisms. The important point is that *the achievement of a well-fitting model is taken, quite properly, to be an exoneration of the measurement base as well as the mobility theory.*

Generative model II

As a second example of generative modelling I want to consider the empirical work of Wright (chiefly 1979, 1985). Once again I ought to bang in a couple of qualifications about the candidature of this work as 'generative modelling'. Wright's work spans a tremendous range; he has tried in many ways to be all things to all Marxists. There is no consideration here of what he sometimes avows to be the principal commitment of his studies, that is to understand the ramifications of the work for political struggle. My interest in his work is rather more genteel, namely to point out that the extraordinary degree of conceptual rigour that he brings to hypothesis making can be carried, in turn, to the heart of measurement systems.

The second proviso about Wright's work is again connected with the breadth of his endeavours, but in a different way. Basically his theoretical commitments lie at the structural level; he wants to know what are the organizing features of the capitalist mode of production. According to his first formulation (1978) capitalism is defined by the way labour is controlled, the way investment is organized, and the way authority is exercised. It is these structural arrangements which lay down the framework of class places. Various combinations are possible with regard to whether or not a position in the division of labour involves control over work, investment, or personnel. Capitalists have power on all three dimensions, labour controls none, the petit bourgeoisie controls the first two. In addition there are three 'contradictory locations' which hold different permutations of power. If you have never had to fathom these out before perhaps it's best not to worry, for in a later analysis these organizing features give way to an 'exploitation centred' definition of class (1985). The crucial axes of exploitation which give capitalism its character are production, organizational assets and skills/ credentials. Out of a consideration of the different permutations of types of exploitation a rather different, twelve-point, typology of class places emerges, which will be examined in detail in due course.

Wright's class schema, then, is well and truly derived from theoretical labours and is much more than a ready-to-hand 'indicator' which conveniently groups or ranks individual cases. Likewise, Wright's understanding of causation is about as far away from the search for regularities between operationally defined variables as one can get. The idea is that these class locations are bound up as a structural totality with the economic structure, the state, political actions and interventions, class identity and consciousness etc. (1978, p. 27). Wright, indeed, goes so far as to break down this notion of structural determination in six further sub-types of causation, which he labels 'structural limitation', 'selection', 'reproduction/ non-reproduction', 'limits of functional compatibility', 'transformation' and 'mediation' (1978, Ch. 1).

I am quite unsure what to make of this morass of social processes and causative forces, but generative model it most certainly is not. However, Wright himself rather disarmingly admits that empirical investigation of this mass of inter-connections would require a comparative and historical inquiry well beyond his capacities. So, in the end, empirical investigation

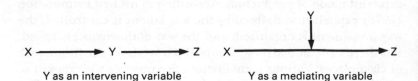

$$X \longrightarrow Y \longrightarrow Z \qquad X \xrightarrow{\quad\downarrow Y\quad} Z$$

Y as an intervening variable   Y as a mediating variable

Figure 6.1   The difference between an intervening and a mediating variable

Source: Adapted from Wright, 1978, p. 25

176

concerns itself with one mode of causation which he calls mediation and defines as follows:

A mediating variable is one which shapes the very relationship between two other variables. Y causes the way in which X affects Z. In a sense a mediating process can be viewed as a 'contextual variable': processes of mediation determine the terrain on which other modes of determination operate (1978, p. 23).

Clearly we are getting close to the language of generative causation here and Wright even produces a little diagrammatic representation of mediation (Fig. 6.1) which is more or less the same as the one I use to portray generative mechanisms (see Fig. 5.1D).

One of the most distinctive features of Wright's research is its use of batteries of hypotheses cast in the form of predictions about the effects of mediating variables. The hypotheses normally have the class location as the unit of analysis and explanation takes the form of how the 'powers' and 'liabilities' peculiar to each location are crucial in such matters as income determination., Reproduced below is a rather splendid diagram which Wright uses to summarize these hypotheses (see Fig. 6.2). More formally, they appear as numbered hypotheses of the following kind (I reproduce only two out of some two dozen).

Hypothesis *The income returns to education will be much greater within the managerial category than within the working class, even after controlling for age, seniority, background, etc.*

Hypothesis *Among proper capitalists, there should be relatively little relationship between income and education; income will be much higher than for any other class position, even controlling for education, age, etc.*

Once again I can only give a glimpse of the generative reasoning that goes into making these hypotheses. If we start with one of the 'contradictory locations' – the managerial class, income determination, claims Wright, is largely a matter of social control. In competitive capitalism, managers must provide responsible and creative behaviour, not simply conformity. Repressive control mechanisms are likely to be counter-productive. Accordingly social control relies heavily on

Figure 6.2 Income returns to education of different class positions

Source: Wright, 1979, p. xxv

inducements of which the main form is the career hierarchy
marked by large income differentials. Such a system is normally
legitimated as a merit system, and the most accessible criterion
for assessing merit is education. It is to be expected, therefore,
that educational qualifications will be closely associated with the
managerial hierarchy and thus income. This relationship should
exist over and above any technical requirements of managerial
posts and of the individual background of the managers
themselves.

If we turn to the working class, a different set of mechanisms
controls the income determination process. Since the working
class are defined in terms of lack of power to control the labour
process, investment, and other agents, it follows that the sale of
labour power to capital is the only available source of income.
Income returns are thus largely a matter of what is available after
capitalists have secured their surplus. Since workers do not plan

or control the labour process, simple conformity is all that is required in the execution of tasks, and social control can thus rely on disciplinary and repressive sanctions. Under certain conditions there can be a shortage of specific categories of skilled labour, perhaps promoted by closed-shop or union training programmes. Hence there will be some income returns to education for the working classes but these returns will be substantially less than for managers. Finally,

> Capitalist income reflects relations of exploitation rather than the reproductive costs of labour power, in any meaningful sense. Capitalist income will, therefore, vary with the magnitude of the capital owned by the capitalist; neither the expected exchange value of capitalist 'labour power', nor the problems of social control within the labour process have any bearing on capitalist income (Wright, 1979, p. 106).

In short, in this position who needs education!

Such is the nature of the explanations on offer. All of it fits quite snugly under the general rubric of generative thinking all right, but is it a *generative model*, or is it *reality-behind-the-appearance hyperbole*, or is it simply description of the *concomitants and contextual accompaniments* to empirical regularities? We can rapidly discount the second possibility since Wright goes to the trouble of checking all the claims empirically; true believers would not go to the bother. There is, however, a reasonable case for arguing that, although the empirical hypotheses are clearly rooted in theory, this theory does no more than describe the background context to a pattern of empirical associations, whose difference is only rather broadly stated. This accords with my definition of explanation-by-concomitants which was criticized in the previous section as providing no worthwhile empirical challenge. It is extremely difficult to argue that Wright's model is about the constitution of the income/education relationship, in the sense of these parameters actually being derivable from the model. Both variables are used in a more or less common-sense fashion, they could be measured according to any ordinary language formulation and on any scale without doing great damage to the reasoning involved and the likelihood of success of the hypotheses

However, such an argument misses the essential conceptual focus of Wright's model which operates much more fundamentally at the level of class locations. So whilst some of the separate hypotheses described above are not particularly explicit about education and income, the totality of hypotheses describes the nature of class boundaries with great rigour. The explanatory mechanisms involved (control of labour, investment and personnel) are turned first and primarily towards the definition of class locations and only then filled out with the details of potential properties and activities of class members which should follow as a result of the causal powers of that class. It is no accident that, in Wright's interview schedules, only one or two questions are required to determine a respondent's income and education, whilst dozens are required to properly situate a class position.

Looking at Wright's data one finds that most of the relationships emerge as predicted, including the education/income regression which reproduce those in Fig. 6.2 to a remarkable extent (save for the cartoon characters). There are exceptions to this, however, such as the predictions relating to the petit bourgeoisie which do not follow the hypothesis at all, and cause Wright to doubt his operational definitions and perhaps even reconsider the basic conceptualization of this particular class fraction. Broadly speaking, though, the treatment of evidence in this work does bear the hallmarks of generative modelling in that empirical research not only verifies the specific substantive propositions but also exonerates the measurement base (at least, that is, that part dealing with class location). Hence, despite the fact that Wright never uses the term, I well and truly declare his work as an example of generative modelling.

Generative Model III

In this case we need have no qualms about applying the label 'generative model' to this particular research programme, since the work I am referring to is that of Boudon (1973, 1974, 1979), who has long been a champion of the strategy. So in this case we have countless examples of generative reasoning to choose from, including a whole book, *Education, Opportunity and Social Inequality*, which is devoted to an understanding of many of the basic regularities of stratification researCh. With the customary proviso that I cannot do full justice to the methodology involved in a couple of pages, I will attempt a brief summary of the logic-in-use underlying his strategy.

Boudon's method normally begins by focusing on a particular expression of inequality and gathering together a range of official or 'bookkeeping data' which tend to show some widespread and recurrent regularity. For instance he provides a range of tables (too extensive to reproduce here) which he believes show that most, if not all, industrial societies experience the following pattern of educational inequality:

- Western societies are characterized by a steady and slow decline of inequality of educational opportunity.
- From a period t to a period $t + 1$, the probability of, say, a worker's son attending high school increases much more considerably than the probability of, say, a professional's son.
- The foregoing observation is also true of college attendance.
- However, from a time t to a time $t + 1$, the additional numbers of high-school students per 100 workers' sons and per 100 professionals' sons are likely to be rather close; the former may even be smaller than the latter.
- At the college level, the number of students per 100 workers' sons is considerably smaller than the number of students who are the sons of professionals (Boudon, 1974, p. 53).

Such are the typical starting points of his analysis. His basic conviction, when faced with the task of having to explain such regularities, is that the data will not speak for themselves, and indeed these findings are properly perceived as the 'remote consequences of elementary mechanisms'. Although no student of realist philosophy he continues in the approved argot as follows:

> [such findings] are the product of the interaction of many factors: inequality of educational structure, extension of meritocracy, change in the social structure and so on. Since we have no data on these variables, a good scientific strategy is to build a theoretical model and observe its behaviour for given values of the parameters (1974, p. 7).

The generative model he produces to meet this end is much more explicit and formalized than is the case with our two previous examples. It consists of a numbered series of axioms detailing those liabilities of social structure and action that might be responsible for the features described in the data above. These axioms describe a fictitious, 'ideal type' society and are stated in an elementary arithmetic form so that it is possible to generate some basic computations about the consequences of the action of these mechanisms. The postulates begin with a description of the occupational and educational system (both three-tiered and pyramidal) as well as portraying the school and college career as a series of selection (or branching) points. The chief mechanisms through which social and educational placement occurs are then formalized as a matrix of probabilities. One such mechanism is described by Boudon as the 'primary' or 'cultural effect' of social background on educational chances. This pools together all the stock-in-trade sociological knowledge about 'cultural capital' and 'material advantages' afforded by the middle-class home. All this is expressed in a simple arithmetic tabulation of the probabilities (fictional remember – this is an unseen mechanism) of the chances of the children of different social background reaching a particular level of education (see Table 6.2).

The second major explanatory mechanism deals with the subjective aspect of stratification. Boudon claims that these should not be envisaged as attitudinal variables dealing with the 'value' of education as viewed by different individuals but, rather, in terms of what he calls the 'utilities' associated with schooling as perceived by the different social groups. It is supposed that

Table 6.2 Generative model of the 'primary' effect of social background on educational achievement

Social background	School achievement			
	R_1 (High)	R_2	R_3 (Low)	Total
C_1 (high)	0.60	0.30	0.10	1.00
C_2	0.50	0.30	0.20	1.00
C_3 (low)	0.30	0.40	0.30	1.00

Source: Boudon (1973, p. 74)

there is a stratified pattern of choices, in which it is possible to associate different 'costs' and 'benefits' of a particular type of schooling as perceived across the different social strata. For instance, for upper-class children the choice of a vocational course would mean social demotion. They (or their families) would, consequently, be more likely to choose a course which tends to lead to maintaining high social status, even if their academic potential is not particularly great and even though the choice might represent a considerable financial cost. On the other hand, working class children have less interest in choosing a prestigious academic course, even if they were reasonably bright, because it would involve greater financial sacrifices and because of peer and family pressures to do so. In such a manner another mechanism governing the allocation of school career places can be formulated in simple arithmetic terms. Although such a mechanism has more affinity with another class of formal models, namely rational choice models, it can be represented in the same social space as the primary mechanism. In this way Boudon fixes a matrix of 'reasonable', if 'arbitrary', values of the utilities of remaining within the high status curriculum and perceived by students with different class and achievement backgrounds (see Table 6.3).

Armed with this package of axioms and mechanisms Boudon is able to generate simulated data showing the potential patterns of association between various items contained in his postulate system. One can illustrate how the model generates such relationships by simply considering the action of this 'utilities' mechanism taken by itself. Boudon, recall, supposes that a child of high school achievement and high social class has a probability

Table 6.3 Generative model of the 'secondary' effect, showing chances of choosing to remain in academic streams for different levels of social background and ability

Social background	School achievement		
	R_1 (High)	R_2	R_3 (Low)
C_1 (high)	0.85	0.75	0.65
C_2	0.70	0.60	0.40
C_3 (low)	0.60	0.40	0.20

Source: Boudon (1973, p. 74)

183

Table 6.4 Exponential effect of the utilities mechanism: theoretical probabilities of remaining in the academic curriculum

	Age			
	15	*16*	*17*	*18*
High class/High ability	85.0	72.2	61.4	52.2
Low class/High ability	60.0	36.0	21.6	13.0

Adapted from Boudon (1973, p. 80)

of 0.85 of staying at school at each of the selection points after the age of fifteen. A child of high achievement but low social class is rated with a probability of 0.60 of staying on at each of the branching points. We can thus generate an exponential model of the over-time rates of school attendance according to the action of this choice mechanism. The probability of surviving beyond the first selection point for the first child is 0.85, the probability of running a further year is $(0.85)^2$, for three years $(0.85)^3$ and so on. A model of the survival rates for both children would produce the contrast shown in Table 6.4.

This, of course, illustrates the action of just one mechanism. The full model of educational and social inequality combines a consideration of the simultaneous effect of the total set of axioms which are hypothesized to control educational and social selection. Boudon's general approach is to go back to those patterns and associations which he deems well-established in the literature, then to suggest those mechanisms from the total list of axioms which he feels are responsible for the particular regularities, and then to attempt to simulate the real patterns found in the data on the basis of deductions and calculations from the mathematical model. For instance, in explaining the last of the regularities from his list printed on page 181, Boudon sets great store by his secondary mechanism of stratification. The fact that the working class have failed to compete for higher educational openings must be largely due to the latter, since on his model the primary effects die out after the early branching points, differences in ability as a function of school background being scarcely observable in the cohorts that do remain at school and college. By contrast the secondary effect repeats itself at each decision point and so is responsible for working-class disadvantage in the higher reaches of education.

In Boudon's case, then, we have the clearest of commitments to the principles of generative modelling. What of my thesis that empirical evidence can only be as good as the generative theorizing that underlies it? The theory in question here systematically relates class and educational places which are filled according to specific selection criteria at specific decision points. Thus it is capable of making a set of empirical predictions at a level which can be regarded as a quantum leap in precision beyond most substantive theorizing. Table 6.4 has shown the exact consequences of educational ability and class locations being related by an exponential function. One must note, however, that Boudon has not attempted to seek an exact empirical match for such theoretical models since his business is to explain regularities across a wide range of national boundaries. The consequence is that the relative exactitude of the conceptual phase of measurement has to be balanced by a certain latitude to account for the conditions of its production. Boudon puts it like this:

> This is exactly the type of situation we confront here: most data were subject to all kinds of errors (heterogeneous classifications, non-simultaneous observations etc). Thus when we found the educational inequality rate was X in one country and Y in another, we translated this quantitatively inaccurate statement into the qualitatively permissible statement 'X is greater (or smaller) than Y' (Boudon, 1974, p. 200).

I thus take Boudon's work as an exoneration of my thesis that the nature of empirical evidence is limited by what theories can discriminate in the first place, though he provides a timely reminder that other factors, too, need to be taken into consideration (which we will pick up in later Chapters). For now, it remains to conclude on the main consideration of this chapter.

6.3 THE NATURE OF SOCIAL MECHANISMS

I will now draw together some of the lessons that can be learnt from these case studies, particularly with respect to what they show about the nature of social mechanisms. The reason for spending such a considerable amount of space describing these three examples of generative modelling is that they will act as anchor points in the investigation of each of the prerequisites and strategies of post-empiricist measurement. I will thus not attempt any self-contained reviews of them as research programmes in their own right. Instead I want to focus here on the immediate problem of how successfully knowledge of generative social mechanisms can be turned to the matter of providing the conceptual parameters that act as the measurement base of empirical enquiry.

Recall my general thesis in this respect. Empirical sociology has traditionally dealt with the meaning of variables at the level of the individual concept. This has simply been a recipe for arbitrary and contested operationalization since measures are based erratically on everyday connotations of the concept in question. I have shown that scientific terms, by contrast, are fixed with great precision because they are developed as part of a generative mathematical model. All the key measurement parameters (units, zero-points, level of measurement etc.) are thus known independently of any operation devised to measure them. In fact the task of measurement is to find operations which correspond to the behaviour of particular properties within these formal systems.

The above examples show that social research can adopt such a strategy to a considerable extent. Substantively, the generative models which are used to establish class categories and boundaries could not be much more different. For Wright class is the context of production which identifies the economic resources and coercive powers open to members of particular class positions. For Boudon class is an emergent property resulting from the cultural assets and patterns of decision making by different groups. For Goldthorpe both class resources and perceptions combine to generate a developing system of hurdles and boundaries which identify the key class positions. Despite these glaring contrasts, these case studies show remarkable similarities in terms of their explanatory and measurement strategies. None of them relies on common-sense categorization in establishing the measurement properties of the key explanatory variables. None of them theorizes in terms of general concomitants and tendencies that engender certain approximately stated class correlates. All of them meet the requirement of defining class positions prior to and independently of any operational criterion. All of them employ an elementary formalism, using axioms and hypotheses to express clear expectations about the empirical consequences of underlying class processes. All develop a model of class in which class positions are understood as part of a system that is constituted by the action of generative mechanisms. All of the theories receive support from empirical data and that evidence exonerates not only the substantive theories but also the measurement and classificatory units that go to make up the theories.

Natural and social mechanisms compared

At this juncture the critic of my thesis will, no doubt, be itching to point out that there is a world of difference between drawing up a list of analogies between generative reasoning in natural and social science and declaring their methodological unity. Whilst one cannot fail to see broad similarities between reasoning which shows how molecular mobility of a gas generates structural properties like temperature, and reasoning which shows how the social mobility of individuals generates structural properties like class position, it is equally clear that there is a limit to such analogies. The most telling difference that remains between the two classes of model is that natural science ones are exact and deterministic, whilst their sociological counterparts yield only probabilistic and conditional empirical predictions. The reasons for this are plain to see in the way basic explanatory mechanisms are construed.

Recall some of the standard physical measures and constants that have been examined in Part 2 (time, length, temperature etc.). These were identified within systems which relied on an understanding of but a few key forces acting as the explanatory mechanism (matter in motion, mechanical force, energy conversion and release etc.). The theoretical framework involved inevitably has a foundation in the likes of basic mechanics, and so submits to exact description in terms of the most familiar mathematical systems such as calculus, geometry, trigonometry etc. It has often been said that such mathematical languages are the very idiom of natural science. This follows from the fact that so many natural science explanations depend upon a description of systems controlled by these elemental generative forces. It is the nature of such mechanisms, then, that gives rise to the way they are theorized, and it is the ability to formalize this theory which gives rise, in turn, to the character and significance of natural science measurement. The basic mathematical systems referred to above are deterministic; that is to say the relationships, hypotheses and laws expressed in terms of them obey an exact function between two or more continuous variables. It follows that empirical tests which have to confirm and duplicate such relationships will automatically constitute the exacting and formidable hurdle provided by having point predictions of one variable against another.

If, by contrast, we turn to the trio of generative sociological models, it is quite plain that they do not establish an understanding of class formation that yields up precise, determinate relationships. Despite the fact that they are models of clarity compared with most of the rest of sociological theory prevailing in the field, these models always end up with conditional statements about observable outcomes: It is a matter of classes being distinguishable in terms of broad levels of mobility that they exchange with one another. It is a matter of classes being distinguishable in terms of broad, over-time probabilities of surviving in high-status educational curricula. It is a matter of classes being distinguishable in terms of broad shifts in income returns to education. Obvious differences follow in terms of the discriminatory powers of the derived measures of social class, and thus of the very significance of the tests that empirical evidence can provide.

So what is it about elemental social mechanisms and the way we construe them that produce sociological models which are 'conditional and probabilistic'? By this phrase I simply mean that sociological theories inevitably take the form of specifying the groups into which society is divided, identifying the properties which differentiate those groups and explaining why these properties are apportioned in different degrees. Given their diversity of theoretical (and political) standpoints, our three case studies provide ideal vantage points from which to study the manner of the operation of those mechanisms which sociologists claim underlie the constitution of the class system. A close study

188

of the explanatory vocabulary involved will inform us of the nature of these mechanisms, and thus of the subsequent limits on type of model and mode of measurement. In returning to these three examples I want to look again at the expression of the explanatory strategies in a way that reduces this to the bare-bones of their logical structure. Once one 'reads-out' their substantive details, one sees the deployment of remarkably similar reasoning processes in the way mechanisms are perceived and in the conceptual structures used to describe their outcomes.

Wright's basic thesis is that the class structure constitutes the central mechanism by which various sorts of resources are appropriated and distributed, therefore determining the underlying capacities to act of various social actors (1985, p. 31). This central mechanism lies in the mode of production and, as we have seen, Wright has toyed with various permutations of the structuring forces which can be said to extend from the capitalist mode of production. In the earlier versions these mechanisms were a trio of processes associated with *domination,* and in the latter version these were amended to be replaced by three mechanisms of *exploitation.* In general terms, one thinks of 'domination' as a process of one group controlling or constraining the action of another. 'Exploitation' carries a mental map of the welfare of one group depending on appropriating the products of another group. This general imagery of control, constraint, domination, exploitation, appropriation is of course common to the vocabulary expressing explanatory mechanisms in all structural theorizing. The social forces here are thus not at all like the forces of nature that act as the generative process in physical science models. In the latter the active forces are moving objects, the energy of bodies etc., whereas the active ingredient in this type of sociological explanation is ultimately composed of groups operating and responding to social controls. Stripped down to its bare essentials then, the basic social forces of domination, exploitation (etc.) are mechanisms of social division and the conceptual structures that result from the action of these generative processes are simply the groups and sub-groups that emerge from these transactions.

This brings us to the way further properties in the social system are conceived. Wright's model (like others of its ilk) goes on to explain the effects of the mechanism of social division on the action of the groups so formed. The basic idea is that group membership (class location) limits the capacities for action of the various groups. Again the explanatory vocabulary is instructive; social constraints do not enforce any definite, unique set of actions, they merely limit the possibilities. This can be seen quite readily in the specific examples of domination and exploitation mentioned already. Of a group of workers deprived of control over the manner of the execution of their work tasks, one can say they will not only be deskilled, but also more open to forms of domination, one aspect of which will be the loss of capacity to bargain for high wages. The model, however, does not determine action, it does not fix and thus allow predictions about exact wage levels. All it can do is tell us of broad capacities for action across the lines of domination. The dominated group will have less income than groups who retain control over the execution of work. This example indicates the typical scope of empirical evidence relevant to generative models based on mechanisms such as exploitation and domination. Such forces act in ways that limit the capacity for action of various groups, and the model explains only broad asymmetries in the social properties that result from this action.

Let us move now to Boudon's understanding of the nature of the social mechanisms which lead to perceivable regularities of class and educational inequality. Boudon is, of course, a leading advocate of methodological individualism, so his perception of the way the social world goes round could hardly be further removed from that of Wright. Methodological individualism involves the principle that sociologists must employ explanatory strategies which regard individual actions as the basic atom of social inquiry, or, as I should now perhaps put it, as the source mechanism of all societal forms. The idea is that even macro sociological problems of social and institutional change are only intelligible if the analysis comes down to the perceptions and actions of individuals. Even so, we shall see that Boudon's theories have similar discriminatory powers, occupy corresponding conceptual structures, and so can be mapped into identical data forms as those of 'structuralist' sociology.

As we have seen, the distinctive element of Boudon's theory about the allocation of social and education positions is his use of mechanisms describing choice and decision making. Again the task here is to strip the processes described of all substantive detail in order to reveal the underlying conceptual parameters. How does Boudon reconstruct and represent the decision-making fields in question? Once again, one has to risk banality to report that the fundamental social processes involved do not remotely resemble the action of elemental generative processes in natural science. A minimal description of decision-making obviously requires two basic ingredients, namely a person doing the choosing and a set of choices (minimally two) from which to choose. It follows (and this is no masterpiece of logic!) that basic to any model of the social implications of decision-making will be a set of categories describing the agents involved and another set describing the options open to them. The basic conceptual space created by decision-making models can thus be thought of as the set of cells or boxes formed by the matrix of agents and options.

Boudon actually describes such a model at one point as a 'box model', and goes on to suggest that sociological theory can be thought of as a process akin to filling in such conceptual boxes (1974, p. 122). For example the set of boxes describing social position can be thought of as the social structure; structural change can be represented by altering the number and size of the boxes; mobility and competition can be portrayed as processes of allocation to the boxes and so forth. His rationale is precisely that supposed here, that data forms take their shape from theory. Simple as they are, these conceptual structures are very close to that used in sociological theory. Thus if we think in boxes, then we must box our evidence.

More particularly Boudon reckons that the notions of costs, benefits and utilities comprise the central mechanisms controlling allocation to these social boxes. As we have seen in the examples relating to the curricula preferences of different social classes, the notion of 'best choice' is poorly defined and so can only be given a probabilistic representation. According to Boudon there are several habitual features of social decision-making which are responsible for this; (i) although methodological individualism lays great stress on the agent's understanding there is no reason why parents and children should have complete knowledge of the social and cash value of different curricula and careers; (ii) for the outcomes of choices

191

to work in the expected manner depends on the action of other agents making the same choices – again knowledge of this is imperfect; (iii) a certain pattern of choices can lead to unintended outcomes as when too many people choose a certain educational path and so devalue the benefits that once occurred – again knowledge of changing utilities can be laggardly (Boudon, 1979, Ch. 8; 1982).

In these models, then, sociological theory is perceived to occupy the same conceptual space as the agent's decision fields. At its most basic this gives us a structure in which certain elements can be clearly categorized and defined (curricula forms are closely institutionally sanctioned, class groupings less so) and in which others can only be described in conditional terms (costs, benefits etc. can only be specified probabilistically). The important point to note is that this mirrors exactly the 'ontological' form of Wright's model – we end up with a classification of a range of social positions distinguished by certain conditional capacities to limit action. Formalizing such theories involves simply the fixing of certain probability levels representing the different liabilities for action of the respective groups and then generating hypotheses about the consequences of this action (cf. Wright again). The empirical evidence pertinent to such models involves the operationalization of the categories of agents and options and counting the cases falling into each (cf. Wright again).

Social constitution and sociological measurement

We now have a rather significant result. The general thesis here is that sociological theory determines the conceptual structures of explanation, which in turn determine the measurement parameters into which we should encode empirical evidence. If one looks at two markedly different traditions of sociological explanation, when analysed down into their basic generative structures, they produce models which demand exactly the same data forms. I will not delay matters further by showing that the same applies to our third example of a generative model. Goldthorpe's mobility theory, using the underlying mechanisms of the 'resources' and 'desirability' associated with different class positions, calls once again on this 'box and probability' type theorizing to explain observations in the boxes found aplenty in the mobility matrix.

What is happening in these examples is that the models are displaying something very general about the nature of social mechanisms. These selfsame conceptual and data forms keep turning up over and over again because they are revealing something elemental about the constitution of society. The fact that a theory of exploitation and a theory of decision-making (not to mention a theory of market position) generate conceptual spaces that are formally identical allows us to venture some absolute statements about the nature of empirical evidence required to substantiate sociological theory.

As a first step one should note that the identity of analytic structures in these case studies provides some evidence for the claims of all those meta-theorists, most notably Giddens, who have been attempting to persuade us for years that the so-called explanatory dualisms of structural and interpretative sociology should instead be regarded as a duality, representing but two sides of the same social process. For instance, of structural explanation he argues that it is necessarily incomplete without reference to the actor's reasoning and knowledge.

> Structural constraints do not operate independently of the motives and reasons that agents have for what they do. They cannot be compared with the effect of say an earthquake which destroys a town and its inhabitants without their in any way being able to do anything about it. The only moving objects in human social relations are individual agents, who employ resources to make things happen, intentionally or otherwise. The structural properties of social systems do not act, or 'act on', anyone like forces of nature to 'compel' him or her to behave in any particular way (Giddens, 1984, p. 181).

Likewise purely interpretative explanations are incomplete because actions logically presuppose the possession of some power or resources which enable the deed to be done, and once carried out the action will automatically work towards the reproduction of wider structural features and resources.

Accepting this general picture explains neatly the analytic similarity of the two generative models described above. At whatever point one begins sociological explanation, one is drawn into this cycle in which the properties of social systems are to be regarded as both the medium and outcome of agency. If, with Wright, one starts with the power to exploit and dominate identified with certain societal forms, it is always necessary to consider how this power is exercised in terms of the choices and actions of the people identified with different resources. Thus, in the end, structural explanation will take the form of specifying broad limits placed on the choices of the members of identified groups. If, with Boudon, one starts with choices expressed by different social groups, one has to understand that these decisions have to be made within limits imposed by the resources of that group and within the bounds of the group's understanding of the outcomes of their action. Thus in the end, agency-centred explanations take the form of specifying broad limits placed on the choices of members of identified groups. The two explanatory forms are thus one.

I have taken a reprehensible amount of time digging out these basic analytic structures which are characteristic of all sociological theory and explanation. However, it is worth risking the charge of pedantry here since these conceptual structures are the key to the whole body of investigation, affecting inquiry right through to the point where empirical evidence is manufactured. If the above analysis is correct, a major limitation on sociological method follows; namely that inquiry must function with only the simplest measurement structures and operations. The elemental form of the sociological hypothesis is a statement about the probabilities of certain types of action in certain social groups. Framing the appropriate evidence will take the form of operationalizing these categories, counting the cases falling into the categories and comparing this to the probabilistic estimates. In short conditional and probabilistic modes of theorizing call upon categorical scales and counting operations.

One could describe this claim as arguing for the restriction that nominal (and possibly ordinal) scales are the obligatory level of measurement for social properties. Whilst this is certainly true in one sense, you may recall that it is a formulation that I do not exactly admire. There are indeed no underlying mechanisms in society which create social systems in which properties interact in an exact, continuous and determinate fashion. There are simply no social theories which enable us to make point predictions of the value of one variable against another. Thus whilst it is simple enough to conceive any number of social variables as having interval level characteristics, this degree of precision is quite irrelevant to any hypotheses that we are able to construct. However, I take exception to the 'nominal scales only' formulation, simply because it evokes some of the fallacious arguments (discussed in section 2.2) about the inherent nature of social properties. Theories concern the way generative processes govern the way that systems move from one state to another. Likewise, evidence should be regarded as holistic, expressing the interaction of whole systems of properties, and not be declared valid or invalid at the level of individual variables. Hence there is no reason why sociologists should not utilize 'ready-made' interval scales even though these inevitably will be put to use in evaluating more broadly stated theories (cf. Wright's income variables).

The limitations on measurement uncovered here should be understood more widely and relate to the matter of the discriminatory power of empirical evidence in sociology. I have argued that the construction of meaningful data requires attention to the operations of classifying and counting social properties, but the point is really about the nature of the test constituted by such data. Sociological theory is conditional and probabilistic; it can do no more than foresee broad limits to the number of cases that will occupy certain given social categories. Boudon (1974, p. 199) refers to this as hypothesis-making of the 'more or less' type, and our range of examples follows this format of defining a matrix of social groupings and showing that a certain property or pattern of properties will crop up rather more frequently here, rather less frequently there and so on.

In terms of evidence this means that there will be a whole range of empirical findings that can be considered confirmatory, and likewise a range of disconfirmatory data with a somewhat arbitrary dividing line between the two. To put this critically one might wonder whether the practice of making 'more or less' predictions, followed by data which 'more or less' interpret them, isn't 'more or less' always going to be successful. Without going this far, one must acknowledge that these limitations do mean that the observational hurdle to be leapt by successful sociological theory is relatively reduced. But on the other hand, fit with data is not the unique, be-all-and-end-all requirement of theory, and must be balanced by other logical and conceptual constraints. There is no reason, of course, to suppose that this balance should remain identical across all of the empirical sciences.

Chapter Seven

CLOSURE: ACTUALISM VERSUS REALISM

This chapter examines the utility of the notion of closed system inquiry in quantitative sociological research. In Chapter 5 I have argued that in natural science the importance of closed system investigation (i.e. experimentation) followed closely from the basic realist premise that events in the physical world are conjoined because of the action of some underlying process. The purpose of experimentation is to provide a context in which the key generative mechanism acts as purely as possible to produce a given regularity. The investigation of the applicability of this idea to a non-experimental science like sociology faces several problems which I need to introduce here in order to establish the framework for this chapter.

The explanation of closure developed in Chapter 5 was, naturally enough, a realist model. It must be acknowledged, however, that there are other models of closure which have been developed in alternative accounts of the scientific method and, since it is these further accounts which have been influential in sociology, I need to give them voice here. Following Bhaskar (1978), I therefore distinguish two accounts of closure, the *actualist* and the *realist*. The actualist account differs from that described above in that it supposes that closure refers to the total isolation of a system, so that the effect of one variable on another can be studied in the absence of all other variables. There is thus a preliminary task to be performed in evaluating these accounts, and the first section of the chapter will demonstrate the advantages of the realist account in both logical and descriptive terms.

In the second section of the chapter I turn to an examination of closure as applied in sociological method. The most direct application of the closure theme is upheld in those methods of statistical control which are said to imitate the logic of experimentation in physical science. Although the limitations of elaboration techniques, partialling methods, path analysis etc. have been much debated at the technical level, an essential failing in the basic strategy has gone largely unnoticed. Closure is perceived on the actualist account as a matter of isolating the effects of one variable on another in the absence of any other influence. I am thus able to show how the logical failings of actualism work their way through as practical defects in the statistical approach.

The possibility remains of organizing social science around a realist understanding of closure. In the second section of the chapter I go on to give examples of work in other schools of empirical sociology which use a method of closure which is more akin to the realist notion. These are none other than the family of 'generative models' I introduced in the previous chapter. Closure in these cases is considered a matter of identifying the precise blend, composition and manner of operation of the mechanisms which constitute the observed regularity. The means to this end involves the incorporation of longitudinal and comparative designs in quantitative analysis.

7.1 CLOSED SYSTEMS IN SCIENTIFIC METHOD

Actualism

All accounts of scientific investigation recognize the importance of the discovery of empirical regularities. However, much debate has ensued on the matter of the relationships between such regularities and empirical generalizations and scientific laws. Of central significance in unravelling these questions has been the concept of closed system inquiry. Bhaskar (1978) has provided us with the most complete account of the idea of system closure in natural science in his comparison of two accounts of closure – the actualist and the realist. 'Actualism' is just Bhaskar's word for empiricism, and in this context it refers to the doctrine that laws are simply relationships between observable events. These events, in turn, are supposed to constitute the basic or actual units of our experience.

198

Strong actualism (read crude empiricism) identifies, for Bhaskar, that proposition which requires that the search for empirical regularities must end in the discovery of generalizations that are *universal*, since it is only then that they can qualify as *fundamental* laws of science. He shows that such a chain of reasoning is completely unrealistic, for it fails to acknowledge that the discovery of the regular sequences of events, on which the whole argument is based, is in practice dependent on the experimental activities of the scientist. If it is necessary to produce experimentally controlled and closed systems to observe empirical regularities, it is quite clear that such regularities cannot also be universal. The trouble with the doctrine is the strong requirement that *unconditional* sequences of events are presupposed in the construction of a law. With the possible exception of the observations of interplanetary motion in astronomy, such regularities are unknown to science.

This completes stage one of Bhaskar's argument, which does no more than point out that human interference is normally a condition of producing the closed system involved in the observation of empirical regularities. There are a number of potential ways out of the paradox that science apparently seeks out regularities to form the basis of universal laws and explanations, and yet can only discover them in closed and artificial situations. Before he calls upon realism to solve the riddle, he allows actualism a final stab at bringing consistency to its methodological pronouncements, under a slightly modified set of assumptions he refers to as 'weak actualism'. It is worth biding our time here since we will meet many a weak actualist in our subsequent visit to sociological methodology.

Weak actualism retains much of the basic metaphysics of empiricism. It still works with the basic unit of actual events which we supposedly register as direct observation. Some of these events are still presumed to be locked in law-like relationships with other events. The basic task of science is still reckoned to be the discovery of these basic regularities. The only difference between strong and weak actualism is that according to the latter the everyday world consists of an infinite flux of events with the result that certain regular sequences can frequently be disguised because of the action of further events. It is assumed that multiple causation is the rule and that a whole series of

199

relationships may act upon any single object at any instance. Under normal conditions of observation one causal influence can overlie, distort, nullify, or even perhaps exaggerate the effects of another one. This notion is depicted in Fig. 7.1a, in which a regularity between X and Y is masked in real world observation because of the extraneous influences A, B and C. The consequence of this is that rather extraordinary conditions of observation are required to observe a pure causal sequence which boil down to cutting off that fragment of the world containing the regularity from all other influences. This is depicted in Fig. 7.1b, in which the effects of A, B and C are physically removed so as not to distort the observation sequence.

In short, the imagery of a closed system assumed under this modified empiricism is of a totally isolated system in which all other potential causal factors are removed or assumed constant. Following on from this one can construe the weak actualist understanding of experimentation which simply duplicates this exclusionary principle. The experimentalist would be responsible for isolating an independent variable, causing it to change, observing its effect on a single dependent variable, making sure that all other potential external influences were excluded. Such a view of 'successful' experimental practice leads to much more restricted sense given to the law statement in which the notion of a causal law is tied entirely to the realm of the closed system. Universal laws of the 'whenever this, then that' formula serve no practical purpose, rather laws should be

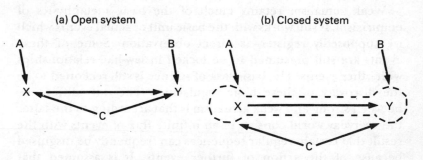

Figure 7.1   Actualist causation and closure

expected only in the *ceteris paribus* usage – 'whenever this, then that, excluding the other'.

Bhaskar goes on to argue that weak actualist understanding of closed systems is also unstable. Basically the problem is that it makes generous use of the *c.p.* clause in formulating the principles of scientific explanation, but leaves us with no means of identifying the conditions to which it refers. If one equates closed systems with mono-causation and open systems with multiple causation a range of contradictions and inconsistencies follow, of which I will paraphrase only two here.

(i) To achieve total isolation of a causal regularity would seem to require knowledge of all other potential causal factors that can influence an object, or in other words ' a complete state-description (or complete history) of the world'. The experimentalist requires this knowledge in order to control potential external factors and failing this has to rely on the assumption that such factors are inactive or constant during the period of observation. Since we cannot achieve knowledge of the laws of science without this complete state description, and we cannot achieve a complete state description without knowledge of all laws, scientists are forced to assume that uncontrolled external factors are irrelevant. The decision on when a closed system is achieved is thus simply an arbitrary or pragmatic one (cf. Bhaskar, 1978, p. 77).

(ii) Suppose a law is established as in (i) and suppose it is found to be inapplicable in some subsequent observation. One cannot know with certainty whether the law has been disconfirmed or the *ceteris paribus* conditions have not been fulfilled. If one presumes that the *c.p.* clause was not satisfied, one is simply presupposing the truth and applicability of the law. If one admits the law is false, one acknowledges the law to be based in the first place on arbitrary judgements about what constitute its closed system of operation (cf. Bhaskar, 1978, p. 93).

Realism

The background to the alternative conception of closure in terms of realist notions of causation, experimentation and explanation has already been developed at length in Chapter 6. The first important idea to recall is that the constant conjunction of events is understood to be a consequence of some underlying mechanisms which connects them. Explanation begins with a theoretical model which shows how changes in the generative mechanism bring about changes in the interrelationships between constituent properties in a system. These conceptually-closed systems are thus the targets for empirical research and the means of testing such hypothesized models is to show that they can be realized through the production of corresponding empirically-closed systems.

This difference in explanatary fundamentals leads in turn to a totally different understanding of the nature of experimentation. Under the actualist model, experimentalists isolate and then stimulate the independent variable and then observe its effects on a dependent variable which is also shielded from other extraneous influences. In realist experiments the researcher builds an entire physical system, every aspect of which is controlled. A context is created and manipulated so as to achieve empirically a system in which two component properties behave in a manner expected by the conceptual model. The actual manipulations involved are thus considerably different. Under normal (open system) conditions the two variables under scrutiny are involved in a range of simultaneously occurring physical systems, each under the control of different mechanisms. In non-experimental conditions no regularity will be observed between two variables due to the action of this whole set of mechanisms which may override and counteract one another in different ways (Fig. 7.2a).

Performing an experiment thus consists of what Bhaskar refers to as the dual functions of experimental *production* and *control*. The first stage consists of triggering off an underlying mechanism to ensure that it is active. To repeat his own illustration of the Ohm's law experiment, this would consist of such matters as building an electric circuit and generating a current within it. The second stage consists of preventing any interference with the action of this mechanism, which in the said example might consist of maintaining the appropriate resistance levels and the shielding of any extraneous magnetic fields. In short realist experimentation consists of the conjoining of three elements,

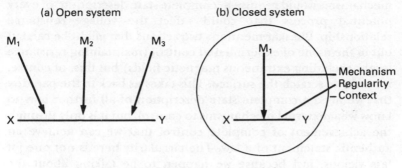

Figure 7.2 Realist causation and closure

whereby an experimental *context* is created by isolating a known *mechanism* to produce a given *regularity* (Fig. 7.2b).

Realist closure boils down to the matter of ensuring the two requirements of production and control are 'in phase'. Explanation, on this view, takes the form of telling us that events happen because something possesses a structure which gives it the power to generate these happenings, if the appropriate conditions obtain. Closure is thus a process of matching up a generative mechanism to environmental conditions which allow the action of that mechanism in all its purity.

Whilst this chapter is primarily concerned with the applications of these ideas, some brief comments on the authenticity of the realist version of closure are in order. In some respects they bear a remarkable and awkward resemblance to the empiricist principles of closure which Bhaskar so conclusively rejects. His notion of experimental control is resonant of the aim of 'isolation' from external causal factors in the weak actualist model. To be sure, there is a major difference in that one refers to the control over confounding variables whilst the other is concerned with warding off extraneous generative mechanisms. However since they are both concerned with potential (i.e. unknown) threats to closure they both require huge doses of pragmatism to put them in practice. The arbitrariness involved in declaring a system free of external constraint can be made into the subject of a range of paradoxes and contradictions noted above. To use Bhaskar's own example of Ohm's law experiment, it would seem necessary that experimental control of external mechanisms would require a 'complete state description' of every potential process that could affect the voltage/resistance relationship. Bhaskar mentions two actions that might be carried out in the name of experimental control (maintaining resistance levels, excluding extraneous magnetic fields) but this, of course, is hardly to scratch the surface. This takes us back to the paradox that we need a complete state description of all further laws to know what external mechanisms to control, but it is only through the achievement of complete control that we can achieve an authentic statement of a law. The circularity here is not one jot less vicious, just because we happen to be talking about the control of mechanisms rather than variables.

Supporters of Bhaskar may claim that he is well prepared to meet this point. Repeatedly he stresses that law-like statements 'speak of structures not events, the generator not the generated' (1978, p. 102). In other words laws are conditional statements which assert the form of the regularity which would come about supposing that a particular generative mechanism comes into operation, undisturbed. Thus it is not the business of a law to speculate about the conditions in which its mechanism will operate. Generative process and thus laws occur in both open and closed systems, and what we must be careful about is confusing laws with empirical regularities and indeed with the whole business of predicting one event on the basis of another. This presumably would be taken to answer the paradox posed above in that the situation is only paradoxical because it supposes that the meaning of a law is tied to a particular experimental outcome.

Such reasoning undoubtedly serves a useful purpose. It gets us out of the empiricist dilemma that laws only exist in totally isolated systems, and thus allows for the possibility that our knowledge of laws can be applied to open systems (engineering becomes possible after all). However the argument that laws are quite independent of empirical statements pays no heed to the significance of experimentation in the rest of the realist model. So whilst he scornfully dismisses the identification of laws and empirical generalizations, Bhaskar does allow that laws can be 'independently and well confirmed (under experimentally closed conditions)' (1978, p. 101). In short realism seems to hurtle between idealism when it comes to describing the function of laws and verificationism when it comes to describing the function of experiments. So whilst the general run of empirical relationships may not be significant for the veracity of a law, the predictions involved in experimental hypotheses are vital and so too must be our worries about the practicalities of achieving experimental closure.

Note that I do not consider such objections fatal to the realist project. Much of the problem seems to me to be inherent in the adversarial style of prescriptive methodology which Bhaskar deploys. He comes to the formulation of the rules for realist closure by the conventional and outdated tactic of trying to provide correctives to the logical pitfalls of what he refers to as actualism. We all know by now that there are paradoxes aplenty in what the rest of us would call positivism, but we also should know by now that it is impossible to derive any set of methodological prescriptions which do not at some point rest on actions open to the judgement of scientific actors. As soon as this is pointed out the argument can be run back to show that the principles are incomplete, inconsistent, paradoxical etc. One might say that since Bhaskar is prepared to live according to the reasoning process of this system then we should be prepared to kill him off under it. Once again however my preferred approach is to abandon the purely prescriptive level and look for the pay-offs of this approach to closure at the level of logic-in-use. What is important about the realist conception of closure, and what I would like to retain for comparison with sociological method, is this pincer movement of matching up mechanisms to environmental conditions.

One can see the vital difference in the actualist and realist approach to experimental closure by re-examining an example much discussed in part 2 on the regularities of pendular motion. One could attempt to describe the system in actualist fashion, as a series of variables (time, gravitational force, pendular length etc.), and carry out controlled experiments to establish regularities in their relationships. Closure under actualism would consist of isolating the variables in question and warding off potential disturbing influences. This might lead to eminently sensible precautions like encasing the pendulum to isolate the system from extraneous air currents. However, it immediately becomes obvious that the real business of control in this system is applied to mechanisms and not variables. The experimentalist is simply not interested in tracking down and controlling all the potential correlates of the variables within the system. It doesn't matter for instance, that time is involved in a whole range of physical laws to do with the diffusion of gases, the rate of cooling of liquids etc. It does not matter, that gravitational force is involved in laws of planetary motion and the control of tides. Quite clearly it would be ludicrous to control for tidal conditions in an experiment on pendular motion. Note, however, that we only know it to be ludicrous because we know the crux of experimental control depends minimally on 'isolation' and almost entirely on understanding how the mechanism controlling the system works in a particular experimental context.

For instance in the pendulum experiment, I have already shown (in Chapter 5) how the amplitude of oscillation was an unrecognized ambient condition in early investigation. The balance of forces controlling the period of oscillation itself changes with angular deflection (see Fig. 5.5). Eventually a simple control process was utilized which suppressed the difficulty by recognizing that a different pattern of forces regulates large as opposed to small amplitude oscillations and thereafter constrained investigation to the latter. Note that control here is a matter of re-specifying and re-making a new experimental context, rather than somehow erecting a physical barrier to ward off the influences of unwarranted external complications. Other subsequent improvements in experimental control in the same context, such as the change from simple to isochronous to compound pendula, need to be understood in exactly the same vein.

It is at this practical level that the differences between actualist and realist notions of closure present themselves most clearly. Actualism lacks a notion of experimental context; it lacks a theory of experiments as physical systems. Control is thus a matter of *isolating* external variables rather than a *matching* process whereby a context is identified to harness the mechanism which produces the observable regularity. Real experimental control is thus principally achieved in a process which, for want of a better term, we can refer to as *recontextualization*. As we shall see it is this opposition between closure as 'isolation' versus 'contextualization' that will exercise us most as we move now to the application of the idea in sociological research.

7.2 CLOSED SYSTEMS IN SOCIOLOGICAL METHOD

Given sociologists' obvious inability to manipulate people's characteristics and social conditions, no one has ever suggested seriously that *experimental methods* can find broad application in social research. However, in so far as methods textbooks are a guide, it seems that it is a very rare exception that dismisses the possibility of applying *experimental logic*. Naturally enough the quasi-experimental approaches prescribed carry a different notion of closure, which consists of swapping the notion of control by physical manipulation for the idea of statistical control. A variety of techniques and procedures are used in the name of statistical closure but they share a basic understanding of the problem which has been characterized thus: 'In one form or another the control approach is viewed as a way of determining the influence some specific characteristic has on a dependent variable net of the influence due to other characteristics' (Lieberson, 1985, p. 120).

Actualist closure

The goal expressed in such a strategy is none other than the weak-actualist version of closure, that is to say the aspiration is the complete isolation of a causal regularity by way of the elimination of all other potential causal factors. Such a conception is expressed directly in the elementary elaboration techniques which form the logical basis of the entire family of modern multivariate methods. The basic approach is to begin by observing the joint occurrence of two properties which are expected to form a causal regularity. At the same time the researcher observes the behaviour of a third variable which is suspected of being capable of influencing the basic properties under study. Since it is impossible to control physically for this contaminating effect, all that can be done is to hold the third variable constant statistically. This requires that the researcher inspect the hypothesized causal relationship in conjunction with all the different values of the third variable. If the initial relationship remains constant, the extraneous factor turns out to have no influence. If the initial relationship disappears then the hypothesized relationship is considered spurious and brought about entirely by the action of the third variable. If the initial relationship changes according to the value of the third variable, a partial relationship is said to hold, whose effect can be calculated. This process is repeated for any number of perceived potential extraneous influences. An array of 'third' variables is examined until the researcher is satisfied a closed system is achieved whereby the effects of extraneous variables are calculated out, discovered to be insignificant or simply assumed to be constant or unimportant.

Since the heyday of elaboration techniques the statistical methods used in these tasks have, of course, changed but the logic-in-use remains intact. All that has changed is that it is now possible to apply controls simultaneously, to work with multi-causal systems, to utilize the methods at different levels of measurement, to apply them using multiple indicators of 'difficult-to-measure' concepts and so on. All of this leaves the notion of closure unchanged. Basically what has happened is that more and more variables can be incorporated in a causal model, the all-time record I believe being pushed to the century mark. Once the various influences have been apportioned the researcher declares the system closed under the assumption that all further causal factors are random, minor or subject to little fluctuation (e.g. in path analysis this formal assumption takes the form that all residual terms are uncorrelated).

Bhaskar probably perceived weak actualism to be a somewhat idealized philosophical stance (and a straw-man to boot). In fact, we discover the method to be alive and well in much causal analysis in sociology. Quite naturally one discovers that this form of social research is driven into exactly the same problems and paradoxes noted in Bhaskar's critique of the general philosophical position (and a few more besides due to the inability to achieve direct physical control). The most obvious difficulty is the necessarily arbitrary decision involved in declaring statistical controls complete so that closure is achieved. To control all extraneous variables adequately requires that they be included in the initial survey hypotheses, which requires in turn that the researcher possess a 'complete state description' of all possible influences. This runs us around the same old circle that if the discovery of a law presumes knowledge of all other laws how does one come to possess an understanding of any law in the first place. Social researchers would probably be more inclined to express the problem in a practical way thus:

> In one form or another, we constantly encounter the following argument: 'The investigator did not control for X_{14}; had such a control been made, then the influence of X_8 on Y would be quite different from the results obtained by the investigator'. In addition, if control variable X_{14} cannot be measured adequately or is not used for some other reason, someone disinclined to accept the empirically determined influence of X_8 can claim that the observed effect would be radically different if only X_{14} were tossed into the statistical hopper (Lieberson, 1985, p. 121).

This problem of making arbitrary decisions on closure is made all the more pernicious because statistical controls are applied, quite literally, after the event. In experimental science the function of actualist closure is quite clear: having decided upon the variables in the experimental hypotheses all other influences need to be physically excluded. Suppose, for instance, we suspect that extraneous air currents are disturbing the regularities of pendulum motion; we can entirely remove the problem by encasing the instrument. So whilst there is going to be a degree of arbitrariness engendered by knowing what to control, the meaning of closure as the system resulting from the complete exclusion of external physical forces is crystal clear.

By contrast, suppose we were investigating the relationship between 'type of school attended' and 'educational achievement', it would no doubt be suggested that some type of control be applied to account for the influence of 'parental status'. Now, since controls of this type are applied to data rather than to the event itself, we have more than one way of conceiving the nature of closure. Firstly, one can envisage the closed system as referring to a purely conditional situation, taking the form of a statement saying that x is the relationship between school type and achievement that would occur if one supposes the absence of all other influences. Secondly one might argue that since in the real world 'parental status' will always have an effect on achievement, that the best course of action is to incorporate it alongside 'type of school' and indeed any other significant variable in some overall model of 'educational achievement'. In this case one is using an alternative image of a closed system as referring to actual outcomes and based on the idea of portraying the overall pattern of influence on any dependent variable. Here, closure is portrayed as a segment of the real world in which the behaviour of individuals, or at least part of their behaviour, is controlled by law-like relationships connecting certain social properties. One concludes that not only is statistical closure arbitrarily drawn (the X14 problem) but the dilemma over whether to 'partial out' or 'calculate in' the effects of additional variables leaves us with ambiguity over the very meaning of a closed system.

This brings us to the second paradox involved in the weak actualist usage of a closed system, concerning the idea of replicability. The issue involves the choices open under the weak actualist version of closure when a causal regularity discovered in one setting does not apply in another. For the philosopher (Bhaskar) this problem drives the researcher into one or other of the unpalatable options which can be rephased for the social research context as follows. One either asserts that the original causal relationship (or model) is true and claims that additional influences prevail in the second instance which have not been picked up by statistical control. In this case one simply assumes the truth and applicability of a particular empirical result. The alternative is to admit that the original relationship carries no general weight and is itself based on an arbitrary notion of statistical closure in the first place.

Oddly enough, sociologists have not gone to the barricades with respect to these alternatives. The expectations regarding the likelihood of exact replication of findings from one study to the next are remarkably low. For instance, in comparative studies of mobility rates or longitudinal studies of the status attainment process, there is simply no expectation that mobility or path coefficients will be identical from context to context or from time to time. Neither would there be any anticipation that increasing the number of variables modelled, or increasing the complexity of statistical control, would render up identical coefficients describing the same law-like regularities. So in fact the only puzzle in the sociological context is why researchers keep faith with the notion of statistical closure when they have so little regard for its power?

Rather than address this sociology of sociology question directly, it is preferable to examine the perceived reasons for the limitation of the notion of statistically closed systems. One can spot this immediately by way of the reaction of any half-decent substantive sociologist when it comes to explaining why the so-called controlled empirical regularities that apply in one context do not occur in another. The answer would not take the form of drafting in further independent variables which would differentiate the two situations but would call upon some contextual mechanism to explain why the empirical relationships themselves were limited and conditioned in different ways. For instance, if there was a need to explain why individual mobility rates varied across space and time, reference would be made to such factors as ideological and political pressures protecting or eroding class boundaries, technological and economic change modifying occupational openings, difference in meaning structures determining the expectations and climate for mobility.

This brings us to the formal reason why statistical closure cannot be achieved, which is that there is a whole range of such contextual mechanisms which profoundly shape the empirical associations uncovered in research, but which cannot be represented, let alone controlled, in the standard statistical models. A number of authors have made this particular point about the representation of the 'status attainment process' in the form of path or causal models (Pawson, 1978; Crowder, 1974; Boudon, 1974). Taking their lead from Blau and Duncan (1967), the idea of such models is to explain occupational status as the product of a number of regular influences which are traceable through a person's career (parent's occupation, parent's income, educational status and so forth). Each linkage is treated (as in actualism) as a direct causal influence of one discrete property on another, and the aim is to decipher and quantify the precise pattern and contribution of each factor on the dependent variable, occupational status. The substantive omission in such models is that such matters as the changing structure of employment opportunities obviously place limits on any relationship describing occupational attainment but cannot be represented in such a model since it is not a property of an individual. The core of the problem is that the occupational structure cannot be construed as an independent variable influencing the dependent event, since it works by placing limits on the form of the relationship between individual properties. What is worse, the influence of occupational structure can destroy the whole point of looking for constant relationships between individuals' qualifications and their jobs. The range of individuals sampled in a path model will typically have attained their occupations at different points in time and, under these different employment regimes, the same individual characteristic (say, educational qualification) can carry a totally different value when it comes to actual job appointments.

This problem of fitting employment structures into path models of status attainment is but a small example of the range of social forces which are omitted in the attempt to follow the doctrines of actualist closure. Once again the failure is due to the lack of any notion of the context which locates the mechanisms which determine the regularities between component properties. Statistical control works entirely within the 'isolation' model of closure and all that can be excluded (or included) within such systems are a range of variables, all conceived and measured on the same unit of analysis that the researchers happen to have had the forethought to include in data collection. What is required in sociological method is a strategy of closure which treats the central issue as the 'contextualization' of regularities, and it is thus to the potentialities of the realist approach that we must now turn.

Realist closure

It would be quite wrong to conclude on the basis of the problems with statistical control that sociology should be regarded as an open system discipline charged with a completely different set of ambitions from the experimental approaches. The critique above relates solely to the defects in the actualist conception of closure which are mirrored in its embodiment within statistical method in sociology. Since actualism offers a complete misreading of the nature and function of closure, it is quite reasonable to retain a solicitude for a sociological method along natural science lines by investigating the possibility of conducting closed system inquiry in the realist mode.

Whilst it is probably true to say that there are no examples of research which have been explicitly conducted employing a realist conception of closure it is quite possible to decipher the elementary forms of the idea in the work of those researchers whose investigations carry a commitment to generative reasoning. Inspecting these will create at least a few expectations about what realist closed system research might look like, especially by way of its contrast to the defunct actualist version.

The realist notion of closure as described above consists of an amalgam of several components. Such a programme adopted for sociological research would, I believe, pursue approximately the following strategy. Firstly, any empirical relationship requiring explanation would be interpreted as the consequence of the action of a *generative mechanism*. Secondly, since it is assumed that all generative mechanisms are localized in their action it is necessary to specify the *social context* where the particular mechanism is expected to operate. This would involve close definition of the social characteristics of the group or location to be studied, rather than simply assuming that mechanisms (and thus laws) act uniformly across general population samples. Thirdly, since it is assumed that the action of a mechanism can be obscured by other mechanisms, some method of controlling the effects of these further constraints on the relationship under inspection is required. Since the physical and statistical elimination of these confounding mechanisms is out of the question, some kind of comparative or longitudinal research design is called for in order to at least recognize their action. Between them, these strategies can approximate what I have characterized as the realistic pincer strategy of achieving closure by matching mechanisms to environmental conditions.

As to the first of these requirements, the alacrity with which sociology can adopt generative explanatory forms has been demonstrated in the previous chapter. Hence it suffices here simply to resume the analysis of the generative models in question in order to see how they tackle the second and third desiderata of closure. Two of the research programmes in particular are well suited to this task, so let us see how Wright and

Goldthorpe use a contextualization strategy in the explanation of class and mobility.

Contexts

The first requirement specifically oriented to realist closure is the identification of the context in which the explanatory mechanism is deemed to operate. This is very much the natural obverse of generative thinking and could even be said to be the chief preoccupation of these particular examples. Readily achievable as it is, this still counts as a key point of distinction from the traditional concerns of quantitative research, which frame inquiry around samples of individuals within a national or local population, and it is these which tend to be treated as the context under investigation.

Recall that the key explanatory mechanisms present in Wright's work concern how the forces of exploitation and domination in capitalism differentiate the opportunities for action of different social classes. These mechanisms are used to explain why income determination is different across the social classes. In the previous chapter I detailed his argument showing how repressive social control was likely to be counterproductive in the managerial class, and that a system of control via merit/education would be more fruitful. Hence income returns to education for this class would be considerable. Workers lack power on all the mechanisms of domination, and their income in general as well as any income advance accruing with education is likely to be low. In this manner, Wright proceeds to build up models of the empirical regularities (concerning income, education, attitudes) that are likely to follow from the mechanisms that operate in each class context, the tale of the development through a six-fold to a twelve-fold class schema being too elaborate to tell any further at this stage.

The key point, however, is that not only does the model explain the interrelationship of various properties, but also it defines the boundary within which they should operate. This gives us for the first time a reasonably clear idea of a closed social system. The researcher does not set out to seek the constant conjunctions that occur in general population samples but actively breaks down the population, identifying those contexts

214

where a particular mechanism operates producing certain observable regularities. Unlike actualism/variable analysis this approach allows the researcher to work across different units of analysis. So, for Wright, class is not a property of an individual nor even a collection of individuals with the same social characteristics, but it is the context in which different structural mechanisms operate to regulate the characteristics of its individual members.

This gives a completely different focus to empirical inquiry on matters like income determination and in Wright's exposition of the strategy he spends an age trying to convince his American readership that class should not be treated as an individual-level property which could be explored and controlled alongside education and other significant variables as a potential determinant of income (1979, pp. 75-8). Since information on class position is acquired, like any other variable, at the level of individuals' responses to questionnaire items then the custom is to treat it as an explanatory variable, alongside others (as in Fig. 7.1). However, by treating class location as the contextual boundary to a regularity (as in Fig. 7.2) allowance is made for those social features which cannot even be represented in the actualist version. Wright's analysis takes the form in which the same relationship is investigated repeatedly through different social contexts and through this we are able to take some account of these changing structural forces. Such a strategy will become *de rigueur* as the significance of 'contextualization' of social regularities is appreciated. One might express the vital difference about Wright's method as the attempt to 'hold constant' class mechanisms rather than variables. This is done through precise definition of the contexts in which these mechanisms operate and then studying these contexts with American capitalism at a particular moment in history (cf. Wright, 1979, p. 63).

Despite the fact that both its data forms and analytic techniques differ totally from Wright's case, Goldthorpe's research is also notable for its emphasis on the contextualization of empirical regularities. The relationship in question is the intergenerational mobility ratio and, once again, the variable/path analysis approach, in which father's occupation would be seen as but one possible influence in a multivariate model of son's occupation, is rejected. Instead the approach used centres on deciphering the underlying mechanisms which give rise to the particular mobility flows between different social classes. The generative forces are conceptualized as the 'desirability' and 'penetrability' of the various class locations. Specific examples concerning the economic and educational requirements and the social costs and benefits of membership of the seven different class locations were outlined in the previous chapter. The key methodological point, once again, is that in stipulating the class barriers to mobility and the social expectations bound up in the different class groupings the model is effectively building up a close definition of the characteristics of each class *context*. When it comes to the actual analysis it is these contexts and not other individual-level variables that are held 'constant'. Goldthorpe's study, too, ends up as an analysis of but one empirical relationship (father to son mobility) in a range of different contexts because it is the variation of these contexts which allows us to address the real explanatory mechanisms.

This research also goes beyond empiricism in its ability to span different units of analysis. Thus the class categories in Goldthorpe's model do not simply identify a set of occupational characteristics which allow us to locate individuals and measure their mobility. Rather it is the powers that come with class membership which provide the resources for individuals to attempt social promotion (or resist demotion) and it is the pattern of such mobility which constitutes the class structure for the next generation. Such logic-in-use moves us far beyond the actualist expectation that universal social laws will be found connecting the various components of social action. On Goldthorpe's model, certain regular flows of human conduct are expected, but these are merely internal, pivotal processes which move the class structure from one state to another. Such models are portraying in an elementary way the notion that class structure is both the medium and outcome of mobility processes. There is no universal pattern to social mobility but we can understand certain much-recognized local trends by this careful contextualization of particular regularities within the overall flow.

Let us pause, briefly, to take stock of the argument. I have shown that the forgotten key to experimentation is the business of devising and manipulating the contexts in which law-like regularities occur. Sociologists need to be equally aware of the same 'forgotten key', namely that accruing evidence is the search for regularities in their context and this will necessitate, in the minimum, that researchers be as painstaking in the operationalization of contexts as they are in the measurement of so-called dependent and independent variables. There are a great many further practical upshots of this change of emphasis. Perhaps the most consequential is that research should take the form of examining the single empirical relationships in a great many contexts rather than the current practice of examining a great many relationships in the single context.

Control

I have yet to consider the second element specific to the realist programme of closure, that is to say the various treatments and conditions applied in the name of experimental control. Following Bhaskar, recall that there are in fact two aspects to what we might more properly term 'experimental manipulation', namely *experimental production* (activating the generative mechanism) and *experimental control* (eliminating other mechanisms): 'The former is necessary to ensure the satisfaction of the antecedent (or stimulus) conditions, the latter to ensure the realization of the consequent' (1978, p. 53). It is in consideration of these functions where the analogies between natural and social science method begin to crumble. However closely the social researcher sticks with the realist closure formula of matching *regularity* to *mechanism* to *context*, the simple fact is that knowledge of all three elements depends on *observation* rather than *production* and *control*.

The examples of generative modelling we have examined follow a strategy which involves the prediction of certain empirical regularities across a wide range of contexts. If the outcomes are as predicted then the hypotheses about what mechanism must have applied in what contexts are considered to be supported. Such inferences tend to be made despite the fact that the researchers have not activated the mechanism supposedly responsible for the observed outcome, nor suppressed any alternative mechanism which may have influenced it. The evidence on which these models rest is thus entirely limited to identifying a pattern of empirical regularities in a variety of specified contexts. To many eyes such a strategy of theory confirmation rests on quite fallacious logic, namely *the fallacy of affirming the consequent.*

This fallacy occurs when attempting to construct, and make inferences from, propositions of the 'if *p* (antecedent), then *q* (consequent)' form. The criticism simply says that since social researchers cannot engage in experimental production there is no satisfaction of the antecedent. It is a fallacy to accept the full (if *p*, then *q*) proposition given information only on the consequent *(q).* The error flows from the fact that there may be other unknown and unconsidered mechanisms that cause the recorded consequent. Going back to our actual examples one can proffer a range of potential antecedent mechanisms that could be responsible for certain regularities observed. For instance one could dispute Wright's claim that the high income returns to education of the managerial class are a result of capitalist control mechanisms and argue that the true cause was the rationalization and bureaucratization of the office. One could dispute Goldthorpe's claim that the passing down of economic resources was the key mechanism accounting for high levels of self-recruitment in the petit-bourgeoisie and substitute the spirit of independence engendered in small family concerns as the key generative process. In general one can argue that without control over antecedent conditions an infinite variety of explanations can be called upon to explain supposedly consequent conditions.

Although sociology faces enormous problems here, it is unnecessarily gloomy to accept that the lack of the facility to produce antecedent mechanisms means that any explanation of a given social regularity is as good as any other. One needs to recall, in this respect, two lessons from the earlier investigation of closure and control in the natural sciences. Firstly, experimental control is always provisional and often imperfect (e.g. an early unrecognized force in early 'controlled' investigation of pendular motion was amplitude). Secondly, control is a matter of re-specifying and re-making a new experimental context (e.g. the subsequent limitation of pendular investigation to small-amplitude oscillation). Control, in short, is something that is steadily won; and won, moreover, by theoretical understanding as much as erecting physical barriers to ward off the influences of unwanted external complications.

Such a perspective on experimental control throws new light on the equivalent function in social research. The statistical interpretation of this matter as the recognition and 'partialling out' of external influences is not only unworkable but, we can now appreciate, misrepresents the very idea. Sociologists need to pay more heed to that formulation which represents the function of control as the 'recontextualization' of the mechanisms which govern regularities in a given context. Now whilst there is nothing quite like physically redesigning an experiment to accomplish this, the elemental idea can find application in sociology. What is required is not only the close specification of the context in which certain regularities are expected to occur but the systematic exploration of different contexts in such a way as to tease out the nature of the underlying explanatory mechanisms. In practice this will involve a renewed appreciation of the importance of *comparative* and *longitudinal* inquiry in sociological investigation.

For the most dramatic illustration of the tension between statistical control and what we might term contextual control, we must leave class analysis for the moment and turn to Lieberson's (1985) account of racial inequality. He provides the following example in reasserting the importance of an historical dimension in quantitative analysis. Suppose an investigator wants to know just how much of the racial gap in occupational attainment is caused by educational differences, research employing statistical control at any one time might be quite misleading:

Let us visualize a situation in which investigators at different times look at black–white differences in the proportion who are physicians. At the time when slaves were initially brought over, there would be no evidence of discrimination in the marketplace; differences in formal education could account for the fact that all of the physicians were white. At the time of Emancipation, the conclusion would still not be that different; since such a large percentage of blacks were illiterate, a substantial part of the racial gap is accounted for once education is taken into consideration. During the decades since then, as blacks made educational progress, the relative influence of education on the racial gap would have declined and one would have to deal directly with discrimination (Lieberson, 1985, p. 194).

So he is arguing that racism is institutionalized in quite different ways in different historical periods. Education may appear to be the significant causal factor under 'controlled conditions', but even if educational differences are then diminished, the occupational gap may not be. Discriminatory forces can reassert themselves in other ways with the regression and partial regression coefficients for individual-level variables changing over time. One can only understand the changing (or constant) linkages of the superficial causal patterns by having a theory of their context and examining them with longitudinal data.

Note that I am not setting up here a total opposition between statistical control and contextual control but merely asserting that the former, by itself, is insufficient. As in experimental closed systems there is a balance to be struck between investigating things in the right contexts and holding things constant. Another aspect of Wright's research provides a useful example of how comparative analysis can be combined with statistical control in order to imitate certain aspects of realist closure. Part of his work shows how class consciousness varies systematically with class location. In this case we are dealing with the formulation of class position based on his latter 'exploitative' model in which a dozen class locations are identified according to whether groups are owners/non-owners, whether they have skills or credentials to exploit, or whether they have organizational assets and positions to provide class advantage. The measure of consciousness is a simple attitudinal scale varying from +8 (maximally pro-working class) to -8 (maximally pro-capitalist class). In both Sweden and the USA his data show that attitudes change monotonically from pro-working class to pro-capitalist class as one moves along from exploited to exploiter on each of the three dimensions (Wright, 1985, pp. 260–1).

Table 7.1 **Class attitudes by class location for union and non-union members, United States and Sweden**

I. United States

Assets in the means of production
Non-owners (wage labourers)

4 Expert managers O−1.46 U−0.53 (3) N−1.52 (55)	7 Semi-cred. managers O−0.34 U+1.31 (13) N−0.59 (78)	10 Uncred. managers O−0.29 U−0.16 (3) N−0.31 (31)	+
5 Expert supervisors O−0.78 U+2.14 (1) N−0.85 (53)	8 Semi-cred. supervisors O−0.24 U+2.19 (16) N−0.68 (85)	11 Uncred. supervisors O+0.54 U+1.87 (16) N−0.29 (86)	>0 *Organization assets*
6 Expert non-managers O−0.09 U+1.06 (4) N−1.18 (47)	9 Semi-cred. workers O+0.78 U+1.17 (58) N+0.60 (124)	12 Proletarians O+0.78 U+1.68 (144) N+0.50 (450)	−

+   >0   −

Skill/Credential assets

II. Sweden

Assets in the means of production
Non-owners (wage labourers)

4 Expert managers O − 0.70 U + 0.04 (36) N − 2.47 (15)	7 Semi-cred. managers O + 1.03 U + 1.55 (41) N − 2.00 (7)	10 Uncred. managers O + 1.81 U + 2.90 (21) N − 0.83 (9)	+
5 Expert supervisors O + 0.07 U + 0.17 (39) N − 0.71 (5)	8 Semi-cred. supervisors O + 0.74 U + 0.93 (35) N − 1.35 (3)	11 Uncred. supervisors O + 1.98 U + 2.51 (29) N + 0.12 (8)	>0 *Organization assets*
6 Expert non-managers O + 1.29 U + 1.47 (64) N − 0.55 (16)	9 Semi-cred. workers O + 2.19 U + 3.06 (182) N + 1.20 (28)	12 Proletarians O + 2.60 U + 2.99 (395) N + 1.29 (118)	−

+   >0   −

Skill/credential assets

O = Overall, U = Unionized, N = Non-unionized

Numbers in parentheses are weighted numbers
Entries in the table are class attitudes, +8 (pro-working class) to −8 (pro-capitalist class)

Source: adapted from Wright, 1985, pp. 260, 261, 270, 271

Having established the simple bivariate regularity Wright is then faced with the question of controls. He provides information on this following the actualist strategy by treating class position as an individual-level variable alongside a range of other such properties in a multivariate regression explaining class consciousness. A number of other variables seem to have greater explanatory power than the class variable, and in fact controlling for 'unionization' reduces considerably the predictive power of the class variable, especially in the Swedish case. The problem here, of course, is that with simple multivariate control one is stuck with simple (and quite misleading) information about the relative explanatory power of different variables. We should now anticipate that such regularities will turn out quite differently according to context. Wright is able to show that the effect of belonging to a union on class attitudes in fact varies with class context and national context, as can be seen in Table 7.1.

This table reproduces the data for the non-ownership classes, the bourgeoisie not being noted for their possession of union cards. We can see that union members are emphatically more pro-working class in every cell and that union membership increases as we progress to the working-class corner of the tables. However it is the different distribution of attitudes and unionization that tells the tale of contextualization. If we look at the cells as a whole we see that, in the United States, managers and supervisors of every grade are 'firmly integrated with the bourgeoisie ideologically'. In Sweden it is not until we reach the 'expert manager' level that we have such identification. This latter line of demarcation can be seen particularly in this cell with the non-unionized experts being particularly pro-capitalist in their attitudes, whilst the unionized, even at this level, show the opposite attitudinal alliances.

The explanation for these differences is of course a matter for the political histories of the two countries. In America union activity has not been class-based, there are legal obstacles to unionizing management and the result is, of course, very few union members in the non-proletarian cells. In Sweden the very language of politics and unionization is much more class-based, with the result that the demarcation point of class attitudes shifts to a top management/middle management boundary. In short it is not simply individual class and union experience that gives rise to consciousness, and we should expect no consistent regularity between such variables. The whole pattern of attitude polarization and lines of demarcation of attitudinal loyalties is shifted according to national contextual mechanisms and it is these that need inspection in quantifying the individual-level regularities.

We can return to Goldthorpe's mobility research once more for a final example of the need for contextual understanding as the prerequisite to the discovery of empirical regularities. The basic explanatory form, as we have seen, is to hypothesize those mechanisms which have operated in the context of a particular flow from class X at time t_1, to class Y at time t_2. As is well known, there is much scope here for the misidentification of these mechanisms because of the way data are collected. The typical father-to-son mobility table is constructed by sampling the current workforce in order to gain information on their class positions, which are then related to those of their fathers. The problem is that the current workforce will typically span a large age range and the information relating to their fathers thus will not refer to a single generation that existed at some earlier point in time. The possibility looms large, therefore, of an unrecognized change in the mechanisms controlling a particular mobility flow. Some underlying force (such as economic recession, war etc.) may intervene across the years to alter the desirability and accessibility mechanism which theorists like Goldthorpe use to explain the overall pattern of movement. One can in fact *control* for such a possibility by performing a 'cohort analysis' on the mobility data and break down the overall mobility table into a series of matrices relating to the mobility experience of people in given time intervals (Goldthorpe *et al.*, 1980, p. 68).

I cannot pretend here that this example is problem-free. Rarely is cohort analysis preceded by any explicit theorizing about the way mobility mechanisms will vary, over time, between the classes, and so the end product is often little more than descriptive. Problems also remain regarding the adequacy of the control strategy. Comparing the present-day class positions of cohorts born in, say, the 1930s and the 1950s would still leave the researcher the problem of distinguishing between 'age effects' and 'period effects' when attempting to decipher the mobility

223

mechanisms (Goldthorpe and Payne, 1986, p. 1). These difficulties apart, the example provides another glimpse of what
control should mean in social research in that this particular
longitudinal design leads to a closer and closer specification of
the context in which a particular mobility mechanism operates.

The object of the exercise is precisely that expressed in realist
control terminology, namely to prevent misidentification of the
generative mechanisms that control a regularity in a given
context. In experimentation, control of generative mechanisms
proceeds via a process of re-specifying and re-making
experimental conditions. In social research the equivalent
function will require the increasingly detailed specification and
comparison of the social contexts that will reveal particular
generative mechanisms. In general, this means that the function
of control will be carried by longitudinal and comparative
designs rather than statistics. In common with the general thrust
of this section one is looking once again for the ever-closer
specification of the social context of regularities to approximate
to realist closure. The means of achieving this in social research
amounts, of course, to but a pale imitation of experimental
closure, but at least this is preferable to a close imitation of a
parody of the method.

Chapter Eight

EXPLANATORY NETWORKS: THE CONCEPTUAL DOMAIN OF CLASS

Thus far we have seen that significant changes for the better can be wrought in quantitative sociology by the incorporation of generative thinking and revised closure strategies into the research process. This leaves for consideration the third of the broader prerequisites of the realist strategy for measurement, namely the *network structure of explanation*. In brief, I shall be asking in this chapter whether sociology can adopt this mode of explanation and testing which is based upon a network of scientific discourse in which connections are made between relatively speculative ideas and certain other concepts which are understood well enough to control and measure. To what extent can sociology develop 'knot concepts', which are commonly identified by many theories and many instruments and so perform a key systematizing role when it comes to the testing of new theories?

Much of the promise of the network model, I believe, stems from its immediate descriptive appeal, and it is perhaps appropriate to recapitulate the essential idea by way of an example. One can find resonances of the network theme as soon as one ponders any of the standard physical science concepts. So if one thinks about the concept of length, gone is the need to argue for its unique capacity for fundamental measurement (rulers embody rules of transitivity, association, commutation etc.) and gone is the need to give undue emphasis to the power of a particular operational definition (all hail to the metre rod in Paris). Instead one can acknowledge the obvious scope of the concept through its identification in a range of theories, laws and instruments. Hempel provides us with a quick-fire list of just some of the best-known:

the lawful decrease of barometric pressure with altitude is the basis for barometric altimeters in airplanes; underwater distances are frequently measured by determining the travel time of sound signals; the distance of globular star clusters and of galactic systems is inferred, by laws, from the period and the apparent brightness of certain variable stars in those systems. The measurement of very small distances may involve the use, and presuppose a theory, of optical microscopes, electron microscopes, spectrographic procedures, X-ray diffraction methods, and many others (Hempel, 1966, p. 94).

Such a catalogue, of course, omits all the everyday devices and ideas involved in length measurement and perhaps rather more significantly all those mathematical systems in which the concept of length is integral (geometry, trigonometry, calculus etc.). One should not take too much persuading, therefore, that what is really significant about length is its systematizing role in scientific discourse.

In seeking analogies with the network structure of explanation, it must be made clear from the outset that the referent here virtually amounts to the nature of scientific activity as a whole. To make the task of the chapter more manageable, and any parallels drawn less facile, I will concentrate here on the network model as a theory of discourse or a theory of meaning. A number of different perspectives have evolved in the attempt to understand the roots of concept or discourse formulation in sociology. The opening section of the chapter considers four such perspectives (operationalism, reconstructionism, contestabilism, formalism) and makes out a case for the latter as the authentic strategy for those seeking to construct a realist science of society.

Hitherto the debate on the conceptual forms appropriate to sociology has run along rather predictable lines which actually misrepresent the choices open to the discipline. Most of those attempting to construct a scientific sociology have admired the clarity and precision, and thus what they assume to be the closure, of scientific terms. This guiding instinct has led to calls for *operationalism* and *reconstructionism* in the attempt to arrive at the definitive base for sociological concepts. Against such a position are marshalled the arguments from the hermeneutic schools which presume that sociological discourse is based on natural language and is thus forever mutable, vague, indexical etc. Pushing hardest in this direction are the *contestabilists*, who use the ordinary language arguments plus a few more besides about the appraisive and ethical nature of sociological discourse to claim conceptual closure is an impossibility.

The point, however, is that contestabilism has seemed such a credible position because it is mounted against the quite incredible assumptions of the closed-definition doctrines. As can be seen in the length example above, conceptual closure is the exception and conceptual extension and change is the rule in natural science. The need for an alternative model of scientific discourse is thus evident and this can be found in the network model which assumes a *formalist* strategy of concept formation. Concepts are understood relationally as part of mathematical models of physical systems, and conceptual growth involves the business of making deductions from these models. These extensions, however, are not uncircumscribable, as in everyday discourse, but are limited by the formal rules governing the mathematical systems in which they are located.

In the second part of the chapter I go on to assess the potential for formalism within sociology by examining the conceptual developments associated with the notion social class. No one can deny the 'confused' and 'contested' nature of the concept of social class, and there will always be good reasons why sociology will gravitate to theorizing through ordinary language networks. However, I will make a case that sociology can and should make at least a restricted use of formal networks. The germ of the idea can be found in the generative models which employ a simple formalization of the action of the underlying mechanisms that bring about social regularities. The network strategy can be evoked by attempting to rework the models of these generative processes so that they explain a range of different regularities in a range of contexts.

8.1 OPERATIONALISM, RECONSTRUCTIONISM, CONTESTABILISM, FORMALISM

Parsons (1938, p. 18) had it just about right when he pointed out that 'mathematics in its application to physics is theory'. This is a rather daunting thought for anyone set upon the creation of a scientific sociology, and before contemplating any analogies with sociological discourse it is necessary to have at least an elementary grasp of the functions of formalism within scientific discourse. I will identify two roles for mathematics here. The first is that formal theoretical discourse carries with it an 'abstract calculus' which acts as the logical skeleton of the explanatory system. One can think of scientific theories as being composed of relatively descriptive, substantive terms like 'gas', 'pressure', 'pendulum', 'length' and so forth, as well as a series of relatively abstract, formalized terms containing only logical terms like 'and', 'or', 'not', including mathematical terms like '=', '+', '-', '%' and so forth. It is these latter uninterpreted axiomatic systems which have a key role in defining all scientific terms. Nagel explains the idea thus:

> the fundamental assumptions of a theory constitute a set of abstract or uninterpreted postulates, whose constituent nonlogical terms have no meanings other than those accruing to them by virtue of their place in the postulates, so that the basic terms of the theory are 'implicitly defined' by the postulates of the theory. Moreover, insofar as the basic theoretical terms are only implicitly defined by the postulates of the theory, the postulates assert nothing, since they are statement-forms rather than statements (that is, they are expressions having the form of statements without being statements), and can be explored only with the view to deriving from them other statement-forms in conformity with the rules of logical deduction. In short, a fully articulated scientific theory has embedded in it an abstract calculus that constitutes the skeletal structure of the theory (Nagel, 1968, p. 91).

His example of an abstract calculus is Euclidean geometry, in which postulates are stated which connect expressions such as 'point', 'line', 'plane', 'lies between', 'congruent with' and so on. More descriptive concepts like distance and length have connotations associated with everyday spatial experience but within a system of geometry such ideas receive meaning according to their place in a network of formalized axioms.

Similarly,

> the theory of mechanics seeks to provide a completely
> general analysis of the motions of bodies which is
> independent of the actual state of experimental technology;
> and the theory aims to formulate the structure of relations
> that characterize bodies at all points of their motions
> (Nagel, 1968, p. 161).

So again we have a series of concepts like 'speed' which have meaning in everyday contexts as when something falls or a race is run, but in science the concept takes its meaning as part of an extended and extendable postulate system. Thus speed as 'average velocity' is understood as the ratio of distance over time. And with the invention of differential calculus the notion is extended to include 'instantaneous' speed which takes its meaning alongside other terms like 'acceleration'.

This idea is depicted as the *formalist* theory of meaning in Fig. 8.1c. The meanings of terms are established not by closed definition, but by their place in a postulate system. Thus what is

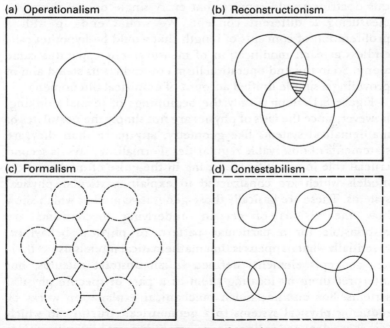

Figure 8.1   Theories of meaning

specified is only the structure of relations a concept may enter, and not the substantive character of any particular property. The descriptively empty concepts in such reasoning are thus marked by dashed circles and the propositions which connect them are marked by the connecting threads of the deductive network.

Such a conception is perhaps most intelligible by way of its contrast with the *operationalist* theory of meaning as in Fig. 8.1a. In the latter, the hallmark of scientific discourse (depicted by the oblong) is that a concept has a clearly specified meaning (depicted by the circle), and is understood in exactly the same sense by all those who use it; all of which supposedly stems from the use of agreed-upon and replicable operational definitions. Now everyone, apart from a few laggards in the humanities and social sciences who have not really looked to see what is happening over the other side of the fence, knows that operationalist closure is the classic example of the false methodological prescription. If one thinks of all the various devices and formulae for length measurement mentioned above, this doctrine would require that every single one of them was measuring a different concept. We would end up with a proliferation of concepts of length that would be hypothetically endless as each modification of measurement apparatus came along. So in the end operationalism contradicts its stated aim of providing a simple unified account of empirical phenomena.

Figure 8.1c depicts only the beginnings of formal thinking, however, since the laws of physics are not simply the postulates of mathematical systems like geometry, any more than they are statements of observable regularities. Formalism plays its second crucial role in scientific reasoning in the guise of mathematical models which are constructed to explain particular physical systems. These are basically those generative models which show how the actions of certain underlying mechanisms are responsible for a particular pattern of physical behaviour. Essentially what happens is that mathematical models use as their key concepts elements defined in an abstract calculus, but interpret them by locating them as a part of specific physical systems. For instance much mechanical explanation works by reducing physical systems to a geometrical structure in which forces are depicted as lines or arrows applying at particular points in a spatial diagram. Simple mechanics are then used to describe the resultant forces applying in the system.

For an elementary example of this idea refer back to Fig. 5.5, in which pendular motion is described as a system of forces acting along the arc of a circle and the vector addition of forces is used to describe the variation in the inward acceleration of the bob. Exactly the same format of force diagrams is used to describe other forms of motion, such as that of projectiles. If one examines Galileo's diagram for the motion of a body projected horizontally (Fig. 8.2), he assumes that it is acted upon by the constant horizontal force of the initial projection and the constantly accelerated force of gravity. Thus objects moving to the left in Fig. 8.2 cover equal distances such as ab, bc, cd, de, in the same time periods, whilst downward travel will cover the distances bo, og, gl, ln, in the same intervals. Conceptual extension is routinely produced in such models, the curve ah traces a form of 'parabolic' motion, a concept which finds usage in describing further types of motion. Experiments with real projectiles, in the meantime, replicate these mathematical models and the usage of mechanical calculation in instruments to set the range of field guns etc. ties another kind of linkage back into the formal network of ideas.

The end result of such a theory of meaning is that when interpreting concepts like 'temperature of a gas' or the 'oscillation of a pendulum', all reference to ordinary language conceptualization is dropped in favour of elucidations using such notions as 'kinetic energy of gas molecules' and 'point acceleration', which are in turn traceable to the elemental units

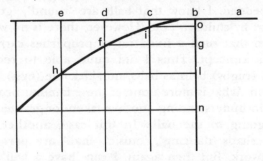

Figure 8.2 Galileo's diagram for the motion of projectiles
(*Source:* Willer, 1984)

231

of the *same* mathematical (mechanical) system. Thus in scientific discourse, although we are dealing with a mass of quite diverse entities in quite diverse contexts (formal systems, experimental systems, measurement systems), it is quite possible to traverse the network because the various components will share (often quite distantly) this formal substructure of discourse. From this base stems the network model of theory testing described in Chapter 5, in which knowledge grows with the *entrenchment* of new concepts and regularities into the core structure of ideas.

The theory of meaning which applies to ordinary language can also be described as a network model, but one which operates in complete contrast to formalism. The meanings of terms are still learned holistically; we come to understand concepts via the utterances, propositions and relationships in which they are embedded. The key difference is simply that no formal system, no abstract calculus, no codifiable set of rules governs the correct usage or extension of a term. This state of affairs has been characterized in many ways, as the 'open-texture' of natural language, as the phenomenon of the 'incompleteness of description', but is perhaps best known in the guise of Wittgenstein's (1958) 'family resemblance' theory of meaning. In Chapter 3 I have quoted his famous excursus on 'games', which demonstrates that concepts are associated with an ever-changing network of properties which do not possess a common denominator of meaning.

Let me remind the reader of the basic idea, modifying the reference from 'game' to 'ball', by way of a change. We learn the meaning of terms through the network of properties in which they are embedded. I know that balls are 'round', 'good for kicking', 'liked by children', etc. However, there is no way that one can claim that such a fixed set of properties carries the meaning of a concept. Thus I am quite able to recognize non-spherical (rugby) balls as balls, non-kickable (eye-) balls as balls, and so on. What is more none of these familiar properties are required in understanding another taken-for-granted usage such as in 'going to the ball'. In this case, another set of properties, perhaps 'dancing', 'music', 'hall' are part of the preferred network. But then again, I can 'have a ball' in the complete absence of the latter properties. Similarly I can make a 'balls up' of things in which the resulting muddle has none of the aforesaid characteristics, save perhaps an allusion to certain non-spherical balls of the testicular kind. To compound the confusion I can attend a play called *Having a Ball* in which the reference is not to pleasure, nor even dance, but goes back to vulgar usage and the fears of attending a vasectomy clinic. In practice, of course, there is little confusion, nor even much judgement to be exercised in deciding upon such meanings. Applying terms is done unthinkingly and confidently without the need for (or the possibility of) tracing meaning back to some essential core. So whilst future proper usage is indeterminate and open-ended, correct interpretations are supplied by knowledge of the social context in which a particular usage is likely to be appropriate.

I would not dream of questioning one word of this as a description of ordinary language usage; the difficulty arises when such a formulation is applied lock, stock and barrel as a theory of meaning in sociological discourse. I will refer to such a perspective as the *contestabilist* theory of meaning (Gallie, 1956; MacIntyre, 1973; Care, 1973; Connolly, 1983). The rationale of the essential contestability thesis consists of a series of ideas bearing a family resemblance which I will attempt to summarize as follows. First is the standard argument of interpretative sociology that ordinary people's actions constitute the way the world is, which is said to require that second-order sociological discourse be based on the talk and terms of first-order language. Second, we have the point that ordinary language terminology is not fixed but has constant innovatory shifts because the struggles and oppositions of everyday life are in the last analysis struggles to assert meaning. Third, it is supposed that social scientists in the act of reflecting on this conceptual contestation are themselves part of the process of the normative appraisal of terms; their own terminology may thus be purloined for everyday usage and this itself creates conceptual (and possibly social) change.

The end result of all this is that, when it comes to understanding a social science concept like 'democracy', we are supposedly in much the same position as someone using the ordinary language term 'ball'. Both refer to a network of characteristics bearing only family resemblance. In the case of democracy, Oppenheim puts it like this:

One may define 'democracy' by a combination of criteria such as periodic elections, competitive parties, representation, freedom of expression, diffusion of political power, implementation of collective preferences; but the presence of all these traits is neither necessary nor sufficient to characterize a given political system as democratic (Oppenheim, 1981, p. 183).

The contestability thesis can be depicted in general terms as in Fig 8.1d. There will be many distinct usages of the term (represented by separate circles), some of which may share certain common ideas but not others (represented by overlapping circles). Thus writing in the traditions of western 'democracy' and soviet 'democracy' might both acknowledge the role of elections in the democratic process, but the former would suppose elections involved a competitive party political system whereas the latter would see them as the final detail of the implementation of preferences within a collective state. Such a set of properties and assumptions might recede completely when it comes to conceptual contestation on 'democracy' within a particular political system. In this case protagonists might share certain principles such as the idea that democracy involves 'representation', but one might express this as following the majority view, whilst another might take it to mean the toleration of minority views. Such viewpoints and characteristics are, further, only considered temporary constructions which will change according to the shifting context of the discourse (marked by the dashed oblong). Thus in time of war many of the basic mechanics of democracy might be deemed unworkable and unnecessary; even, in the very limit, the absolute need for democracy coming into question (cf. Connolly, 1983, p. 33).

Is social science discourse necessarily open-ended and uncircumscribable in the manner suggested by contestabilists? Well, it is and it isn't. It is open-ended and uncircumscribable all right, but the basis of the argument is quite misplaced. What I want to do here is to show that the contestabilists' arguments are not so much wrong as misdirected. As a matter of fact, I believe that the trio of justifications for contestabilism presented above are no more than a series of vague generalities and half-truths. So, in passing, it should be said that it is not the case that the

234

social world is entirely constituted in people's conceptualizations and actions. The outcome of people's collective experience is important but sociology needs to observe a balance in the consideration of agency and structure. Similarly, conceptual change might be the engine of social change but the world isn't so plastic as to follow our every perception; choices (conceptual or otherwise) are not made in conditions of our own making. Thirdly, I take with a pinch of salt the idea that social science conceptualizations have been a major shaping force in social change (though I could be persuaded of one exception to the rule). The fact that such terms as 'role-model' and 'institutionalized racism' have filtered into everyday discourse is no more significant than you and I speaking about 'nuclear fusion' or 'acid rain'. For social science to have an effect back on its subject matter requires the impact of a totality of propositions and not just the odd word.

I might add, still in passing, that lurking behind such arguments and counter-arguments is the conundrum that any attempt to set forth a rationale for the doctrine of essential contestability must by its own premise be essentially contestable. All the above arguments about agency, structure, social change etc., and all the above examples about balls, democracy, role-models and so forth contain terms which, by the lights of the perspective, are contestable and so, therefore, must be the arguments which are marshalled using them. In this respect contestabilism is in much the same position as any quasi-relativist perspective, the status of its own justification remains something of a fog.

Fortunately we need not explore these metatheoretical mysteries a moment further, since my opposition to the contestabilist position stems from a different issue. Contestabilists have not earned their academic spurs simply by making the point that social science terminology is beset with confusion and contestation. Such an essentially defeatist position has only found merit within the discipline because it is mounted as an attack on the prospects of the closure of social and political concepts. Thus contestabilism is best understood as an essentially critical point of view which opposes the operationalist mentality which, as we have seen, believes social science can only be an objective, empirical science on the basis of having singular and consensual definitions of terms. To be precise, contestabilism opposes the view of *reconstructionism* (Sartori and Riggs, 1975; Sartori, 1984; Oppenheim, 1981). The latter seeks conceptual closure, but not by the pre-emptive strike of defining some unique operation along which to channel all empirical work. Rather they operate at the level of discourse and indeed assume most fields are plagued with conceptual ambiguity and inconsistency. Their point is that the way out of the morass is to try and recover as usable a concept as possible from the existing literature. This is depicted in Fig 8.1b, in which several general conceptions are examined in the belief they will share some core theme (represented by the intersection of circles) which can then be used as a reconstituted and transparently clear basis for all future usage.

The result of all this is that the 'problem' of concept formation as it is presented in the literature is very much one of *contestabilism versus reconstructionism.* Bryant (1987), for instance, has produced an exacting review of the issue precisely along this divide. Given the choice between these two, my money would very much be on contestabilism (as is Bryant's, incidentally). The key point, however, is that this misrepresents the real choice. Operationalism and reconstructionism only have any currency because of the misplaced belief that they provide the path to conceptual rigour and consensus which are assumed to be the building blocks of the scientific method. However, as I have demonstrated constantly throughout this book, conceptual certitude, measurement, empirical validity and all the other hallmarks of scientific method cannot be achieved by attention to singular terms, be they relatively empirical or relatively conceptual. Scientists are confident in their usage of particular terms, not because they have some once-and-for-all conceptual anchorage, but because they are entrenched in a formal network of concepts. Faced with a plausible rival theory of meaning (namely formalism), we can judge many of the contestability arguments for what they are (namely an excuse for sloppy thinking). So when a contestabilist says something like 'complete agreement on concepts would bring history to a close', a formalist could only shout, 'hear, hear!'. Complete agreement on the meaning of scientific terms is a dangerous irrelevance since it would also bring science to a close. The very medium of scientific growth is the extension of the network of ideas leading from a concept, and all the major concepts have enjoyed a continual metamorphosis (e.g. Bachelard's, 1968, discussion of the 'epistemological profile' of the concept of mass). When a contestabilist says something like 'it is in the nature of argument that innovatory and unpredictable conceptual moves can occur', a formalist can only reply 'I told you so'. To be sure a formalist has a couple of particular innovatory moves in mind. One is the application of the same formal system to new substantive fields, i.e. what Schon (1963) calls the displacement of concepts (e.g. the metaphorical extension of the laws of mechanics into the molecular field). The other possibility is the extension of the formal system by mathematical innovation as described above. Such innovatory moves cannot be predicted in advance, and are in fact largely driven by the interests and competitive situation facing particular groups of scientists.

Having dispensed with what can now be seen as the smoke-screen opposition provided by operationalism and reconstructivism, the way is clear to give a genuine appraisal of the conceptual structure of sociological theory. The question of whether our theories possess the requisite structure to act as the foundation for a measurement language, and thus empirical research, turns out to be a matter of *formalism versus contestabilism.* We can return to our example of social class analysis and ask whether theorizing about class takes the form of formal networks of co-ordinated reasoning or whether it merely resembles a labyrinth of disconnected, appraisive, assertions.

8.2 IS CLASS A KNOT CONCEPT OR A CONTESTED CONCEPT?

Is class a knot concept with roots traceable to some elemental social process which ultimately connects to all others, or is it a contested concept which operates in linguistic structures developed on the you-pays-your-money-and-you-takes-your-choice principle? If I was to ask this question in the form of a survey of sociologists' opinions on the matter or, more to the point, a survey of their actual usage of the concepts, the answer couldn't be much clearer. Wright's often-quoted remark to the effect that 'class is not simply a contested concept but an essentially confused concept' probably sums the matter up. In fact if one looks at two recent attempts to circumscribe the conceptual universe of class their conclusions are simply variations on the contestability theme. Calvert (1982) actually uses Gallie's famous five criteria of contestability, and despite some gyrations caused by the contestable nature of the criteria themselves (see the note on relativism above) manages to force the concept into some sort of compliance with all of them. Martin (1987) concludes that social class is essentially a 'common-sense' idea as opposed to a scientific one, and thus can only prompt one of sociology's classic disputes rather than objective research.

The reasoning behind all this is plain enough to see; one is greeted by a rambling mass of dimensions, measures and meanings that come and go as soon as one begins to scan the social class literature. Thus there are 'ownership of the means of production' definitions, 'market position' definitions, 'authority and control' definitions, 'productive work' definitions, 'surplus value' definitions, to name but a few. Arguing that any one of these is criterial would seem to amount to rather a similar claim to one urging the 'good for kicking' definition applied to all usages of the term 'ball'. Correct usage, as in everyday discourse, would seem once again to be a matter of local custom and practice; that is to say one needs to understand whether a particular corner of the sociological community is Marxist, neo-Marxist, Weberian, American empiricist and so on to be able to situate the appropriate usage.

What is clear, however, is that few sociologists in the business of concept formation are happy with the full relativist implications of the contestabilist position. So whilst most sociologists would perhaps acknowledge contestabilism as an adequate description of the terminological turmoil of the discipline as a whole, few would regard conceptual indiscipline to be a feature of their own composition of theory. I would go so far as to claim that most social theorists hanker over a modicum of formal rigour in their own work, even if they might be quite loath to use such a term to describe their goal.

What I have in mind here is a form of reasoning that is in fact quite commonplace in sociology, most especially perhaps in our area of substantive interest – class analysis. Routine as it is, it is hard to give it an authoritative name. Wright (1985, p. 20) simply

calls it the logic of concept formation, Althusserians have made
it into the sole basis of a methodology under the name of
'discursive practices' (Benton 1984, p. 193), but perhaps the
most approachable label is Kaplan's (1964, p. 64) term, 'systemic
meaning'. His point is that there are terms which require, for a
specification of their meaning, not one sentential context, but
the context of the whole set of sentences in which they occur.
Most social science terms are thus located in what he calls a
'conceptual structure' or an 'horizontal articulation'; that is to
say 'a whole set of independent terms, that is, the terms not
strictly defined by the others, used in the theory presupposed in
and emerging from the enquiry' (p. 74). His example is 'family
budget' studies, which might include in their conceptual
structures terms like 'income elasticity of demand', 'liquidity
preference' and 'external economies of consumption'. In the
limit systemic meaning can extend to cover a whole body of
literature and in this sense one frequently hears claims to the
effect that what Marx meant by class or what Durkheim meant by
anomie can only be understood in respect to the whole corpus of
their writing.

The idea of systemic meaning undoubtedly forms the bread
and butter of theoretical discussion in sociology, and has been
seen by some as providing the basic rules and goals of concept
formation. Wright expresses the essential idea (with appropriate
caution) as follows:

> concepts have theoretical presuppositions. In some inst-
> ances the presuppositions function as explicit, systematic
> theoretical requirements imposed on the production of a
> new concept; in other instances, the theoretical presuppos-
> itions act more as unconscious cognitive filters implicitly
> shaping what is thinkable and unthinkable by the theorist.
> In either case, such theoretical presuppositions determine,
> if only vaguely and implicitly, the range of possible concepts
> that can be produced (Wright, 1985, p. 20).

A good name for what is being suggested here might be
'linguistic formalism'. Conceptual adjustments and extensions
are perpetually made in the name of 'theoretical consistency'
and 'logical coherence', thus evoking some kind of formal rules
of construction for sociological discourse.

The major question, of course, is whether they are doing anything of the kind. Are we dealing with some embryonic proto-formalism or is it a case of pseudo-formalism? For an answer we need look no further than Wright's own work, for he (characteristically) has pushed the development of 'systemic meaning' to its limits in attempting to codify the explicit rules of concept development associated with it. His logic of concept formation (1985, Ch. 2 and Appendix I) can be paraphrased as follows.

(i) Assert a set of authoritative, irreducible core ideas which identify the abstract structure of a particular body of theory.
(ii) Extend or transform certain of these concepts to deal with concrete instances of the social world in such a way as some of the essential raw materials go into the production of new concepts.
(iii) Whenever a concept is modified in such a way, there should be some kind of exercise in reintegration by examining the consistency of the new concept with the totality of existing elements.

Although these are brave words (and ultimately important goals), I want to argue that they are stated in the absence of any formal abstract calculus which is needed to accomplish them. The result is that Wright's rules are prey to interpretation in dozens of ways, giving the possibility of making hundreds of conceptual transformations to adopt them to a specific circumstance, thus leaving us with not one, but a thousand explanatory networks. This can be seen quite clearly in relation to Wright's reconstruction of the development of his conceptual thinking about class (1985, part I), which is supposedly regulated by the rules above.

Wright begins at rule (i) with the identification of what he considers to be the six key conceptual constraints on the development of any authentic class model. It must assume (a) the class structure has primacy over class formations, class consciousness and class struggle; (b) the class structure shapes the range of possible variations of the state, ethnic relations, gender relations etc.; (c) class is a relational concept and not a gradational one; (d) class interests are intrinsically oppositional and antagonistic; (e) exploitation and not inequality is the reason for class antagonism; (f) the fundamental basis of exploitation is to be found in the social organization of production. These are assumed to be axiomatic propositions and one vital test of any conceptual development is that it remains true to these principles. The obvious problem, which Wright admits but takes no action to circumvent, is why these six principles are chosen? So one might ask how can the list exclude the materialist theory of history, why is not the labour theory of value down there amongst the first principles and so on. Although Wright wisely avoids the mistake of attempting justification through 'textual authority', we are left with the possibility that the whole conceptual edifice is based on contestable building blocks. This is so because the six 'abstract' conceptual constraints on class conceptualization are in fact internally complex verbal propositions which make sense only in relation to a totality of further propositions from Marxist and neo-Marxist theory. It is this propositional or interpreted form of the core axioms that differentiates them from the contentless propositional 'forms' that characterize the abstract calculus of physical theory. Any extension to the original substantive axioms must therefore be substantive, and thus contestable, rather than logical.

This can be seen as we follow Wright to stage (ii) of his concept building process in which he reviews the success of the attempts to generate concepts dealing with the 'new middle class' in so far as they remain consistent with these key principles. This gives him occasion to criticize his first attempt at the problem, namely through the concept of 'contradictory class locations'. Among its problems is its lack of consistency with principles c, d and e. Managers were basically defined as a contradictory location because they were simultaneously *dominated* by capital and *dominators* of labour. Wright now feels that this is merely a gradational distinction; he might be said to dominate his children but it doesn't mean he exploits them. In general, domination-centred class distinctions do not identify the subjectively opposed interests which are the hallmark of antagonistic class relationships.

However, the middle classes can still be identified within Wright's new exploitation model. The vital extension to the model thus involves uncovering the dimensions along which

241

exploitation occurs in contemporary capitalism. The principal axis of capitalist exploitation (remaining close to first principles) is ownership of the means of production. To this, Wright adds that it is possible to exploit workers through the control of organizational assets. By virtue of their place in organizational structures managers and bureaucrats control part of the socially produced surplus. It is possible to capitalize both skill and organizational exploitation and thus after further operational refinement another two dimensions of 'organizational assets' and 'skill/credential assets' are included in the full model of class position as in Table 8.1. But are these conceptual transformations faithful to the set of first principles, especially those that damaged his prior conceptual adjustments? Wright makes a brave fist of arguing their consistency (pp. 78–82) but ultimately it is hard to see how skills/credentials or even organizational seniority, sliced as they are in Table 8.1 are relational and not gradational. It is impossible to fathom why the possession of educational qualifications puts one in an intrinsically antagonistic and exploitative position in relation to the unqualified. As usual, Wright is disarmingly honest about this difficulty (pp. 92-98 and elsewhere), but the issue is really not the extent of his success but whether success is possible at all. He is

Table 8.1 Wright's typology of class locations in capitalist society

	Assets in the means of production				
	Owners of means of production	Non-owners (wage labourers)			
Owns sufficient capital to hire workers and not work	1 Bourgeoisie	4 Expert managers	7 Semi credentialled managers	10 Uncredentialled managers	+
Owns sufficient capital to hire workers but must work	2 Small employers	5 Expert supervisors	8 Semi credentialled supervisors	11 Uncredentialled supervisors	>0
Owns sufficient capital to work for self but not to hire workers	3 Petty bourgeoisie	6 Expert non-managers	9 Semi credentialled workers	12 Proletarians	–
		+	>0	–	
		Skill/credential assets			

Organization assets (right side label)

Source: Wright, 1985, p. 88

trying to adduce reasons for making a constant distinction between exploitation and domination when the rules and tools of verbal reasoning are not precise enough to allow him to do so.

Thirdly we come to the question of the integration of the provisionally complete network of concepts. Is Wright's new ensemble of concepts consistent with the essential doctrines of Marxism? In this case I have the good fortune to be able to allow some of the collaborators in Wright's international project (Rose and Marshall, 1986) to pronounce on this matter. They claim that, in the course of this work, Wright emasculates the Marxist theory of history, he owns up to the fact that classes other than the proletariat have the potential to pose an alternative to capitalism, and to cap it all he uses, as the key explanatory device, mechanisms which are essentially market-based rather than production-based. In short, the conceptual strides in Wright's work integrate just as nicely with some pretty old Weberian ideas rather than establishing the authenticity of a new Marxism. Presumably the respective parties are still slugging this out, and I am happy to let them continue this futile task, since my point is again the methodological one, that there are no logical rules available in sociological discourse which, as Rose and Marshall might put it, allow us to begin to decide who is (W)right.

Once again we are back with the none-too-stunning conclusion that ordinary language reasoning cannot sustain the development of a logically consistent network of concepts. So if we are to find the equivalent of formal networks of discourse in sociology, we must clearly look to those perspectives which carry some commitment to the expression of theory in mathematical terms. There is, of course, a school of mathematical sociology which has precisely this aim, and which one must always be careful to distinguish from the statistical school which uses mathematical ideas only as a tool in the analysis of preconceptualized *data*. I have no space at this stage for anything like a complete review of what has become a totally specialized field, which even its leading Figure describes as 'too complex, too multi-parental in its origins in terms of goals and means for anyone to really take hold of it as a whole' (Fararo, 1984, p. 158). Recall in any case that the network structure of natural scientific discourse stems not simply from the application of mathematical theory, but from the fact that the theory, data, experimental and measurement languages all carry the same structure. So what we require is not mathematical theory for mathematics' sake but the mathematical expression of theory which can be married to the substantive concerns of sociology and which can in turn be subject to some form of empirical test.

Recall that we are looking for analogies with two related functions of formal discourse. First is the 'abstract calculus' with its descriptively empty concepts tied only by logical propositions. Second is the 'mathematical model' in which these concepts are interpreted and extended to portray a range of different physical systems. Sociology, of course, has no use for a ready-made matter-in-motion formal system like geometry, mechanics, calculus etc., but thankfully the potential for formal reasoning begins with far less grand ideas than these. As soon as a sociologist identifies groups, distinguishes the properties and relationships of members of these groups, compares their size and so forth, a series of logically deducible truths can be set down about the system. Perhaps the best-known work of this kind is Blau's *Inequality and Heterogeneity* (1977), in which he derives some 187 'theorems' on the basis of just a few simple assumptions about population differences and distributions. He refers to this as a 'primitive theory' of social structure because it functions in much the same way as the 'empty' structure of mathematical reasoning described above. That is to say, just as such geometrical motions as 'point' and 'line' can receive any number of substantive interpretations, the primitive terms in Blau's theory like 'group' and 'member' can refer to potentially any societal and institutional arrangements.

Blau's theoretical propositions are formal in another sense in that they were developed in a systemic, logical way, consisting of what often seem tautological truths. Consider, for instance, his very first theorem:

> If society is divided into two groups that differ in size, and if there are any social associations between members of the two groups (which is assumed to be the case), it logically follows that the *rate of intergroup associations of the smaller group must exceed that of the larger* (Blau, 1977, p. 21).

Starting with these simple analytical terms like 'size' and 'number', the theory progressively moves to employ other terms like 'status' and 'distribution' from which more complex terms like 'inequality' and 'heterogeneity' are derived. Blau's aim (p. 17) is none other than to develop a general vocabulary of social structure, and for him this involves a proto-mathematical theory in which terms are defined precisely, not through closed definition, but through their place in evolving logical structures.

So what became of this idea? Perhaps I am not in the best position to judge, but I do not get the impression that there has been any widespread adoption of Blau's core terminology across structural sociology. This conclusion would probably be even nearer the mark if his algorithms had been manufactured in formal set theoretical terms from whence many of them hail. However, if one allows for a much more implicit take-up of usage, one finds a spectrum of very similar ideas used as the basis of theoretical reasoning in a wide range of examples. There is a kind of do-it-yourself formalism that can be found at the basis of nearly all large-scale investigations of social inequality. If we return to our three standard examples, the work of Wright is obviously not developed in this respect, but the two other programmes will illustrate what I have in mind. Boudon's theories are cast in the form of what he calls 'box' models, that very name evoking the kind of empty structures that characterize formal languages and which he justified as follows:

> its basic rationale consists in representing any mobility process by the distribution of a population into a set of boxes, according to some inequalitarian procedure. The set of boxes stands for social structure, and the size of the boxes can change over time. Also, the structure of the population competing for a place in the more desirable boxes generally changes over time. . . . The 'box model', although simpler than the refined statistical models currently used in social mobility analysis, has the advantage of being very close to sociological theory. Such concepts as meritocracy, inequality of educational opportunity, and social structure, are directly translatable into operational terms and incorporated into the model. Factors that certainly play a role in mobility, such as discrepancy between educational and social structure, acquire precise operational form in the so-called box model (Boudon, 1974, p. 122).

Similarly the mobility matrices that Goldthorpe (and countless others) employ are rich in formal properties. The cell entries, marginal entries, totals, percentages all lie in fixed relationships following the rules of matrix algebra. This uninterpreted system specifies the structure of relationships that any interpretation of the system must follow. Thus classes, mobility flows, class structures, structural change over time are all formally defined and further derivations to the system can be incorporated in order to distinguish between such factors as structural and individual mobility. Once again such conceptual extensions can be made with greater or lesser degrees of formal rigour (cf. Blau, 1977, p. 40; Boudon, 1973, Part I).

I conclude that at least this initial characteristic of formalism, namely the deployment of empty, relational structures, is available and can be developed by sociology. The problem is that at this level, formalism offers little more than static, abstract, notational schemes, which cannot and are not really intended to go much beyond tautological truths. The network structure of scientific reasoning only begins to multiply in its connections when formalism is applied in generative reasoning. Simply by varying certain of the initial conditions in mathematical models it is possible to utilize a core of central propositions and laws to generate explanations with a large number of outcomes. Thus armed with a few basic laws of motion and certain axioms and notations of geometry, the possibilities for describing different types of matter in motion seem endless. Think of the examples I have used in the proceeding argument: we have had a model for pendular oscillation, a model for the motion of projectiles, motion down an inclined plane can be understood by using the same machinery, and the imagery can be further extended as in Newton's models integrating projectile and planetary motion (see Willer, 1984). The explanatory networks of concepts which follow thus boast scope and precision simultaneously.

We are thus faced with the question of whether the box model and matrix structures which provide an abstract notation to describe social structures in general can be reworked to encompass and explain a whole range of particular situations. Sociology faces serious limitations in this respect, and ends up having to make the stark choice, scope *or* precision. The modelling strategies available in sociology have at their heart generative explanatory structures which I referred to in Chapter 6 as 'conditional and probabilistic'. Thus, whether one's preferred social ontology was structural determinist or methodological individualist, the actual empirical claims made in particular models simply estimate broad levels of probabilities of social action in particular social groups. I have shown in Chapter 6 that this is a fact of life in sociological research.

The consequence of this is that sociological modelling is limited to only qualitative, x-is-greater-than-y type predictions. In extending the scope of social modelling to account for a range of process, the capacity for even this level of precision of empirical test is soon exhausted. In mechanical explanation, the scope of explanation simply stems from the analysis of a particular physical process down into its simpler parts, and these parts are literally combined together under such rules as the vector addition of forces to deal with situations of great complexity. These more complex situations can also be replicated experimentally and so one ends up with a discursive network that is both theoretical and empirical as well as having both scope and precision. In extending a sociological model to cope with a range of different situations one is simply lengthening the string of deductions made with probabilistic mechanisms and any possibility of empirical exactitude collapses. The consequence is that sociological research is involved in a constant trade-off of scope and precision, and the network of discourse associated with each of these goals takes on a different form.

This dilemma is neatly illustrated in the dividing of the ways of two slightly contrasting traditions of generative modelling represented by Goldthorpe's and Boudon's work. To put it crudely, Goldthorpe opts for precision whilst Boudon goes for scope. Thus Goldthorpe's et al.'s (1980) task, as I have presented it in Chapter 6, is to give an account of the mobility densities that portray the movement between the different classes in contemporary Britain. The precision of the analysis is thus a matter of how well his theory is able to identify and differentiate a range of classes in terms of their desirability and penetrability. And increasing the precision of such a task requires that Goldthorpe builds in more and more contextual or historical knowledge. Thus his main theory (pp. 100–4) starts off with what can be regarded as a generalizable piece of sociological wisdom that economic resources can be transmitted intergenerationally more so than other social or cultural resources. Certain 'economically' defined classes are thus predicted for high self-recruitment levels. However, when it comes to making precise claims about the likelihood of demotion from upper class to a range of manual positions, specific knowledge of British workforce practice, such as the requirements that apprenticeships begin at an early age, are brought to bear (p. 101). Similarly when over-time trends in class mobility are explained, specific historical detail, such as the fact that a whole cohort of men were engaged in military service at a particular time, is required to explain the finer points of the changes in mobility flows (p. 69).

By contrast, Boudon's (1974) task, as I presented it in Chapter 6, is to attempt to explain a range of regularities of educational and social inequality, some of which I have reproduced earlier. This decision to concentrate on explanatory scope has consequences for the conceptual forms he employs, which ignore national and institutional peculiarities in order to maintain a relatively empty 'abstract' structure. Thus he speaks of 'higher curriculum schools' rather than 'grammar schools' or 'lycées' and he uses models of class distinctions, assuming only that the class structure is three-tiered and pyramidal. Though his data are derived from information referring to France, Britain, USA, Germany, Norway and many others, his model refers simply to an 'ideal type' Western society. The consequence is that the explanatory thrust of his model relies much more closely on derivations from the simple formal structures that lie at its base. Many of the regularities that he portrays are simply the outcomes of portraying educational achievement as a queueing process and then going back to a knowledge of the mathematics of queueing processes. In general, his explanations turn quite closely on the structures derived in probabilistic mathematical processes like game theory, Markov chains and so forth.

The thesis underlying this chapter is that the form of discourse customarily employed in a discipline will regulate the form of empirical analysis that can be followed. Fields of study using formal discursive networks work by linking conceptual development back to some core propositions. These core ideas become identified in a range of theories and instruments thus allowing the testing of new propositions against empirical replicas of the central axioms. Studies employing ordinary language networks are rich in descriptive resources but due to the open texture of discourse are never able to claim a privileged description of any empirical event. Using these two reference points, I now want to examine the slightly different versions of quasi-formal reasoning employed in these two case studies. Examining them in terms of their general discursive structures will give a good indication of the broad limits of the prospects for exact empirical enquiry in sociology.

Returning to Goldthorpe's model, I have argued that, in following a strategy of generative reasoning, it poses a theoretically justified, rather than an arbitrary, measurement base. Hypotheses about the relative desirability, advantages and barriers carried by each class position not only allow a prediction of likely mobility flows but provide a justification for the class measures in the first place. Thus I claimed in Chapter 6 the modelling process which showed a close fit between the observed mobility densities and those predicted by the generative theory was an exoneration of both theory and data. Furthermore, as we have just seen, basic assumptions of matrix algebra are used to give meaning to various coefficients describing mobility flows. Thus it is so-far-so-good for formalism until we reach a particular point in the argument. The fly in the ointment crops up with the use of local contextual information which is needed to explain the linkages between certain of the elements in the data. I refer to the examples noted above in which classes are defined with respect to specific features of the history of the British workforce. So what we have in this model is something which is absolutely typical of sociological discourse, namely a mixture of formal and verbal reasoning. What follows is that some of the less desirable features of ordinary language discourse work their way into the explanatory structure.

A good example of this is the possibility that exists for the reinterpretation of generative models of the type that Goldthorpe uses. It is quite possible to operate the strategy in an 'upside-down' fashion, that is to say one could create a mobility matrix using any old definition of the constituent classes, observe the resulting pattern of mobility densities and then generate the reasoning why the particular data structures turn out as they do.

In short one can lapse into a *post-hoc* justification of measurement parameters as well as the *post-hoc* development of theory that I have had cause to criticize earlier (section. 6.1). Because the interpretation of data depends in part on such highly contextualized reasoning one lapses into the theory/observation circle. Given the richness of sociological imagination, it is possible to account for almost any pattern of mobility data, often with a range of historical interpretations as candidates for the job. In such cases, data lose their status as a check upon theory. The problem is that it is logically impossible to distinguish *post-hoc* theorizing from a genuine attempt to build a generative model when both rely on specific contextual reasoning to establish the meaning of key elements in the model.

If there is a solution to this question it would seem to lie in achieving a different balance between formal and verbal reasoning and it is the structure of Boudon's model, in this respect, to which we must return. Boudon explains that his purpose is not to describe or even predict particular findings of particular studies in the field of social and educational inequality. Rather he seeks to explain a whole range of regularities that generally occur. The consequence is that the balance between formal reasoning and substantive interpretation changes somewhat. At the heart of explanation of a diverse range of inequalities is thus a series of axioms about the mechanisms which allocate people to the box structures of educational and social positions. The axioms consist of *relatively uninterpreted* statements. These define cultural advantage in terms of probability levels of educational attainment across different classes, a different set of probability levels describing the structure of utilities of moving to different social positions according to one origin position, a set of branching points describing how the allocation takes place over time and so on.

In Chapter 6 I have provided an illustration of how these axioms are used to simulate a general pattern of 'survival rates' of the different classes as they move up the educational ladder. These over-time rates of educational attainment are, for Boudon, largely a result of the effect of the utilities mechanism. This explanation is derived solely in formal terms, being an effect of a utilities structure which disfavours the lower classes being repeated at a number of branching points. This produces an

250

exponential decay in their survival rates, a pattern which Boudon claims is a common feature of such data.

Another regularity that Boudon (1974, 1982) attempts to explain is the stability of occupational mobility within and across Western nations despite the fact that educational provision, attainment levels and aspirations are apparently all changing drastically. Again explanation is a matter of grinding out the consequences of a mathematically constrained generator. I have no space to reproduce the abstract mathematical derivation or the vast mathematical simulation involved here, but (somewhat perversely) I can present a verbal paraphrase of the idea. The occupational structure is taken to be relatively stable over time, whilst a considerable growth in educationally qualified persons is assumed. The consequence is that the 'occupational value' of certain educational qualifications has to decline. The model shows that those with the very highest levels of educational attainment retain their relative advantage in occupational placement, whilst those without educational qualifications are unaffected since they never had access to this rank to high-status occupations. The consequence is a drastic deterioration in the structure of opportunity linked with middle education levels.

These conclusions, as well as a range of others, are basically formal derivations from the mathematics of matrix algebra and 'queueing theory'. Thus what seems to be happening in this example is something much closer to the use of formal reasoning in the natural sciences. In other words, a whole stream of deductions are made from the axiomatic assumptions of the model before attempts are made to interpret them in the findings of concrete empirical studies. It is this approach which provides for the networks of co-ordinated reasoning from which conceptual and empirical certitude springs in physical science.

Life, however, is never as simple as this in sociology, and because Boudon's model lacks other elements present in formal discourse in natural science, we cannot aspire to the equivalent depth of conceptual or empirical rigour. Firstly, there is the problem that the model is (necessarily) probabilistic and so makes essentially qualitative claims about the relationship between variables. Secondly, the business of the empirical confirmation of these models cannot be a matter of manufacturing direct physical replicas of mathematical models since we can only weakly approximate the conditions of experimental closure.

The consequence is that the empirical intepretation (and thus verification) of such models becomes a highly imprecise affair. Boudon scans whole swathes of data looking for examples of the exponential decay of educational survival rates, looking for constancy of mobility rates, looking for non-linear effects of educational qualifications on occupation etc., and, generally speaking, finds them to his own satisfaction. However, to researchers used to much more detailed (if largely descriptive) encounters with data (like path analysis and log-linear modelling) the regularities sought here amount to virtually non-empirical claims. Hauser (1976), in particular, has produced a scathing review of *Education, Opportunity and Social Inequality* in which he asserts that Boudon makes absolutely sweeping claims about the so-called 'official bookkeeping' regularities, which according to Hauser are not universally present or even present in some of the very data in which Boudon claims to find them.

Seen from the point of view of closure, the difficulty is that Boudon declares his theorems to be true of an 'ideal type western society since the war'. Unfortunately, we cannot obtain data on such a society, but only on real societies which have been shaped by historical circumstances such as the intervention of war into the careers of certain cohorts, the timing of training practices of particular occupational strata and so forth. The consequence is that many of the outcomes and even certain of the assumptions of Boudon's model do not show a close fit with the educational and institutional practices of particular societies. For instance, Halsey *et al.* (1980, p. 33) accuse Boudon of deliberately constructing a misleading model with an artificially high number of branching points, so that he is able to emphasize his own pet theory about educational inequality being largely due to choice mechanisms. In their eyes this over-simplification of the generative assumptions of the model is matched only by its erroneous predictions, since their British data fail to show the smooth exponential progression of educational survival rates as forecast by the model.

To my mind these are the inevitable consequences of the task which Boudon sets himself, which in turn mark the limits of formal reasoning in sociology. Boudon (1976) has produced an equally scathing reply to Hauser, pointing out how the latter has totally misunderstood his task and simply applied the defunct standards of local descriptive statistical analysis to an altogether different enterprise. To critics who accuse the box models of operating with over-simple assumptions about status allocation mechanisms, his reply is essentially the same: of course the assumptions are over-simple, the very purpose of formal analysis is to attempt explanatory scope rather than descriptive detail. Indeed sociology faces a rather unenviable choice in this matter. It can combine formal and verbal reasoning whilst never being able to claim the full advantage of the former. One either plumps for statistical precision in the analysis which allows one to include local contextual information aplenty, but this tends to drive the analysis into descriptive forms, for which one can claim no privileged status. Alternatively one uses formal reasoning which, whilst being deductively fertile and linking back to a central core of propositions, is inherently weak in the field of empirical confirmation. It should be fairly obvious that, working from a perspective of scientific realism, I consider the latter to be the lesser of two evils. It seems to me that Boudon strikes about the optimum balance between verbal and formal reasoning. It is equally obvious, however, that there are many constraints in the research process which push local contextual and historical features to the centre of investigation and so there will always be an opposing tendency to see the benefits of the descriptive approach.

Conclusion

What then is the answer to the question posed in this chapter – is class a knot concept or a contested concept? Well, as you know, professor, black and white questions in sociology only ever manage to produce grey answers. It seems to me that sociologists unconsciously aspire to the benefit and goals of formalism even when conceptual development is managed entirely verbally. However, as far as the full-blown mathematization is concerned, the conditional and probabilistic nature of all sociological explanation places irreducible limits on that, and the examples in this chapter indicate important constraints on the expression of theory in terms of formal networks of co-ordinated reasoning.

On the positive side, I conclude that the very medium of class analysis is a language of groups, hierarchies, inequalities, structures, mobility, change and so forth, and thus the term 'class' can act as part of a basic conceptual map of society, if not the knot to which all other concepts are mathematically tied. Much is to be gained by trying to develop a common terminology to act as the 'abstract calculus' linking these and a range of further concepts which are currently open to rather diverse usage. Whether the 'calculus' involved is developed through set theory, matrix algebra, box models, or verbal algorithms is neither here nor there; what is important is to recognize their commonalities. Secondly, the aim of maintaining logical consistency in the development and extension of concepts can be achieved in a much more meaningful way through the device of formal model building than through purely verbal means. Boudon's model is an examplar of how some of the remoter and unanticipated consequences of social action can be tied into a uniform conceptual framework.

On the negative side a number of problems remain which mean that sociological conceptualization will inevitably involve a degree of ambiguity and confusion. I would submit that the reasons for this are not so much a matter of the customary arguments from phenomenology or contestabilism but rather of the necessary limits of formalist concept formation in sociology. The fact that all social data are historically unique means that a certain amount of manoeuvring is involved in applying any formally developed conceptual scheme to specific contextual circumstances. It is the balancing act between formal and verbal reasoning that has to ensue which dictates the degree of clarity of sociological concepts.

Chapter Nine

CHOOSING CLASS CONCEPTS: FROM INDICATOR SELECTION TO THEORY ADJUDICATION

In this chapter we arrive at the most important and most contentious issue in sociological research, that of *empirical adjudication*. Can one really say with certainty that social theory X is to be preferred to social theory Y on the basis of empirical evidence? Thinking of the substantive area that has preoccupied us here, it has been noted over and again that class analysis is almost overwhelmed by a variety of contending theories which produce a remarkable array of definitions of class boundaries, fractions, locations etc. After years of disputation we still have Marxists who perceive the increasing antagonism between capital and labour, and we still have Weberians witnessing the declining grip of the historical classes as exploitation is replaced by the ebb and flow of the competition for market closure. For that matter, we now have Marxists observing and explaining the intrusion of the middle classes into monopoly capitalism and Weberians studying the proletarianization of formerly middle-class strongholds. Thus it is all very much business as usual for class analysis, though one must note the growth of another school of thought which reckons that class analysis is a residual sociological memory, completely unsuited to explain the conflicts of advanced society. Against this background can we look to empirical evidence to evaluate this overabundance of class theory, or do we always end up with data that are constructed on the 'sweet-shop' principle of picking and choosing the empirical goodies which happen to suit our theoretical tastes?

The potential investigative strategy to be evaluated here is that of empirical testing through the *creation of points of intersection between rival theories* (introduced in Ch. 4). I have argued that the

255

so-called incommensurability problem is really the creation of some abstract and (over-) imaginative thinking by relativist philosophers of science and that natural science deals quite routinely with the fact that different theories can generate different empirical programmes. The crucial point was to stop thinking of 'theory' as some kind of singular all-embracing conceptual framework whose every proposition can be tested only by instruments defined within that same framework. Once it is understood that a vast *network of theories* is involved in the construction of even the simplest empirical test, then one can construe empirical adjudication as being manufactured at the point of intersection of rival theories. Scientific theories always have a history; they are always part of some emergent programme and so they are always embedded in a mass of different mathematical models, experimental results, measurement apparatus and so on. It is thus rarely if ever the case that competing theories demand total changes of empirical vision; somewhere along the line the chances are that rival theories will share common assumptions, analytic techniques, concepts, measurement units or whatever. It is by building upon these common assumptions of rival theories, and not by any withdrawal to supposedly neutral and objective observation, that one is able to provide evidence for crucial empirical tests.

Chapter 4 has confirmed the picture that 'hard' evidence is the exception and interpretative flexibility the rule when it comes to the assessment of rival theories. I demonstrated this through an examination of two very different episodes in scientific experimentation. One case considered a dispute, settled long ago, on how best to describe the laws of pendular motion; the other examined a contemporary squabble about the detection of 'gravity waves'. Both examples demonstrate the deep structure of scientific theorizing, and both show that empirical adjudication consists of filtering out superficial self-corroborating observational support and constructing evidence on the basis of certain mutual assumptions of rival potential explanations.

I will not review these cases here but simply remind the reader that there is no set formula for the development of intersectional evidence; we cannot know in advance which of the many sides of a competing set of explanations can form the basis for a common

256

evaluation. My point, however, is that at the heart of scientific practice is constant debate about what constitutes a good experiment, and that this debate is always advanced in terms of discussion about how best to attain intersectional evidence. Hence, in examining this notion in sociology my basic aim is not to attempt a pat statistical formula for its application but to put firmly on the agenda the principle that the construction of evidence is the search for points of intersection between rival theories.

In pursuing this idea I am going to use what will be recognized by now as the familiar format of Part 3 of starting with the bad news before going on to reveal the good news. Given the superabundance of rival theories in all areas of sociology, the potential for building evidence by examining their common assumptions is enormous. However, this option has been almost completely ignored, and the problem of the tendency of different theories to call upon different empirical evidence has been treated as a technical problem of 'measurement error'. In other words it is acknowledged that concepts can always be designated by different indicators, and a range of strategies has evolved to warrant the selection of particular measures. I will show that such strategies are bound to end in indecision and leave the real problem of the interdependency of theory and data completely unresolved. In the second part of the Chapter I turn to the positive side of the thesis and go on to make a detailed study of one of the few rare and choice examples of sociological research, based on the general methodological stance that 'empirical adjudications are always between rival concepts or propositions, not directly between a proposition and the "real world" as such,' (Wright, 1985, p. 189). In the final section I will pass some more general comments on the potentialities and limits of the adjudicatory strategy.

9.1 VALIDATION AND THE SELECTION OF INDICATORS.

The tactic of choosing a single indicator to measure a concept within a proposition under test can in no circumstances avoid the charge of reliance on evidence which is selective and theory-laden. As we have seen this problem is acknowledged in principle even in mainstream survey research which has driven towards a solution by including multiple or alternative indicators of the key research concepts within the basic research design. I have already called into doubt the general wisdom of multiple indicator methodologies in Chapter 2. We are now in a position where we need to examine some of the practical methods whereby choices and preferences are made for particular indicators.

In terms of our interest in social class measurement this matter of selecting and comparing indicators is coming to the boil in contemporary British research. After years of reliance on the Registrar-General's classification (and to a lesser extent on the Hall–Jones scale) we have now reached the point where no new investigative team can resist devising its own scale. Recent productions employing occupational classifications include the Nuffield scale (in several variants), the Cambridge scale, the Warwick Occupational Classes, and the Surrey Occupational Groupings to name but a few. One doesn't even have to belong to a new or ancient university to go in for this sort of thing, since even the old dinosaur, the R–G scale, was conceptually and operationally reworked for the 1981 census. Apart from these, claims for the significance of operationally simpler 'surrogate' measures of class, such as income and housing tenure, have also been pressed on the research community in recent years. Details of the measures can be found in summaries by Marsh (1986a) and Taylorson and Halfpenny (forthcoming).

All this has resulted in a situation where the various research teams have been anxiously looking over their shoulders as each new indicator is published. A period of speculative and informal comparisons has now given way to systematic comparison since it is a relatively simple matter to recode cases from one indicator to another. I only have space here to pause and review one typical case of such investigations. As ever, my aim in doing so is primarily methodological, since I want to show that such statistical comparisons fail to shift research from a basically empiricist mode. What happens is the attempt to resolve our doubts about data by throwing more data at the problem. Hence we remain locked in the whirlpool of the interdependence of theory and observation. Just as evidence can never speak for itself, neither can evidence about evidence lie beyond dispute.

I shall attempt to demonstrate the above using Marsh's (1986b) assessment of the comparative predictive validity of some fifteen potential measures of social class. (The list includes those occupational schemes mentioned above, plus a further range of non-occupational proxy variables.) Her basic idea is to examine to what extent these independent variables are able to predict a range of dependent variables dealing with a range of work and non-work items. For this purpose she uses a multipurpose survey which provides a range of data on the importance of different aspects of the respondent's occupation – job satisfaction, hours worked, chances of promotion, membership of trade unions, engagement in protest activity, as well as attitudinal information on the importance of health, family, neighbourhood, betting and so on.

Running each association fifteen times creates a pile of results which are difficult to summarize, but basically Marsh began by comparing the predictive power of the occupationally based measures across the whole range of dependent variables. Using the simple device of counting those class measures which recorded the greatest number of high-level correlations across the range of independent variables, she emerges with a ranking which places the Hope–Goldthorpe scale (seven-fold analytic version) first, followed by the Hope–Goldthorpe scale (occupational standing version), following by the Registrar-General's classification, followed by the Cambridge scale and so on. If non-occupational measures of class are included the picture changes completely with six of the so-called 'proxy' measures of class (wealth, state or private employment, job autonomy, individual income, family income, terminal educational age) having more predictive power than the occupational variables. These rankings of predictive power change again if a statistically more sophisticated stepwise regression analysis is used as the basis for calculation. Marsh uses this method for calculating the relative importance of each class measure in relation to each individual dependent variable. Taking the occupationally based measures first the Cambridge scale predicts the non-work-dependent variables somewhat better. However, the pattern is much harder to discern for the work-related variables though the Hope–Goldthorpe (occupational standing) version shows some form. Adding the

259

non-occupational, class variables back into the picture complicates the matter further (I hope you are following this, dear reader). Basically different variables or sets of variables prove to be significant predictors as the range of matters to be explained varies across people's attitude to promotion, their perception of the importance of family life, the number of hours they worked last week and so on.

For reasons which escape me, Marsh, considers this a 'pleasurable picture of construct validity' (1986b, p. 21) and on the basis of this and further analysis goes on to make a number of recommendations. These operate within the fairly anodyne framework that 'different measures have been used for and appear to perform best at different tasks' (1986a, p. 142). More specifically she ventures,

> Those who want a measure of social status/lifestyle, or for whom an interval scale is particularly important may find that the new version of the Cambridge scale is the most useful. Those who require a variable whose explicit focus is on differences in the work situation will probably find that some version of Goldthorpe's class scheme is most suited to their needs. But so long as OG and employment status have been coded, none of the Registrar-General's schemes are ruled out; researchers could easily check their results against a variety of official data sources, for example (1986a, p. 143).

Though rather contradictorily we have,

> The traditional defence of RG as an explanatory variable in the face of attack from theoreticians worrying about its construct validity, has usually been a metaphorical shrug of the shoulders: 'It just *correlates* highly with things'. This will not do as a sole defence at the best of times, and is baseless when other, more carefully constructed measures correlate better (1986 b, p. 24).

Despite the significant showing of the non-occupational measures, Marsh considers that it would be wrong to conclude that occupational detail was an expensive extravagance. None of the 'proxy' variables is thus singled out for special praise and the empiricist's love for the safety of numbers comes out once again in the final recommendation, 'the safest conclusion is to collect them in addition, rather than in preference to, occupational measures' (1986a,p. 144).

The task undertaken in this paper could not be more important. Marsh is perfectly correct to deplore the situation in which 'There has not been a more concerted effort among social scientists to get together to debate what different schemes are actually measuring and to work out a better system for general use' (1986b,p. 24). Unfortunately I have to declare myself none the wiser with regard to this worthy goal even with the benefit of having studied the mass of information in this paper. The natural terminus of such studies is not so much more certain conceptualization but complete vacillation. Marsh's indecision is shown in the recommendation, already quoted, that we should measure everything, just in case. To understand why the method does not in fact produce a better measurement system for general use, one has to look first to certain technical problems and then beyond to the basic methodological error implicit in the strategy.

Clearly the technicalities of the way in which the data are reclassified and reanalysed has consequences for the predictive power of the recorded associations. One important factor of this kind is simply the *number* of class groupings defined as we traverse from measure to measure. Clearly the simpler classification systems which employ fewer categories are going to have more potentially distinguishable social groupings lumped together, and this will be reflected in the predictive power of each indicator. For instance, a variable like 'housing tenure' in Marsh's analysis simply divides the population into two rough halves of 'owner-occupiers and mortgagees' versus 'the rest', and not surprisingly it fails to match the predictive power of these occupational schemata which have five, six and seven sub-classes. Such a finding, of course, is more informative about elementary statistical theory than any genuine sociological theory.

Another problem with the predictive validity strategy is the lack of agreement on the *scope* of the predictive associations to be examined. In some of her analysis Marsh seems to assume the goal, noted previously, of finding a 'better system for general use', and to this end she inspects the predictive power of the class scales across a range of a couple of dozen work and non-work variables. In other respects she assumes something nearer the 'horses for courses' formula and seeks the best single measure for pursuing particular lines of investigation. Though both of these goals are perfectly intelligible within the overall logic of comparative predictive validity, alas they are often quite contradictory, as can be seen by the comings and goings across the various league tables of predictive power presented above.

The matter is further complicated if we ask of the first of these strategies (general predictive power), what range of dependent variables should constitute the appropriate target for the test of predictive power? It is not unreasonable to assume that a different set of dependent variables will alter the predictive power of the contending class measures. Marsh's selections in this respect range across the varied and in some cases quite exotic shores of a general-purpose survey; the class measures being asked to predict, amongst other things, if people had ever laid a bet (a question that probably did not occur to even Marx or Weber).

Even if we stick to predictive power measured against the single dependent variable such agonies do not disappear, since we can always query what would happen if we selected a different indicator of one of the concepts in the particular relationship deemed to be vital. For instance, Marsh's indicator of 'wealth', like all the others, is chosen for her according to the questions posed in the survey which provides the validity data. She acknowledges that the 'savings' index actually used is horribly crude. This, however, is to miss the point since selectivity rather than crudity remains the problem. One could readily formulate alternative indicators of wealth in terms of 'property' or 'possessions' and, be they crude or sophisticated, the chances are one could manufacture a completely different range of predictive powers for 'wealth', when the alternative measures were plugged back into the validity exercise.

There are further contentious technical matters which could be discussed, such as the variation in predictive power caused by the choice of statistic used to display the validity coefficients. Without going into this one can already see that the notion of comparative predictive power turns out to possess a range of different interpretations. The end result of course is that having endured the validity exercise we end up slap bang in the original problem. Since we can pick and choose between the different interpretations and expressions of predictive validity, we end up, as ever, by picking and choosing our measures. Instead of directly selecting our measures, arbitrarily or by theoretical fiat as the case may be, the problem is kicked upstairs for the meta-analysis of a validity exercise. However, validation itself can end up as a matter of arbitrary arithmetic preference or be manipulated so that a preferred indicator is statistically warranted. The maxim that observations never speak for themselves, applies equally to the validation as to the use of data.

Even in their own terms, it is clear that such exercises in comparative predictive validity cannot be judged a success. The real problem is the highly limited understanding of the interdependence of theory and observation assumed throughout the method. The 'theory' at work takes the form of low-level generalizations in which it is supposed that class influences (or causes) several aspects of work and non-work behaviour. These theories are not remotely challenged in the course of the analysis; it is simply taken for granted that 'class position' will affect 'income', 'education', 'attitudes to promotion' and 'family life' and so on. Conversely, it is also clear that the differences in the data do not require us to rethink our theories. The simple fact is that all of the causal hypotheses just mentioned would be exonerated regardless of the indicator chosen. If we scan Marsh's results as a whole, and indeed other such exercises in comparative predictive validity (Arber *et al.*, 1984, 1986), one notes little major variation in predictive power across entire ranges of class indicators. The arguments about interpretation that do remain are thus simply disputes about arithmetic; arguments, in fact, about second decimal places (cf. multiple-indicator models in Chapter 2). Whilst it would be nice if our theories did stand or fall at this level of accuracy, the fact is that the causal theories under consideration here are entirely untouched by the process.

At this stage we can begin to introduce a genuine solution to the problem, the background to which I trust has been well rehearsed by now. Theorizing is not a matter of making provisional statements about empirical relationships, but is a matter of framing generative explanations about the mechanisms that produce these regularities. Social regularities must be viewed as the distant outcome of scores of social processes. What offers real scope for the theoretical reinterpretations of data is not the problem of how to express a regularity, but the problem of deciding which social mechanisms have brought it about.

Given this, one can see that the validation approach misses a golden opportunity to put to use the information generated by the cross-coding of cases into different measures. Rather than resting content with the simple arithmetic answer to the question of explanatory import, the real problem is to explain why different indicators give rise to different results. By asking the pertinent question we are driven away from the idea that class indicators are simply flags of convenience for grouping and ranking occupations in different ways, to the notion that measures contain implicit theories about class formation. A measure of social class is only really successful to the extent to which it identifies groups whose actions give them a class identity. The relative predictive performance of the various indicators is thus a matter of how well each measure is able to locate and differentiate the social contexts which give rise to concerted class-related actions. It is this genuine theoretical question we need to put to data and one which, we shall see, data may well be able to help resolve.

9.2 ADJUDICATION AND THE INTERSECTION OF THEORIES.

We cannot allow simultaneously the proposition that all observation is theory-laden and the notion that theories are corroborated by empirical evidence. In order to understand the undoubted centrality of the role of empirical evidence in the production of scientific knowledge we need to appreciate that it performs a function other than that of the straightforward verification (or falsification) of theory. I have argued that empirical evidence in natural science is marshalled with an eye on *adjudication*, that is to say its role is to compare the relative support for rival hypotheses rather than simply acting as the 'data' against which we test 'theory'. In this section I will attempt to show what the logic of theory adjudication might look like when applied to sociological research.

When it comes to concrete application of this idea in the area of stratification research, I find, to the best of my knowledge, that

I really only have one example to ponder. This occurs in Wright's (1985, Ch. 5) empirical adjudication of certain Marxist concepts of class position. The choice of this example is by no means self-evident. *Classes*, even in its own terms, is primarily a work of conceptual refinement and has received most attention for its attempt to shift the explanatory thrust of Marxism away from domination to exploitation, and from structural determination to game theory. Its empirical aspects have received far less comment and superficially at least look quite conventional – the data base, for instance, comes from a large-scale survey and a telephone survey to boot, which only in America is taken at all seriously.

None of this matters much, however, because I come to praise Wright as a methodologist, for my money his work will become a lasting contribution for its development of a unique research strategy. In fact it is precisely because he is a theorist and not a surveyer or a statistician that he has a different understanding of the significance of data. This means he has the inclination to allow a complex family of theoretical assumptions to order the data, before asking that data to make explanatory decisions for him. For once in quantitative work, the tail does not wag the dog.

The logic of adjudicating class concepts

In order to understand how the logic of comparison in Wright's research differs so markedly from what has gone before, it is necessary to remind ourselves of his basic explanatory account which is retained from his earlier work. Re-establishing how it is founded in the realist style of generative explanation will then allow us to make the step to appreciating why empirical evidence must be constructed within an adjudicatory strategy. Wright's basic endeavour remains that of finding clear demarcation criteria for identifying different social classes. In the 1985 model there are twelve such classes which are established by a complex pattern of exploitative mechanisms. In terms of the exploitation of capital, this identifies a group of owners and non-owners of the means of production. In terms of the exploitation of skills/credentials, we have the formation of three divisions of experts/semi-credentialled/uncredentialled. In terms of the exploitation of organizational assets, this splits the class structure into three divisions of managers/ supervisors/workers. The permutation of possible class locations laid down by the combination of the exploitative processes has already been set out in Table 8.1.

Methodologically, the important point is that the class locations become the unit of analysis in all subsequent hypothesis making. The mechanisms of exploitation which identify the different class locations endow the classes with a set of 'liabilities' or 'powers' which give rise to a further set of properties that are associated with that class. Wright puts it like this:

> Definitions of specific classes can be regarded as a particular kind of proposition. All things being equal, all units (individual and/or families, depending upon the specific issues under discussion) within a given class should be more like each other than like units in other classes *with respect to whatever it is that class is meant to explain* (1985, p. 137).

Already at this very first stage the model has important differences with the more customary usage of class measures within variable analysis. This can be seen simply at the level of presentation of the various schemas. If we refer back to Arber and Marsh's work all the measures discussed there are presented simply as a series of ordered and sometimes nominal categories which together comprise the class variable. Wright's schema, as in Table 8.1 is a *typology* depicting the mechanisms of class location. Taken to the level of explanation the comparison becomes even more obvious. In variable analysis the list of class

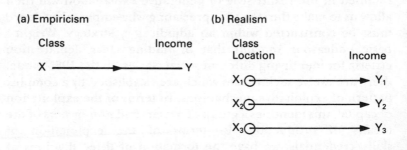

Figure 9.1 Empiricist and realist explanatory strategies

categories becomes, naturally enough, a variable, and that variable as a whole is taken to be the causal factor influencing another dependent variable. We end with an explanatory format in the form of the time-honoured causal diagram (Fig 9.1a). Wright's realist explanation treats each class as a separate context, identifiable by certain underlying processes which have systematically different influences on other dependent variables. In short, the causal hypotheses take on the familiar trinity of realist components linking mechanism to context to regularity. Diagrammatically this can be represented in contrast to the causal model (using income as the dependent outcome) in Fig. 9.1b).

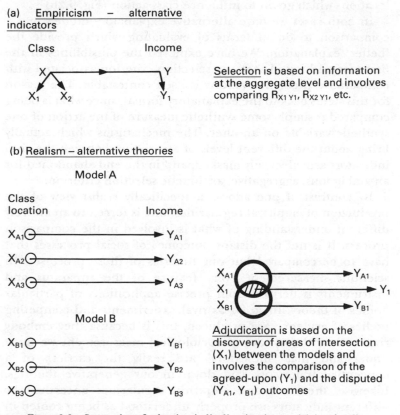

(a) <u>Empiricism – alternative indicators</u>

Class   Income

Selection is based on information at the aggregate level and involves comparing $R_{X1\,Y1}$, $R_{X2\,Y1}$, etc.

(b) <u>Realism – alternative theories</u>

Model A

Class location   Income

Model B

Adjudication is based on the discovery of areas of intersection (X_1) between the models and involves the comparison of the agreed-upon (Y_1) and the disputed (Y_{A1}, Y_{B1}) outcomes

Figure 9.2 Strategies of selection/adjudication in empiricism/realism

If we are operating within the empiricist mode, then such differences in explanatory strategy would be quite inconsequential: these would simply be two different ways of displaying the fact that income varies with class position, which we know already. If, however, we try to allow for the problem of interpretative flexibility, the two modes of explanation begin to differ markedly. On the variable analysis model the problem is that we can represent class by different indicators, and so we have the problem of choosing which indicator is most causally efficacious (Fig. 9.2a). On the realist model an alternative conceptualization of class involves more than the potential replacement of one *indicator* by another, but involves the rivalry of a whole set of *theories* postulating the mechanisms which identify the class locations which go on to influence class action (Fig. 9.2b)

In both cases we have alternative explanatory models and a comparison to do in terms of evaluating which provide the 'better' explanation. We have explored the possibilities in the first case and found that any selection criterion associated with comparative predictive validity is itself contestable. The reason for this stems back to the explanatory format, since what is being compared is simply some synthetic measure of the action of one synthetic variable on another. The mechanisms which actually bring about the different levels of association between the rival indicators are effectively masked, and in the end abandoned for an ambiguous, aggregative, arithmetic selection criterion.

By contrast, if one adopts a specifically realist view of the production of empirical regularities, one is forced to an entirely different understanding of what is involved in the comparison process. It is not the distant outcomes of social processes that have to be compared but our theories of those processes. In scientific measurement every feature of the apparatus and instruments is derived from precise applications of particular bodies of theory. In so far as rival experiments and competing bodies of evidence are produced, this is because they embody rival sets of theory. So, in sociological measurement we must understand that 'indicators' are really the carriers of a conceptual framework laid down in our generative theories. Likewise, the alternative empirical regularities unearthed by different indicators are properly understood as being rooted in alternative explanatory theories.

268

An adequate understanding of the comparison of class concepts would thus have us retrace our steps from empirical outcomes to their theoretical base. The first step is to set out the alternative models of the mechanisms which identify the class context in which certain empirical regularities are expected to be found. In the case of Fig. 9.2b we depict two theories each trying to explain the association between class and income, each one proposing an alternative set of class categories with certain powers or liabilities with regard to income generation. Given the theories in question are likely to have been generated by reference to, and in criticism of, other theories, there is a large probability that these theories will overlap, they might agree on the criterion for the identification of certain classes and disagree on others, they might locate identical personnel in certain classes and not in others.

Here, then, is the opportunity to begin to evaluate the respective strengths of each model according to an intersectional strategy. Because the nature of the explanatory categories is immediately open to inspection we can begin a systematic exploration of the areas of correspondence and non-correspondence between the respective models (Fig. 9.2b). At its simplest what is being proposed in such theories is that people who fall within a particular class categorization will have a higher probability of behaving in a homogeneous fashion than persons who fall into different categories. Alternative theories will set up different lines of demarcation between the respective classes. This is unlikely to render the theories incommensurable however, for, as I have just argued, the rigid specification of the theoretical format plus the inquisitorial habits of the sociological community mean that it is likely that there will be overlap in the explanatory categories.

Wright takes up precisely this line of argument in his Chapter on the adjudication of contending definitions of the working class:

> If definitions are propositions about lines of demarcation
> for homogeneous effects, then this suggests that the
> appropriate strategy for adjudicating disputes over
> definitions of class is to focus on those cases where one
> definition places two positions on different sides of the line

of demarcation whereas the rival definition treats them as homogeneous. These are the cases where the differences in definitions have different empirical implications (1985, p. 137).

Picking up on the previous diagrammatic representations, let us suppose that theory A has a particular definition of the working class which is in some respects, but not entirely, equivalent to the definition of the working class in theory B. Let us ignore the other class identifications the theories might make and simply regard cases who do not fall into the working class as 'middle class'. A comparison of the two theories permits the classification of individuals into one of four categories which Wright presents in the form of Table 9.1.

Table 9.1 Categories in the adjudication of contending definitions of the working class

		Definition A	
		Working class	'Middle-class' wage-earners
Definition B	Working class	[1] Agreed-upon working class	[2] Disputed category 1
	'Middle-class' wage-earners	[3] Disputed category 2	[4] Agreed-upon 'middle' class

Source: Wright, 1985, p. 138

One can think of this as a representation of the simplest possible case of theory intersection. In general I have argued that one does not arbitrate between theories by aspiring to some *independent* body of evidence but by searching for the area of *interdependence* between contending theories around which one can build a common criterion of empirical adequacy. Table 9.1 is an exemplification of such a strategy and Wright codifies the logic of the adjudication as follows,

> Cell I in this table consists of positions which both definitions define as working class. Cell 4, on the other hand, consist of wage-labour positions which both definitions see as 'middle' class. Cells 2 and 3 are the disputed categories. Definition A argues that cell 3 should

be much more like cell 1 than it is like cell 4, and cell 2 should be much more like cell 4 than it is like cell 1, whereas definition B argues that cell 3 should be basically similar to cell 4 and cell 2 should be basically similar to cell 1. The empirical adjudication of these contending definitions of the working class consists of seeing whether the disputed categories are closer to the agreed-upon workers or to the agreed-upon 'middle' class in terms of criteria on which both definitions agree the working class and the 'middle' class should differ (1985, p. 138).

Wright, of course, is justly famous for being 'admirably clear in setting out his arguments and spelling out the details of his analysis' (Rose and Marshall, 1986). In this case he has achieved more than clarity. He has codified a general methodological strategy which hitherto had been exercised only in a completely *ad hoc* and unsystematic fashion. His logic of empirical adjudication could act as the basic strategy in all quantitative work, and to this end some suggestions will follow at the end of the chapter.

Before I proceed to lay down the law on these matters, it is wise to acknowledge that there is a world of difference between devising the foundations for an empirical strategy and applying it. In Wright's research the next stages consist in operationalizing the various class positions as well as defining standards for what constitutes 'similarity' between the disputed and agreed-upon categories in the above logic of adjudication. These are themselves contentious matters, and it is to these further troubled waters we now turn.

The practice of adjudicating class concepts.

Wright's own empirical work, following the logic of adjudication, seeks, naturally enough, to proclaim the advantages of his exploitation-centred definition of the working class derived from the typology above. The adjudication concerns two further potential definitions, Poulantzas's 'productive-labour' definition and the 'manual labour' definition obtained from using a conventional blue collar/white collar occupational breakdown. As noted above the 'dependent variables' used in these 'comparative predictions' are 'income' and the aggregated scores from a set of Likert scales which are taken to measure 'class attitudes'. The actual adjudications are advanced in the form of a dozen or so formal hypotheses, stipulating a set of agreed-upon and disputed categories between two definitions, and then going on to predict that the two forms of class-dependent behaviour in the disputed locations should follow more closely that in Wright's preferred categorization.

We can briefly analyse here the fate of just two of these predictions. First let us compare Wright versus Poulantzas on income distribution. The results are set out in Table 9.2. There are some small departures from the basic logic which should be attended to first. Wright argues that his exploitation-centred definition includes a specific acknowledgement of certain 'marginal' class locations. These are people from cells 9 and 11

Table 9.2 Adjudication of Wright's and Poulantzas' definition of the working class with respect to income

Entries in cells of table:
Means
(Standard deviations)
Number of cases (weighted)

Exploitation-centred definition	Productive labour definition		Row totals
	Working class	'Middle' class	
Working class	[1] $13,027 (7952) 143	[2] $10,241 (6921) 340	$11,065 (7344) 483
Marginal working class	[3] $19,285 (8441) 55	[4] $13,822 (7757) 192	$15,032 (8217) 247
'Middle' class	[5] [Empty cell]	[6] $19,843 (12422) 335	$19,843 (12422) 335
Column totals	$14,760 (8543) 198	$14,744 (10476) 867	

Source: Wright, 1985, p. 164

272

of the main typology, i.e. wage-earners having limited skills/qualifications or basic supervisory tasks (but not both) and who are thus not expected to be unambiguously working or middle class in their actions. As a result they have to be recorded in the results, even though the genuine theoretical disputes to be adjudicated lie in the 'corners' of these tables. In terms of the specific adjudication, we see that Wright is exonerated. Category 2, which Wright takes to be working class and which Poulantzas reckons to be middle class, is much nearer to the income levels of the agreed-upon working class (in fact, more working class

Table 9.3 Adjudication of Wright's and the 'manual' definition of the working class with respect to attitude scores

Entries in cells of table:
  Means
  (Standard deviations)
Number of cases (weighted)

Exploitation-centred definition	Manual-labour definition		Row totals
	Working class	'Middle' class	
Working class	Agreed-upon working class [1] 1.12 (3.17) 344	Disputed category no. 1 [2] 0.27 (3.42) 250	0.76 (3.30) 593
Marginal working class	[3] 1.44 (3.34) 154	[4] −0.50 (3.03) 130	0.55 (3.34) 284
'Middle' class	[5] Disputed category no. 2 −0.28 (3.13) 111	[6] Agreed-upon 'middle' class −1.62 (3.57) 280	−1.24 (3.19) 391
Column totals	0.95 (3.26) 609	−0.68 (3.51) 660	

Source: Wright, 1985, p. 175

than the working class). Category 5, the other potential point of dispute, is in fact empty; there are no folks whom Wright considers middle class whom Poulantzas would not also.

Let us now consider Wright's specification of the working class versus that in the 'manual' definition, as adjudicated by attitudinal scores. The results are set out in Table 9.3, in which values on the class attitude scale go from +8 (maximally pro-working class) to -8 (maximally pro-capitalist class). In this case the disputed category no. 1, people who are not manual workers but whom Wright judges to be working class, turns out to reveal attitudes which are significantly closer to the agreed-upon working classes. In the case of disputed category no. 2, people who are manual workers but middle class by Wright's standards, in fact have attitudes falling about exactly between the agreed-upon poles.

There are further such exercises in which the analysis edges still closer to the data, by way of comparing single attitude items, separating male and female workers etc., but the analysis as a whole conforms remarkably closely to the pattern presented here. Wright is thus able to conclude that his own view of the working class as uncredentialled, non-managerial employers received more empirical support than Poulantzas' view of the working class as productive labour. Similarly the behaviour of most non-credentialled, non-managerial white collar workers puts them much nearer their blue collar equivalents and so gives added support to Wright's criteria. Credentialled, managerial, manual workers, however, fail to provide evidence to arbitrate between Wright's and the class-by-collar distinction.

9.3 THE LIMITS OF THEORY ADJUDICATION IN SOCIOLOGY

Wright forwards these empirically based conclusions with all the caution of a man who has survived an argument or two about class being objects-constituted-in-thought. Taking on board the qualified and conditional nature of his claims for these results, it is nevertheless important to try to ascertain whether one can properly declare such adjudications a 'success' or whether these results are also ripe for perpetual reinterpretation in the manner of all the other sociological data we have encountered. If we can discern any clear answer to this question in this example we might then be in a position to do a little methodological adjudication of our own and decide whether sociological research programmes will forever remain incommensurable or whether we may yet hope for a hint of 'progress' in sociological explanation.

In terms of the possibility of reinterpreting Wright's results we shall find that the short answer is that there is no denying the golden rule that evidence never speaks for itself. More considered reflection, however, will show that the manner of the reinterpretation is limited. So whilst adjudicatory research cannot produce final answers, there may be something akin to the processual narrowing down of possible explanations that may be observed in experimental science. In order to appreciate the difference alluded to here it is useful to split the reinterpretative possibilities into different types and examine to what extent they apply to Wright's research. To this end I will distinguish between (i) operational reinterpretation, (ii) conceptual reinterpretation, and (iii) paradigmatic reinterpretation.

(i) Operational reinterpretation.

It would be quite possible for someone to accept both the way in which rival concepts had been specified and the logic of the adjudication strategy outlined above, but still want to challenge the results on the grounds that the actual operationalization of the concepts was faulty. Wright himself is briefly one such person, when he engages in some speculative self-criticism in order to rescue that portion of his hypotheses which proved indecisive under adjudication. Recall that the class attitudes of credentialled, managerial, manual workers (disputed category 2, Table 9.3) forwarded the case for neither Wright's nor the collar-colour definition of class. Wright suggests that some 'over-stringent' operationalization may have had the effect of enlarging that category at the expense of his working and marginal working class. At the conceptual level occupations are classified middle class if they are 'supervisory' and have 'skills/credentials'. Wright suspects that his operationalization of supervision – supervisory jobs involve the capacity to impose sanctions on subordinates – may not carry the correct emphasis. To capture the 'exploitative' aspect of supervision may require indicators tapping some kind of minimal participation in managerial decision-making. The result of such operational adjustments, Wright supposes, would be to reduce the membership of the disputed category and presumably leave those that remain with a class orientation nearer those of the undisputed middle class.

Is this simply another case of the opportunistic, *ad hoc*, theory-saving adjustment which always seem to lurk ready to undermine any case that may be made for the objectivity of an empirical strategy? I want to answer my own question here negatively, partly on simple practical grounds and partly on more hypothetical judgements on the role of empirical evidence developed in Part 2. At the practical level we are dealing in this example with something much more akin to instrument 'noise' in measurement apparatus. That is to say, the issue concerns the relative precision of the results rather than their theoretical implications. The key point is that the conceptual categories utilized in the adjudications are the carriers of specific theories and not arbitrary operational compilations. Consequently it is impossible to bring about major changes in the empirical content or membership of each category without altering the conceptual base of that category. For instance, consider the problem of reshaping disputed category 2 in the adjudication of Wright versus Poulantzas (Table 9.3). In the above analysis this potentially disputed group turned out to be like the working class *but more so*. To transform the category into one favouring Poulantzas' criteria would require moving virtually all of its present membership and replacing them with personnel drawn from Wright's 'side' of the divide. In short, it would require not so much an operational modification but the total replacement of the productive labour definition by one usurping some of Wright's criteria.

So am I saying that this sort of operational tinkering that Wright is contemplating here is a legitimate part of sociological measurement strategy? Indeed I am, in a qualified way. The point, as Popper might say, would be for Wright actually to run an adjudication of the two operational definitions of supervision. Thus, rather than speculate to save a theory, one needs to demonstrate the general superiority of the 'decision-making' definition of supervision across the full range of hypotheses under investigation. This would not, of course, make the conclusive case for that particular operationalization; it may yet receive its come-uppance in further adjudications. Nor would such a tactic constitute a lapse into verificatory, as opposed to adjudicatory, research, since (as we are about to see) the latter strategy never lies in the hands of the single researcher.

(ii) Conceptual reinterpretation.

It is at the level of conceptual adjudication that Wright states his claim for his research, and so it is this level that requires the closest scrutiny in terms of the possibility of reinterpretation of his results. Can we really say, on the basis of this evidence, that the 'exploitative' concept of class is superior to the 'productive labour' definition and the 'manual/non-manual' formulation. What undermines the validation strategy, examined previously, was the ever-present possibility of calling up a host of alternative explanatory mechanisms to explain the predictive ability of different class indicators. The comparisons themselves needed explanation. Now, in the adjudicatory strategy, by contrast, the class categories are deemed to carry the explanatory mechanisms, so what is being compared is, or should be, clear from the outset. What is more, concepts (and thus explanatory mechanisms) can only be compared two at a time, and so the influence of other potential mechanisms relating class to the dependent variables is irrelevant.

The act of so tightly circumscribing comparisons cuts both ways, of course. It might be that we consider another class conceptualization, say a Weberian identification of a set of different market positions, as a superior way to partition the mechanisms of class advantage. The adjudication Wright engages in cannot help us one jot in evaluating this belief. The adjudicatory model places the onus on the Weberian (or Wright if he wants to enlarge his claim) to produce a whole new body of intersectional evidence. Put into practice systematically, such a strategy would amount to a revolutionary inversion of the way theory feeds upon evidence in social research. When the focus of evidence is on particular empirical regularities then there is little to prevent a plurality of theories growing to interpret the evidence. When the focus of evidence is established by the intersection of theories, we have a continuing narrowing down of explanatory possibilities, rather in the manner of those explanations which survive the test of large scale experimental programmes in natural science.

It follows that the feasibility of such a research strategy depends crucially on the authenticity of the notion of *intersecting evidence*; it requires the potential for clear agreement on precise areas of correspondence and non-correspondence between our explanatory categories. Figure 9.2 and Table 9.1 represent the logic involved in its ideal form but beg a rather important question; namely, how securely can we gain agreement on what constitutes an 'intersection'. This can hardly be taken for granted given that the interests of the different camps involved would colour their perception of this matter, just as they sensitise them to different explanatory categories in the first place.

For instance, to my eyes Wright is guilty of taking liberties with the adjudicatory categories in the inclusion of the 'marginal' working class categories in much of the above analysis. What is supposedly happening in adjudication of social class concepts is that mechanisms of class advantage are compared so that, ideally, each category in the analysis should identify a separate mechanism (or, at least, a clearly defined package of mechanisms). Without this we are back to the 'guessing game' conception of theory and have to speculate why a certain concept has explanatory advantages. Now in Wright's analysis the definition of the working class can be said to meet the requirement of clarity of specification. However, because the whole analysis works from this working class corner of the table the remaining classes lack conceptual coherence precisely because they are the remainder. So the middle classes consist of a jumble of six other locations identified in the main body of the theory (cells 4-8 and 10 in Table 8.1). Worse still from the point of view of the adjudication is the designation of a 'wastepaper basket' category of marginal class position (cells 9 and 11 in Table 8.1). Wright, of course, justifies this by saying that his explanatory mechanisms of class advantage identify class position along a continuum rather than as specific polarities. Apart from sitting rather uneasily beneath a class concept labelled 'exploitation', this gradualist conception of class position allows him to play the 'cutting-point game'. By chopping his class categories three ways,

278

they automatically have a head start in any adjudication with a two-class model. The rival class definitions would no doubt fare better had they been granted an in-between category for mopping up ambiguous cases. Once again there is danger of a statistical artefact being mistaken for a substantive finding about class position.

In fact it would be quite possible to include such a marginal category in a more demanding adjudication of class definitions, provided it was preceded by a more exact specification of the mechanisms which identified the group and a series of hypotheses about how these mechanisms affect the dependent variables. Such matters are conspicuous by their absence in Wright's analysis; this class is just in-between in terms of supervision, in-between in terms of skills/credentials, full-stop. This lack of coherence in the specification of the structural position of the marginal class is demonstrated by the lack of a consistent pattern of their behaviour across the totality of adjudications. Wright actually chooses to call them 'marginal working class' and indeed they sometimes act in a rather working class fashion (e.g. cell 3, Table 9.3). Oft-times, however, they are distinctly closer to a marginal middle-class (e.g. cell 3, Table 9.2). Wright himself notes the lack of homogeneity in their attitudes in one particular comparison (cf. cell 3 and 4, Table 9.3) One concludes that in so far as Wright's adjudication leaves his definition victorious, and I still believe it does, it is merely a points victory which owes nothing (conceptually) to his liking for all manner of contradictory, in-between and marginal classes. Others, I know, would go further than this and consider it an empty victory, on the grounds that the vanquished consist of most commensensical and un-theorized conceptions of class, together with the notions of one of the looniest theorists of the left.

Should we take all this to mean that the notion of intersectional evidence is itself incoherent? Will it not always be possible for adherents of a particular theory to add a category here and fudge a category there in order to improve the showing of their own favoured hypotheses? Will not particular schools of thought always pick and choose their opponents? Can we trust one school to represent the conceptualizations of other viewpoints with even-handedness? In the face of all this should we

not turn on our heels and say, 'welcome back, incommensurability – all is forgiven'.

Stout adjudicationalists need not be so easily moved. At the
level of doctrine, all of these objections mistake or misrepresent
the principles of adjudicationalism as I formulated them in
Chapter 5. Adjudication is the medium and outcome of research
practice and not its rulebook. There are no given and grossly
apparent points of intersection between rival bodies of theory. If
this were the case then a strategy of adjudication could be applied
mechanically and we could map the future course of science as a
series of flow diagrams predicting the points of collision between
the major theoretical programmes. The real roots of the strategy
lie in practical concerns. I have argued that, since alternative
explanations will always emerge for a given body of empirical
information, scientists will routinely look for further evidence
which can narrow down the theoretical choices, and this is done
by *constructing* data at the point of intersection of those theories.
We can thus dismiss the idea that every adjudication becomes a
crucial experiment. Adjudications can always be challenged and
alternative points of intersection identified. Experimentalists
spend their lives not only doing experiments but also arguing
about their significance. The consequence is, of course, that the
adjudication process is perpetual. We would anticipate the
construction of a whole series of experimental adjustments
before we saw the smallest shift in prevailing wisdom.

Much the same applies to my comments on Wright's
adjudication. If I were a determined follower of Poulantzas, I
could run a further adjudication in which Wright's classes were
forced back into two categories and in which the productive
labour definition was applied with an intermediate category for
'service workers' and/or 'productive administrators' between
labour and the new petty bourgeoisie. One would not be
surprised if doubts, rather the reverse of those criticisms above,
were expressed about the authenticity of this adjudication.
Someone else might argue that justice would be done by running
the adjudication with both definitions as dualisms. The Wright
group might come back with a more clearly conceptualized and
operationalized notion of the marginal working class. In general
there could be a great deal more adjudicatory work concerning
the fine tuning of operationalizations and the clearer

identification of the social context (space/time/gender etc.) in which the mechanisms operate. In short, I find myself arguing that more research is needed. Lest you find that unbelievably hackneyed, let me add that I refer only to adjudicatory research; we have had more than our fill of the verificatory stuff.

(iii) Paradigmatic reinterpretation

Work done within an adjudicatory strategy, like any other in sociology, will eventually have to face that line of criticism which says, 'well, what you are doing is all very interesting but it is bad sociology because it ignores X'. For 'X' read any of the key ontological or epistemological propositions around which the major sociological perspectives are formed. Has the adjudicatory strategy anything to offer in the face of this ingrained paradigmatic incommensurability that bedevils sociology? Don't worry, I am not about to claim that we can adjudicate between, say, structural and interpretative sociology, or any of the variants thereof, by identifying intersectional domain assumptions, apportioning representative research to agreed-upon and contested categories, inspecting whether the contested research betrayed one leaning rather than the other and end thus declaring a winner to the paradigm wars.

What I would claim, however, is that the adjudicatory strategy has a flexibility considerably beyond that illustrated in this example which has deliberately stressed the finer points of the method. Thus it is possible to extend the adjudicational model to disputes within perspectives which assume markedly different types of explanation from the theme of capitalist exploitation which runs through Wright's work. These possibilities arise not because of the adjudicatory strategy itself but because of the models of concept formation and explanatory adequacy upon which it is premised. Adjudication is possible because the models work with 'realist' rather than 'nominalist' concept formation and a 'mechanism' ontology rather than an 'event' or 'property' ontology. Realist research categories consist of well-defined theories which identify a context within which the action of a mechanism produces regularities of behaviour in that context. As we established in Chapter 6. This means that realist class categories can be constructed assuming the structural

281

determination of class position, or from a decision-making model based in methodological individualism, or assuming that the influence of structure and action exist as a duality.

This means we can take empirical adjudication to disputes which have hitherto taken the form of ritual displays of the respective domain assumptions of each perspective. One of the many such oppositions which has grown up in social class research is that between the so-called 'positional' and 'trajectory' theory. The former has it that class positions are regulated by wider social and economic conditions. The latter believes that incumbents come before places and that class identification will depend on such matters as individual mobility between classes. This debate began to polarize in Goldthorpe *et al*'s (1980, p. 24) critique of Poulantzas, assumed trench-warfare style with Stewart *et al.*'s (1980) formulation of the trajectory assumptions, and works its way into the research we have been discussing with Wright's adversorial message to potential critics that 'positional analysis . . . is a logical pre-condition for the exploration of the trajectory approach to class' (1985, p. 186).

Once again we find much ado about ontological priorities when there is no irreducible irreconcilability between structural maps and trajectorical flows. The example always quoted in this dispute is whether clerical work should be considered 'proletarian' or 'pre-managerial'. On the one side 'positional' evidence is brought forward concerning conditions of work, autonomy, pay etc. On the other side we have 'trajectory' evidence used about educational origins, age profiles, promotional prospects etc. In fact it is not at all difficult to imagine an adjudication which would examine the behaviour of a group composed of clerical positions in comparison with that of agreed-upon 'proletarian' and 'managerial/supervisory' categories. Running the adjudication in the context of different sub-groups (age-cohorts, gender) would allow a fairly comprehensive answer to the problem.

Conclusion

What are the prospects for empirical research turning to an adjudicatory mode? I can think of a rather long list of reasons why research will carry on in the customary descriptive and verificatory manner, which concern the fact that most social research is problem-centred, government-funded and busy enough in the first place with providing a picture of contemporary social change. Basic theoretical concerns such as how best to characterize the class structure will inevitably be short-changed in such a climate. Leaving aside these external conditions let me concentrate on the rather formidable practical requirements of the adjudicatory strategy itself.

The basic requirement is to have data available in such a form that they can be used to express rival theories so we can go on to adjudicate them. Alas this makes it somewhat unlikely that we can use existing data for such purposes since the power to express the nuances of different schools of theory about class formation is simply not a feature of general-purpose surveys. For instance, even simply to locate people in Wright and Poulantzas' classes, information on occupational title, qualifications, job autonomy and industrial sector would be a minimal requirement. What is more, it is not just the availability of these complex operationalizations that is required. The attempt to replicate such comparisons means forever going back to the original 'unit record'. That is to say, the furtherance of adjudications concerning comparisons of, say, productive/non-productive or credentialled/non-credentialled workers cannot work by nominating their indicators afresh in each investigation but must ensure exactly the same codings are used (cf. Goldthorpe, 1985; Rose and Marshall, 1986).

In short, the problem goes beyond what can be retrieved in data banks; we need the equivalent of 'coding banks' and in particular 'hypotheses banks'. What I am talking about is very large-scale collaborative research in which data are collected in such a way that existing concepts and operationalizations can be repeated alongside those of any rival hypotheses that the investigator wants to add to the adjudication process. The crucial point is for research to follow a *programme of reproducing and transforming existing conceptual schema.* Such a process is routine in experimental research and is achieved at a stroke by the modification of experimental design, whilst leaving intact much mutually agreed theory in the form of the standard equipment and apparatus. In sociology, data have always to be built from scratch and so such a programme would require a degree of co-operation hitherto undreamt of. The fact is, of course, I am not really dreaming any of this because as I am writing this, Wright's research has proceeded well into a series of international comparisons, some of which are carried out by collaborators who, whilst closely replicating Wright's survey are seeking to extend the adjudication process into the territory of Weberian theories of class formation (Marshall, *et al.*, 1988).

Unfortunately, it is too early to measure the possibilities of success of the larger programme, but I should finish here with a few speculative comments on what 'success' might look like in a broad adjudicatory strategy. I have expressed enough doubts about Wright's manipulation and interpretation of his own results to suggest that adjudication is not just something that can be mechanically applied by attending to the distribution of data in 2 x 2 tables. Even though it uses the same raw materials, adjudication should not be confused with any of the statistical modes of comparing indicators; there is certainly no way of increasing its exactitude by such means as the '*t*-tests', which Wright applies to establish the statistical significance of the proximity of the contested and consensual classes.

The ultimate limits to adjudication are set in the probabilistic nature of generative modelling discussed in Chapter 6. There I suggested that, whatever the nature of the class mechanism supposedly at work, we would end up expressing hypotheses in a highly *conditional* form. The syntax of sociological theory, whatever the substantive area, comes down in the end to statements about the probability of behaviour in context X being different from behaviour in context Y. Thus, for Wright, the theory of class exploitation states, in part, that the earning capacities of members of class X are similar, and different from those of class Y. In addition, if certain members of class X also happen to be black, female and so forth, then we know a different set of mechanisms will influence their income. Furthermore, the earning capacity of members of class X will be influenced by their likelihood of moving from class X. Since any hypothesis-about class liabilities is going to be problematic in at least these three senses then there will be clear limits on our ability to identify intersecting classes in rival theories and in the empirical significance of those identifications.

Several results flow from this. The first is that one should expect no wholesale 'winners' or 'losers' in these exercises, in the sense, say, of being able to show that a Weberian conceptualization of the class structure as a whole is superior to any particular Marxist schema *in toto*. This is going to be jolly sad for all of those battle-hardened troops trained in the ancient rivalries, but can be seen quite clearly in the adjudication exercise above, which only established some provisional results about one of Wright's twelve class locations. The fact is that if we attempted to compare his entire typology with some other complete schema then it would be likely that we would fall at the first hurdle: that of identifying systematically all the areas of correspondence and non-correspondence between the categories involved. For instance, starting from an 'exploitation' theory Wright identifies distinct classes of non-expert supervisors (classes 8 and 11), whilst Goldthorpe, starting from a Weberian perspective of 'market position', locates a class of manual, technical and supervisory workers (class V). Now whilst the content of these groups can be expected to overlap, it is far from clear, given Wright's difficulty in defining these marginal levels of supervision, and given Goldthorpe's reliance on operational codings to implement the fine details of his schema, whether we may assume that any group with personnel in common is thereby identified with an agreed-upon explanatory mechanism.

One further interesting corollary stems from the 'triple' problematic level of hypothesis-making noted above, which is that our main problem in trying to compare rival concepts and theories is more likely to be *indistinguishability* rather than *incommensurability*. The explanatory power of any one class category will turn on the matter of how well it distinguishes behaviour in that category from that in any other. Since these differences apply only within broad bands of probability it might well follow that making a minor modification to a particular category will not register any great change in the empirical distribution of the results. Wright, for instance, notes (in a footnote, 1985, p. 187) that the major overhaul in terms of Marxist theory, in changing from a 'domination' to an 'exploitation' perspective makes virtually no difference in the matter of who gets assigned to the working class. I do not think we need be particularly shamefaced about this; the discipline is full of brazenly contradictory theories so we still have plenty of work to do. This limit on the discriminatory power of empirical evidence is simply a consequence of the general explanatory power of sociological theory, which we will have to learn to live with. This should not, however, detract from the important point about the adjudicational strategy, which is that it offers a practical solution to a discipline which has far too easily been terrified by the incommensurability problem. To adapt a comment that was made about Wright by his collaborators (Rose and Marshall, 1986), but which I would prefer to reserve for the adjudicatory strategy he initiated – it ensures that we need not talk past each other, and thereby presents a challenge to us all.

Chapter Ten

CONSTRUCTING CLASS DATA:
IMPOSITION AND CONTROL
IN THE INTERVIEW

Our search for parallels between the construction of empirical data in natural science and sociology reaches its conclusion as we now come to consider the actual act of data collection. When comparing the specific measurement operations of physical and social science, one's first (and quite possibly second) thoughts must be to admit defeat and abandon any pretence that there are worthwhile analogies to be drawn between what are essentially disparate practices. Natural science measurement, as we have seen in Chapter 4, consists of a whole series of physical manipulations, the crucial one being the transformation of the property to be measured into some other form of energy. This *transduction* process enables investigation of the measurand via its action on further properties under the closed conditions created within the measurement apparatus. Any notion of social measurement in the form of energy transfer, instrument construction, signal transmission, pointer reading and all the rest is patently fanciful. Sociological data will always emerge in an interactional phase between researcher and subject (directly in the case of interviewing, indirectly with the use of official data). Accordingly, measurement in social research will always be primarily an act of *translation*. There will always be a need to square the conceptual elements established in relatively closed theoretical models, with the reasoning and language of the respondent, which operates routinely in much more open conceptual systems.

In these introductory remarks to this chapter I want to begin to chart the main consequences of these inevitable differences in measurement practice. We face two important, in fact potentially

287

disastrous, consequences of the fact that sociological data are produced in situations which are not linguistically and socially conducive to the production of valid and reliable data. The first problem is that in acknowledging that the actual mechanics of measurement are irretrievably social, I would seem to have let my defences slip against the phenomenological critique of measurement dismissed many, many chapters ago. To the charge that sociological measurement always ends up by using commonsensical categories, the thrust of my argument has been that the slide into ordinary language (and all its associated problems) can be prevented by paying careful attention to the language of theory and the structure of explanation. Whilst this may answer important issues concerned with conceptual development in sociology it does not help us one jot with what are essentially operational problems, since in the last analysis the operational language of sociology is ordinary language.

The first sort of issue at stake with data production is thus something we might regard as a *control* problem. The problem is familiar from all those discussions of the social nature of the interview. The information collected in an interview cannot be simply thought of as a verbal response to verbal stimuli but is actively created in the interaction between the two parties involved. Students of this encounter suspect that a relatively minute difference in the exchange of language can change the course of the interview. The detail of question wording and sequence will have a substantial influence on the data which are generated. Similarly, the information flow in the interview will be affected by the respective social position, character, appearance and manner of the interviewer and interviewee, in a way that cannot be assumed to be held constant from occasion to occasion.

Contrast this with the physical science model in which the explanatory, experimental and measurement systems are entirely equivalent, the significant feature being that they are all closed systems (see Figs. 5.4, 5.7). Recall that the mark of this equivalence was the historical process whereby the theoretical systems become experimental systems and then measurement systems. Whilst the explanatory and survey design stages of social research can approximate to the requirement of closure, the actual measurement operations would appear to contain irretrievably open features. The first problem to be faced in this chapter is to find a way of pressing the rather unpromising linguistic and social raw materials of the interview into service as a quasi-closed system.

Were this not problem enough, the actual mechanics of sociological data collection give rise to the return of a second major difficulty, which amounts to another version of the ubiquitous circularity problem. Recall that I have argued that physical science encounters no routine problems with the theory-ladenness of data because of the transduction strategy, which is at the heart of all measurement apparatus. Circularity is avoided because the theories under test are not transmitted directly into the measurement apparatus. This strategy is accomplished physically by the production of some device which converts the measurand into some other property (usually from one energy form to another). I am quite unable to think, except facetiously, of any social equivalent of this transduction process; we are forever doomed to ask questions in order to produce data.

The second main cost of a translation mode of measurement is thus an enforced return to something akin to a concept/indicator model of measurement. Essentially, we are looking for measures (questionnaire items), to capture the concept under consideration as precisely as possible, and this means that our theoretical assumptions about the concept are carried more or less directly into the data. This can be regarded as the *imposition* problem, the concepts and ideas in the questionnaire items potentially impose a frame of reference onto the respondent's answers regardless of whether the respondent sees the issue in this way. This direct translation of conceptual structures from theory to data languages thus automatically avoids a whole area of potentially falsifying evidence and prompts, once again, the charge that theory testing using survey data is all too often a self-corroborating exercise.

10.1 THREE MODELS OF THE INTERVIEW

The issues which I have described here as the control and imposition problems have prompted yet another polarization of approach in sociological methodology. On the one side we have a broadly empiricist camp advocating a *structured interviewing* style

(a) Empiricism – data collection in the structured interview

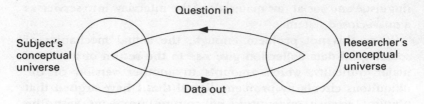

(b) Phenomenology – the joint construction of data in the unstructured interview

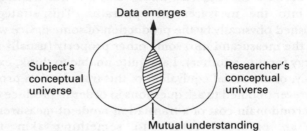

(c) Realism – data construction in the structured interview

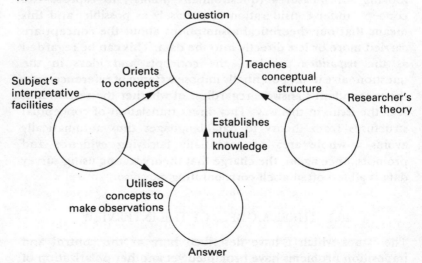

Figure 10.1 Models of the conceptual structures and information flows in the interview

and stressing the importance of precision and clarity in the construction of questions as well as neutrality and uniformity in the conduct of the interview. On the other hand we have the phenomenological view which is committed to understanding the respondent's 'meaning' and so regards data collection as a task for inducing everyday talk within *unstructured interviews* in near-to-naturalistic settings. The trench warfare that exists between these two is well enough documented so as not to require review here. Instead I will concentrate on redrawing the battle lines by introducing a third, *scientific realist*, account of the social and linguistic context of the interview. Note that though I use the term 'realist' again, the purist would be correct in telling me that it is not derived from any known principle of realist philosophy. The term is now simply acting as a useful label for the overall strategy presented in the book. Figure 10.1 represents the conceptual structures and information flows assumed in the three models.

The empiricist or *data collection* model goes back to assumptions about an external world out there, which we inspect and from which we retrieve information. One introduces the instrument of observation, be it a thermometer, a skin response galvanometer, or a questionnaire item and records the response. The underlying principle, as phenomenologists never tire of telling us, is a stimulus–response system (Fig. 10.1a). As a working model, however, the stimulus–response principle is tempered with assumptions about language since both stimulus and response are spoken rather than activated and observed. These assumptions, of course, are that the stimulus question is commonly and identically understood by all subjects and that all responses are intelligible within the frame of reference of the question.

This goal of creating common meaning in the exchange of questions and answers is attacked by what one might refer to as the 'lowest common denominator' approach. Questions are asked in the simplest possible form which will nevertheless remain faithful to the conceptual intentions of the researcher. To these ends, the major effort of this school can be summarized in the oft-stated goals that the interview schedule should be clear, precise, unambiguous, intelligible etc. and *not* leading, hypothetical, embarrassing, memory-defeating and so forth.

Great care is also taken over question form, dealing with such matters as whether to phrase questions negatively or positively, whether to include don't know categories, how to arrange the sequence of the questions and so forth. Since the stimulus is compound and includes both the interviewers and their questions, equivalent care is taken to neutralize and standardize social and personal factors which might affect the nature of the response. All of these features have led to a great deal of research on research, which has the aim of minimizing the distorting effects of the language and conduct of the interview (e.g. Schuman and Presser, 1981; Dijkstra and van der Zouwen, 1982).

Whilst these studies demonstrate that so-called positivists are far from blind (or should that be deaf?) to problems of language in the interview, the basic difficulty remains concerning the assumptions made about the nature of the information created. All the attention paid to question and situation management is in aid of gaining knowledge of the respondent's 'true opinion' or a 'true record' of their activities (an idea cherished in the famous notion of the 'individual true value'). In this way the essence of the stimulus–response model is retained in the supposition that the subject matter of inquiry and the subject of the interview are one and the same. It is this seemingly trivial assumption which lies at the heart of this model of the interview that I will wish to challenge in due course.

Phenomenologists have no truck with the idea that language can be thought of as verbal behaviour, and so dismiss any notion of the interview as a stimulus–response system. They assume that even identical, plain words, identically and plainly delivered by identical and plain interviewers can still mean quite different things to different people. This school, however, also assumes that interview subjects are indeed the subject matter under investigation. What is distinctive about sociological inquiry is that human behaviour is intentional and that our subjects are meaning creators. Since it is assumed that the basis of action lies in the intelligibility of the social world to the subject, steps must be taken to ensure that the research act is intelligible to them. In order to penetrate the meaningful world of the subject it is thus necessary for the researcher to engage the subject in a process of joint construction of meaning (Fig. 10.1b). To know how subjects think is to share in the experience of that thought at a certain level.

Such principles demand a rather different kind of practice. Ideally the joint construction of meaning takes place over many months of ethnographic study, although it is sometimes allowed that the informal unstructured interview can act as an imperfect substitute for this. In terms of interview language, apart from the 'topic' of inquiry, no frame of reference is imposed on the subject. There are no dilemmas over question wording and question sequence because the nature of the interview is conversational. Data thus emerge as a narrative and not in the form of ticks in pre-coded boxes. The conduct of the interviewer calls for equivalent informal practices. There is no place for detachment and neutrality; what is required is genuine responsiveness and involvement on the part of the interviewer.

I take the view that these traditional models present a needlessly polarized view of interview possibilities. I am not suggesting that there should be some fuzzy midway compromise in the form of semi-structured questions in semi-formal interviews or some such like. What is required is a clearer view of the aims of the interview and thus a new model of the division of labour in the tasks and responsibilities in the interview. What is defunct in both orthodox models is the view of the respondent as the subject matter of inquiry. Whilst I would agree that there is no other source of information open to the social researcher, this practical limitation has all too often led us to forget what we are really supposed to be investigating – the researcher's theory about certain of the workings of the social world. Neither of the traditional models has an adequate understanding of how the conceptual structures assumed in the theory under test should inform the interview. What is proposed here is an interviewing strategy which places such schemata at the centre of the data gathering process. Once this principle is established, many of the old antagonisms between the basic approaches can be bridged.

Against empiricism, I would agree with the phenomenological assumption that the common meaning of questionnaire terminology is quite problematic. However, as I have argued all along, the root-cause of this is not to do with the nature of language as such, but with the language of variables. That is to say variables are constructed independently, they are rarely locked into the theoretical structures, and so they often lack common meaning for researchers, let alone respondents. The result is that the qualities used to identify the key variables drift into everyday usage, from whence all the problems of vagueness and ambiguity derive. The solution to the problem is indeed to write clear and unambiguous questions. However, the problem with the solution is that it is never quite clear who is to set the required standard of clarity. Are we talking about the respondent's or the researcher's idea of an unambiguous question? I would claim that traditional survey methodology has never got to grips with this distinction. Indeed most of the research on the matter deals with question form (open versus closed questions, order effects, yea-saying and so forth) rather than question substance (the substantive issues actually referred to). I take clarity and precision, initially anyway, to be unequivocally a goal and responsibility for the researcher's theory. Thus, running rather against conventional wisdom, I take the first task of interview to be one of *teaching* the respondent the distinctions involved in the conceptual structure under test (Figure 10.1c).

Against phenomenology, I would agree with the traditional (empiricist) objection that relying on the joint construction of meaning produces jolly nice conversations but ones that are simply not comparable from subject to subject. Since no stimulus is imposed, and there is no systematic recording of answers, there are no measures and reference points available to assess the range of responses, apart (paradoxically) from that imposed by researchers in their summary accounts of these encounters. I thus take it for granted that all inquiry imposes a frame of reference onto the subject matter and for sociology this means a degree of imposition of meaning on to the subjects themselves.

However, unlike the cruder versions of empiricism, we need a model of the subject as something more than a response mechanism which is automatically attuned to the stimulus concept. So whilst I maintain that the question content is unequivocally the researchers' responsibility, there is necessarily a process of question interpretation on the part of the respondents. However, what the subjects should be pondering is not how to make good conversational sense out of some vaguely defined topic, but rather their task is to discover how the question conceptualizes the social world and to see how they fit into the picture. What I am suggesting here is a role of interviewee as *learner–informant*. They have to orient themselves to the model of the social world given in the question categories and to locate their experiences and life-events within it. Armed with the appropriate conceptual orientation, *they* do the observation on behalf of the researcher (Figure 10.1c). Apart from these conceptual and linguistic matters, the realist model also assumes a different view of social interaction in the interview. To put it briefly, the model of the researcher is neither that of the neutral technician, nor all-time buddy, but a guide and interpreter of the interview schedule.

In short, a realist interview strategy involves both the determination of concepts by the researcher and interpretative work by the respondent. What I am trying to suggest is a new and clearer demarcation of where one begins and the other one ends. As a first step, the overall task might be best described as *data construction*, a term I take from Bateson (1984), one of the few survey practitioners to have attempted to move away from the ingrained data collection model. Although I depart from him on many a detail, his basic metaphor for the process can act as a general guide:

> posing a research question . . . in fact *asserts* far more about the social world than it asks . . . It is as though the client has written a book about the social world and the task of the researcher and informant at the data construction phase is to fill in the gaps (1984, pp. 82-4).

Sociological research of course involves rather different personnel than governmental surveys, so if you read 'theorist' for 'client' here and regard the theorist and researcher as one and the same person, you will have caught the gist of the idea.

Attempts to provide general models for a complex research technique like the interview always appear somewhat brutal, and what is needed next is some refinement of the data construction model. What I want to do first is to support some of the assertions made above by looking more closely at the 'meaning imposition' problem. Then I go on to examine the model in terms of some real live questionnaire and interview items and so add some detail as to what question wording and interview context should look like on the realist model.

10.2 WHOSE CONCEPTS (ABOUT WHAT)?

Whilst I hope that it is reasonably clear that the 'realist' model of the interview postulates a rather different pattern of conceptual flows in the construction of data, the utility of such a model depends on how it fares in relation to overcoming the traditional dilemmas of the interviewing method which I have described above as the 'control' and 'imposition' problems. Taking the latter first, the crux of the critique of the interview method in this respect is that the questions dictate a conceptual framework that might or, rather more importantly, might not correspond to the way that the subject normally thinks about the world. I have taken up a seemingly uncompromising position on this matter, that is to say since all observation is theory-laden, sociologists, too, must construct data according to their own theoretical predispositions. What is more I would now appear to be preparing to add a further twist to the conceptual vice by advocating that the subject's task is to assimilate these conceptual structures. The obvious problem here is the more I argue for the priority of sociologist's conceptual universe, the more I would seem to run the risk of imposing an alien framework onto the cognitive distinctions typically made by the respondent. The plot thickens if the reader recalls that I myself have used the imposition-of-conceptual- framework argument as a means of criticizing the path to measurement via scaling techniques (in Chapter 3). If the presumption and usurpation of meaning was illegitimate on this earlier occasion how do I now propose to warrant it?

The answer, in fact, is not so much a question of who does the conceptual imposition (since that is always the lot of the investigator) but what it is that is imposed. So I am saying that the imposition problem turns crucially on what the concepts utilized purport to be about. I want to raise a distinction between 'external' concepts (that is concepts which refer to institutional practices and interactions in the social world) and 'internal' concepts (that is concepts which purport to reflect people's perceptual structures, orientations, values etc.). It will require a whole section to clarify the nature of this distinction, but at this stage I can alert the reader to the denouement of the tale. Imposition is a problem only if the concepts the researcher is using purport to reflect directly the inner perceptual world of respondents. When concepts refer to the mutual knowledge we possess of the external world, their usage does not amount to passing off one's concepts as someone else's.

Similar conceptual distinctions about concepts are made throughout sociological methodology and it is useful to hone the meaning of my external/internal division by way of comparison with other uses. The first such usage that comes to mind in this context is difference between 'factual' and 'opinion' questions, long established in the literature on survey methodology. What would be regarded as a typical 'factual' question, I suppose, would be questions about such matters as 'age' and 'educational qualifications'. Opinion questions would span quite a range from specific 'approval/disapproval' items on particular topics such as the 'right to strike', to abstract questions about basic 'world views' and 'values'.

I will argue that such a distinction marks the vital division but labels it incorrectly, and as a consequence treats the investigation of the two domains inappropriately. The very term 'factual' raises again the empiricist dream of an external world which we can relate to without making any conceptual presuppositions. The whole point of this book is to drag sociology back to empirical inquiry without the need to assume a world of brute 'facts'. Since perception is blind without conceptual support, we need to understand the real reason why certain questions in survey research are considered 'factual'. This is basically because they refer to some *external* standard or practice or institution which is recognized in the public domain. 'Age' is thus external in the sense that it refers to a measure of time (one lap of the sun by the earth) which we all accept as the standard for counting our birthdays and which gives us the conceptual framework to express the idea (years, dates, months etc.). Questions about 'educational qualifications' also presuppose the existence of the external institution and its terminology.

Opinion questions, by contrast, are quite appropriately if rather narrowly, defined. The subject matter now refers to the 'internal' thought processes that the respondent uses in interpreting that aspect of the social world under investigation. Thinking of the subject matter that concerns us here, opinion questions about class would include specific, poll-type items, charting beliefs on snippets of received wisdom about social class (e.g. We are all working class now – agree/disagree). Opinion questions would also cover rather more abstract ideas usually referred to as class orientations, class imagery or class consciousness. This, of course, is potentially a matter of great complexity as we would be dealing with subjects from those whose every thought was steeped in a sectarian political reading of the subject, to those for whom the notion of class was a complete irrelevance. Henceforth I will prefer to use the label 'internal' to cover the entire area from subject's basic perceptual structures to highly specific evaluative activities.

Despite the time-honoured usage of the fact/opinion question distinction in survey methodology, there has been some controversy over whether both are legitimate targets for the questionnaire/interview method. (see, Bateson, 1984, pp. 29–30; Marsh, 1982, pp. 104–24). The prevailing wisdom, as represented by these two authors, would seem to suggest that the distinction between the internal and the external represents a difference of degree. We gather data on them in exactly the same way (i.e. by having the respondent provide the information); all such questions are prone to error, opinion questions merely providing more difficulties with wording and validation. Although such a pragmatic view might be just about acceptable in surveys which are essentially descriptive in intent, I propose that the 'external' questions mark the boundary of utilizable data in explanatory research.

The reason for this is perfectly simple and resides in a paradox contained in the presuppositions of all 'opinion' or 'internal' questions. As I have just pointed out, these items are delivered in the same way as any other in survey research, and therefore make the conventional assumption about question wording, namely that questions utilize a conceptual framework which is common to researcher and subject. 'Internal' or 'opinion' questions, however, make the second assumption that they uncover those conceptual orientations which subjects are naturally predisposed to use. Between the two lies our paradox: the questions are supposedly investigating conceptual structures but in order to pose them we already have to assume a certain conceptual structure is appropriate.

We have already seen this paradox at work in the investigation of scaling techniques in Chapter 3. There, I demonstrated that as soon as one offers the respondent a cognitive structure to work with, one loses, at a stroke, any knowledge of the salience of that cognitive structure. In the case of ranking occupations, one finds that subjects will sift and grade job titles with great alacrity, but there is no telling whether this is how they routinely think about or act towards such occupations. Further, I showed that there is no way to rid such exercises of all presuppositions about the subject's perceptual structures. The more abstract the task, the more the subject will look for clues as to the 'appropriate' cognitive framework in the peripheral structure of the instructions and questions.

Scaling, of course, is distinctive, in that its assumptions about perceptual forms are plain to view, as they form the basis of the respondents' task. However, the same paradox emerges in any direct investigation of people's 'inner' conceptual structures. Perhaps the best example is the complete inconclusiveness of the attempt by a whole generation of sociologists to find some constant pattern in people's class imagery. These investigations were promoted by Lockwood's (1966) famous paper which supposes that the working classes were internally differentiated in their views of the class system, and that three main types of imagery could be anticipated – 'deferential', 'proletarian' and 'privatized'. British sociology, being what it is, sought to study the issue by providing direct empirical evidence for their existence. These investigations proceeded by presenting a range of possible models of the class structure to the respondents and asking them which most nearly fitted their own interpretation. The questions took the form of all kinds of verbal and visual presentations of hierarchies, dichotomies, trichotomies and so forth, which supposedly allowed the subjects to express their own inner cognitive structures (for a summary see Bulmer, 1975; Davis, 1979). Whilst not a few deferentials, proletarians and privates(?) were discovered, the major problem is that different inquiries led to different and sometimes contradictory results, a state of affairs which led some commentators to face the possibility that 'few people apart from sociologists and intellectuals have an image of society at all and that so-called images of class and society are an afterfact of the interview method' (Davis, 1979, p. 29).

I must admit my heart would sink if I were forced to make the following choice:

(i) In Britain today there are basically two main classes, bosses and workers.
(ii) Most people in Britain today belong to the same class.
(iii) There are several classes in Britain.
  Which statement comes closest to your opinion?
  Please say if none of the alternatives comes close to your opinion (Martin and Fryer, 1975, p. 99).

The fact is, given a particular context, I could accept any of the above models as a fair approximation to what is going on. Suppose I felt that Britain was a class–divided society, with a tiny capitalist class, with most people belonging to a huge but occasionally internally divided working class, then I'm well on my way to agreeing with all of these propositions. My answer might depend, therefore, rather closely on the particular terminology involved, in which case my 'orientation' might be dramatically changed by a slightly different version of the same statements as follows:

(i) In Britain today there are basically two main classes, bosses and workers, and these classes have opposing interests.
(ii) Most people in Britain today belong to the same class: the only important difference is how much money they earn.
(iii) There are several classes in Britain today: the upper classes run the country and industry, and this is as it should be (Cousins and Brown, 1975, p. 73).

So I might well have been happy to plump for the safe, 'several classes' answer to version 1 but be put off by version 2 in which the ruling class have somehow inveigled themselves. Regardless of such deliberations, however, the 'several class' answer will put me down in the 'hierarchical view of class' category, and were I working class, I would be well on my way to being labelled 'deferential'. Although the question form is quite different in these examples, the outcome is precisely the same as in scaling, namely that the researcher's categories are being passed off as someone else's.

One objection to the line of argument pursued here is that by concentrating on the content rather than the context of the interview I am directing attention away from the real culprit, namely the highly artificial nature of the linguistic exchange between respondent and researcher. Indeed, it is high time that I introduced the standard response to the 'imposition' problem, which is that the conceptual straitjacket produced by the interview is best removed by abandoning the strict structured question/answer formats for a much more open-ended exchange of language. Let us examine the case for what I referred to earlier as the phenomenological strategy of the joint construction of data. The imposition problem is considered solved in such forms of research because responses are supposedly uncovered in their natural context in the life-world of the individual. The argument goes that we can capture the genuine orientations, attitudes and values of the subject because they are captured 'live', in terms of how they are actually felt and spoken of by the respondent. What is crucial, in this view, is the sensitivity with which the field work or informal interviewing is carried out in order to retain this quality of first-hand involvement with the respondent's understanding of the social world. To use the customary and hallowed example from British research, Spanksy and Joey are reckoned to be the authentic voice of deprived working class lads because, thanks to Willis's keen ear we are able to hear them speak their own inner thoughts (Willis, 1977).

The problem, however, is not Willis's ear but his theoretical predispositions. So what one finds in this and all cases relying on the informal interview is that the imposition problem crops up in another guise. On the one hand the lads speak of the importance of 'having a laff', of the fact that 'all jobs are the same when you'm a grafter', of the likelihood 'that the ear oles will be civil servants, toffs and the lads will be brickies and things like that'. On the other hand Willis informs us that such views can be categorized according to those which are 'penetrations' of capitalist ideological structures and those which bear the marks of its 'limitations'. Thus,

> 'Penetration' is meant to designate impulses within a
> cultural form towards the penetration of the conditions of
> existence of its members and their position within the social

301

whole but in a way which is not centred, essentialist or individualist. 'Limitation' is meant to designate those blocks, diversions and ideological effects which confuse and impede the full development and expression of these impulses (Willis, 1977, p. 49).

The problem, of course, is whether the lads' conceptual forms can ever survive such a jarring change of language. Willis, of course, never makes the final commitment to the joint construction of meaning. For him 'ethnography is a supremely ex post facto product of the actual meaning of life' not to mention it also being 'patronizing and condescending' (1977, p. 194). We are thus left with a real curiosity, the strategy which is supposed to make light of the imposition problem, and the example which is supposed to bear the hallmark of authenticity in this respect, is just as capable of leaving us with the question of whose concepts are remaining loyal to whom.

Whatever proponents of unstructured research have to say about the importance of data being established in forms of discourse shared between the subject and researcher, the fact remains that it is researchers who have at some stage to give a summary account of all the expressions of inner meaning. Given that the nature of the data presented takes the form of the apt quotation and the anecdotal summary, we can see that such a research format allows every bit as much opportunity for the imposing of the researchers' conceptual framework as does the structured approach. I conclude that the imposition problem is a feature of the type of concept that sociologists try to employ rather than a characteristic of certain data-gathering strategies. This allows me to construct the first principle of an alternative approach to data construction, namely to claim that sociological data should refer to what people do and not what they think. I propose that the research interview should abandon attempts to ascertain directly orientations, motivations, values, world-views, evaluations, opinions and so forth and instead concentrate on events, happenings, actions, situations, conditions. Having people say what they do is on the whole more likely to achieve valid and reliable results than having them say what they think. The only way to polish the verbal formulation or mode of delivery of such questions as, 'do you think that class is an inevitable feature of modern society?' or 'how is it that people come to belong to the class that they do?' is to refrain from asking them of the respondent and regard them as problems for the theorist to answer.

Thus far I have tried to establish the importance of 'external' rather than 'internal' events as the focal point of sociological data. I have been careful in the argument to this point to leave these notions in inverted commas and, though I have paraphrased the basic ideas, given a couple of examples and likened the difference to that between the factual and opinion qualities in survey research, I have yet to define the distinction systematically. The concept of externality I have in mind is not of course that of physical externality, in that one could say of the physical world that it would still be there regardless of what one thinks about it. The external social world is thus not independent of our reasoning process as in some of Durkheim's more ruthless maxims on 'social facts'. On the contrary, the apparent externality of social facts depends on shared knowledge of certain ideas.

Thus if we take a concept like income, its 'facticity' depends on the shared intelligibility of the idea, which in turn stems from the coherence of a range of social interactions which sustain it. 'Income', then, is not to be considered a concept external to our thinking because it can be regarded as physical 'stuff' in the form of coins and notes. For most of us, of course, income comes in the rather more intangible form of the transfer of numbers from one bank balance to another. This little process of exchange gives us the real reason why income can be considered 'factual', which is that it is locked into a range of other ideas that are part of our routine practical consciousness. In other words, every one of us would have a reasonably clear idea that income was money paid over for a range of services a person might provide, that it might be paid at regular intervals, that the transactions often involve particular financial institutions and so forth. The mundanity of my description here in a way makes the point for us. Income is factual because of the phenomenon which Giddens (1984, p. 331) calls 'mutual knowledge' or, rather more graphically, the 'acceptance-as-real' that is built into the continuity of interaction in any institution. Giddens in fact uses the distinction between 'incorrigible mutual knowledge' and 'fallible common-sense belief' as an ontological distinction on which to base a critical sociological methodology. I think the distinction is rather more problem-free when used as a basis for establishing the 'facticity' of sociological data. The nearest sociology gets to dealing with hard facts are thus the measures that can be observed from the 'hardened' institutional features of social life.

In general, when I say that sociologists should attempt to measure external social facts I am saying they should make use of the intelligibility of a set of routine social practices to which we are all happy to give broadly the same name. We should use our knowledge of the 'accepted-as-real' as the basic linguistic resource of inquiry. Mutual knowledge is a condition of us being able to communicate, and thus a condition of us being able to generate any social data at all. It refers to the things we treat as knowledge in our daily activities and not our beliefs, values or attitudes towards them. To give an example, suppose we hear or read that 'BP shares will provide a steady income for the long term investor' or that 'lecturers' income has fallen behind that of civil servants by 5% in the last five years', you and I know what is meant because we are roughly aware of the institutions and transactions to which the statements refer. This would be the case regardless of whether we approved or disapproved of the economic order which sustained the types and levels of income.

Note, however, that this notion of mutual knowledge is not the same as that understood in a stimulus–response view of concepts. It is not assumed that the concept speaks for itself and that, for instance, 'income' means the same thing to all persons. The above statements in fact provide us with a clear example of why such an assumption is groundless and needless, since they use the same term but refer to two differing forms of income, namely dividends and salaries. This is not normally a cause for consternation, since mutual knowledge does not refer to a knowledge of terms but a knowledge of the continuity of action which sustains a particular meaning. In different institutional contexts we know that a different spectrum of mutual knowledge is required and assumed. So in some instances, as when I fill in my income tax form, the definition of income might be legally sanctioned; in others I might have reason to defer to a particular usage, as perhaps when being advised by an accountant; in others

I might want to make the conceptual running as when explaining to my son that there are institutions other than my pocket from which he might obtain income. So what is crucial to 'facticity' is not 'fixity' of meaning but knowledge of the bundle of activities and institutional features which sustain a particular meaning.

The very condition of me being able to communicate is the assumption that I have knowledge, with other people like me, about a given order of relationships in the external world. Since all interaction presupposes the 'accepted-as-real' in this manner, I am suggesting that sociology can do no better than to imitate real life in this respect and attempt to construct data at this level. I am not about to suggest that operating within this world of mutual knowledge is a straightforward practical demand on the researcher. Indeed I will examine the problem in relation to question wording in the next section. My aim here is simply to offer the 'accepted-as-real' as the solution to the 'imposition' problem. From the point of view of the respondent, questions used utilizing mutual knowledge will not assume anything about how they regard, value or appraise the concepts referred to. To be sure they will be directed to particular practices, activities and institutional arrangements rather than others. So, for example, picking up the 'income' example again, an interview question on the matter should make quite clear what kind of sources of income are relevant. Thus if the theory under test is investigating the income accruing to various class groupings, and an ownership dimension is considered important in defining class, then specific questions on dividends, interest etc. would be included in the relevant items on the questionnaire. The important point is that this in no way constitutes meaning imposition since I have just described how concepts can assume a place in the accepted-as-real whilst changing in meaning from context to context. Just as an accountant can say this is what counts as 'income', and we are able to orient to this as the appropriate definition without being forever bound to do so, the respondent can accept the researcher's definition of the relevant institutional practices involved in defining a concept without somehow being compromised.

Suppose we assume for the moment that theoretical concepts of the type referred to here can be translated into the realm of the 'accepted- as-real' without befuddling or brainwashing the respondent, is there not still a problem of imposition from a rather different point of view? Even if I could be absolutely sure that no cognitive distortion was involved in the production of a response, am I still not effectively making the respondent the mouthpiece of the theorist at the data construction level? In asking them to follow the conceptual distinctions forged in the theory under test am I not granting that theorists can deliberately choose the ground on which to evaluate their theories? So even if we have good analytic reasons for assuming a difference between externalized mutual knowledge and corrigible internal beliefs, there is still a case to be answered that mutual knowledge is not simply another circular route in which data are preselected to be attuned to theory.

To escape this charge that theory language is simply and surreptitiously 'imposed' rather than overtly and ruthlessly 'imposed upon', we need to consider again how circularity is avoided with the use of theory-laden data in natural science. Theory testing is never a case of a single proposition being tested by a single datum. Rather, producing experimental evidence involves the testing of a proposition derived from a whole series of theories and models using evidence also derived from a whole series of theories and models. The assumptions of the theory under test are thus not driven directly into the evidence. The *channelling* of information required to perform this feat is done at a stroke in the transduction process. Whilst no direct equivalent of such a process is available in sociology we need to think of the translation process involved in data construction in terms of how it can channel the information flow from theory to data in some corresponding way.

To this point I have suggested that the theorists translate their formal concepts into categories describing certain practices and institutions in the social world, which it is the respondent's task to 'orient to'. Whilst such a path might sound like the high road to circularity, what must not be forgotten is that the theories under test here are also not singular propositions but complex models linking the action of generative mechanisms to the production of regularities in particular contexts. Just as the transduction process is selective in the information signals that are passed into the measuring instruments, so too can sociology avoid circularity by preventing the totality of the theoretical structure being translated into the data. In practice this means that a good deal of the theory must be made intelligible to the respondent in order to convey the precise meaning of the terms involved, but that this process can stop well short of informing the respondent of the actual hypothesis under test. It is fairly easy to construct a principle that will allow this, namely that the researcher's task is to conduct an interview in such a way as to reveal the conceptual structure of the theory under test but not its propositional structure. For a clear example of this distinction think of the mobility research examined at several points in this book. The mobility theory makes a whole series of propositions about the barriers and desirability of certain class positions and about how these give rise to differential flows of individuals between the class positions. To construct the data it is necessary to translate in the fullest detail what the theory supposes about the class positions but nothing whatsoever needs to be said about the underlying social processes which distribute people across the class positions.

10.3 LANGUAGE AND CONDUCT OF THE INTERVIEW

In trying to solve some of the traditional methodological problems of the interview I have produced a model of the interview based on a series of relatively novel analytic distinctions, such as that which regards interviewing as data construction rather than data collection, that which regards data as residing in mutual knowledge rather than common-sense belief, and that which seeks data at the level of conceptual structures rather than discrete variables or complete hypotheses. Such considerations are of little use if they remain at the level of principle and metatheory. It is important to be able to set them into practice as technical rules of thumb, and to be able to envisage the principles as a potential outcome of practices already in use. I intend to split this task into two and examine both the linguistic and non-linguistic conduct of the interview. In this case I will use some of Wright's interview schedule by way of illustration, noting of course that it had no pretentions to be anything other than a standard structured interview.

Question wording

I shall begin with the idea that questionnaire items and measures should concern and draw upon mutual knowledge of the 'external' social world. This requires finding a method of writing questions which upholds two principles established above. (a) Mutual knowledge is propositional or relational knowledge and not an ability to recognize and name objects and events. We should thus think of the task of question wording not so much as the operationalization of concepts but the translation of the reasoning in which they are embedded. (b) Mutual knowledge is made not given. The development of such knowledge consists of establishing relationships, utterances, sentences about the institutions and practices in which the concept is located and not just relying on words to make their own good sense.

These principles tell us that we cannot expect concepts, however simplified, to speak for themselves, but that in order to convey ideas to respondents it is necessary to teach them something of the theory. Whilst such an idea of conveying conceptual structures might sound fanciful on first hearing, it is in fact in close accord with everything we know about the linguistic structures involved in translation. In Chapter 3 I have referred to the research which points out that no two languages can be successfully translated on a word-by-word basis. In using a word appropriately in English I call upon a whole range of general knowledge about the context in which the term describes. To translate this into, say, French requires a basis in what Quine calls the shared collateral information between the languages. Failures or problems in translation are not remedied by ever more detailed attention to particular terms but by finding some common ground in the context of ideas in which the term is located. Exactly the same applies in translation from sociological to everyday discourse.

How might we put this principle into practice? To begin with researchers, they should of course be totally clear in the conceptual structure of the terms they employ. Now I have already made great play of the conceptual tightness of realist explanatory structures. A unique propositional structure is employed in which regularities are explained by discovering the particular generative mechanisms which operate in a given social context. When applied to a particular problem like social class analysis, it results in a conceptual structure in which the different classes are identified by particular structuration mechanisms and combine together to form the class structure. To come to a specific example, suppose, like Wright, we are trying to operationalize a particular class position, say 'expert managers'; this is not done by directly stipulating the indicators which identify a particular set of individuals with particular characteristics. Rather 'expert managers' is a category thrown up by the relationships of a range of social structures and processes. Thus the correct operationalization requires a conceptual filtering process which matches and in fact puts into reverse the steps that go towards the creation of his typology of class positions. In other words, to identify expert managers one has to know the twelve-fold structure of class position, one has to know the combination of generative processes which create these positions, one has to designate raw variables to characterize each particular aspect of those mechanisms and finally one has to ask specific questions to gain information on each raw variable. The whole process is depicted in Figure 10.2b. In short (if that is the phrase), to find his expert managers Wright has to ask individuals about their formal position in job hierarchies, whether they supervise or not, whether they take decisions or not, the nature of their occupation, their educational credentials, their autonomy over work tasks, whether they are self-employed or not, and how many employees they have. Each one of these matters can be an issue of greater or lesser complexity. The 'decision-making' item, as we shall see, consists of a filter question and seven others on various aspects of decision-making.

Starting from the respondents' point of view, they too are faced with a kind of filtering process in which conceptual possibilities are narrowed down in the course of the interview. In this case, respondents start with a more or less open-ended understanding of the subject matter of the interview and how they might answer. As the interview progresses there is a process of orientation to certain conceptual categories whilst others are simultaneously foreclosed. It is this process which constitutes the move from the free play of common-sense beliefs to the assumption and use of mutual knowledge. So, to use the same example, Wright's respondents start with the world as their

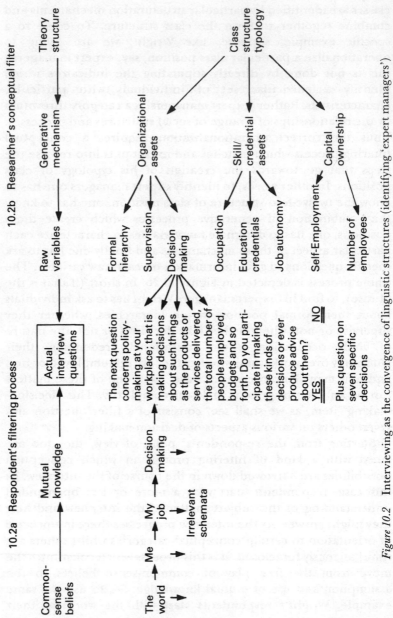

Figure 10.2 Interviewing as the convergence of linguistic structures (identifying 'expert managers')

The image contains the following labels:

10.2a Respondent's filtering process

Common-sense beliefs → Mutual knowledge → Actual interview questions ← Raw variables ← Generative mechanism ← Theory structure

10.2b Researcher's conceptual filter

Me
My job
The world

Decision making
Irrelevant schemata
Relevant schemata

The next question concerns policy-making at your workplace; that is making decisions about such things as the products or services delivered, the total number of people employed, budgets and so forth. Do you participate in making these kinds of decisions or ever produce advice about them?
YES
NO
Plus question on seven specific decisions

Class structure typology

Organizational assets
Skill/credential assets
Capital ownership

Formal hierarchy
Supervision
Decision making
Occupation
Education credentials
Job autonomy
Self-Employment
Number of employees

oyster, they learn the interview is about their social position (and not those of others), they learn that it is about their work (and not other matters such as their social activities), they learn it is about particular aspects of work such as decision-making (and not others such as holiday allowance), they learn it is about particular types of decisions such as budget size (and not others such as when to make the coffee) and so the process continues. This is depicted in Figure 10.2a which, in conjunction with 10.2b, represents the interview as the convergence of conceptual categories.

The process which respondents enter into here is common to all perceptual, understanding and learning processes, and has been characterized by cognitive psychologists and linguists in a variety of ways, all centred on the focusing, or filtering of anticipatory schemes, relevance structures, frames of reference and so on. One can even pick up essentially the same idea from a perspective which is traditionally supposed to oppose the view of interviewing advocated here. That is to say the ethnomethodological notion of 'membershipping' is also capable of fostering a view of interviewing as the convergence of conceptual categories in the development of mutual knowledge. Membership categorization devices are used by conversationalists to search through given utterances for convenient categories that allow them to group certain of its elements together and thereby to establish a frame of reference to understand that utterance. Hence we are liable to understand the phrase 'the baby cried, the mummy picked it up', in certain ways and not others, because we anticipate the relationship between the two characters. Similarly, in the interview discussed above, we 'pair' the concept 'decision-making' with further concepts like 'budget' and 'policy' and so understand the reference is to managerial decisions rather than judgements on individual job routines and the like.

Interviewing then is a matter of attempting to harness these absolutely commonplace elements of the communication process. Viewed as an attempt to encourage the convergence of anticipatory schemata, several quite definite prescriptions can be made about the linguistic structure appropriate to the interview. Above all comes the need for questions to be structured and to offer fixed-choice, closed answers rather than to take on any of the possible unstructured forms. If one examines the transcripts of a typical open-ended interview, what one finds is that the respondent usually engages in a series of queries designed to clarify those elements of mutual knowledge which they assume should be there but are unable to find in the original semi- or unstructured question (e.g. Mishler, 1986, p. 60). Ethnomethodology has taught us that communicants make sense of a conversation by continually thinking forward and backwards though the context of what is said to establish a framework of meaning. They have discovered a whole range of devices such as 'ad hocing', 'letting pass', 'filling in', 'post and pre-utterance pertinizers', etc. which serve the purpose of the gradual establishment of shared conceptual categories. My point is simply that much of this can be cut through in the special context of the interview, since a question prepared with a set of predetermined answers establishes in seconds what the respondent expects anyway, and what the researcher and respondent otherwise have to accomplish at length through the use of other conversational devices.

This continual prospective/retrospective examination of meaning, which is the key to understanding all conversation, is also anticipated in another traditional questionnaire design strategy which makes more eminently good sense with respect to the view of interviewing as a convergent linguistic structure. I refer to the idea of question *filters* and *sequences*, an example of which from Wright's questionnaire is reproduced as Figure 10.3. The sequence of questions and the range of possible answers here does more than simply provide the body of information Wright is seeking. It shows how the distinction between common-sense belief and mutual knowledge is established. The notion of decision-making of itself can call forth an immense variety of interpretations and evaluations, but the phased introduction of the specific practices associated with it, such as work rate, product change etc., establishes the idea in terms of shared assumptions about the work place.

Whilst what I have said to this point can be regarded as a new justification for old questionnaire design strategies, the perspective of the interview as a converging linguistic structure also requires something of a change in priorities within the traditional techniques. Basically what is happening in sociological data construction is the researcher trying to

The next question concerns policy-making at your workplace; that is, making decisions about such things as the products or services delivered, the total number of people employed, budgets, and so forth. Do you participate in making these kinds of decisions, or even provide advice about them?

 YES   NO ➞TURN TO NEXT QUESTION SEQUENCE

Think of your specific place of work. If the organization for which you work has more than one branch, plant or store, think of the specific location where you work. I will ask you about decisions which might affect your workplace. For each, tell me if you are personally involved in this decision, including providing advice on it.

First, are you personally involved in decisions to increase or decrease the total number of people employed in the place where you work?

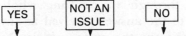 YES   NOT AN ISSUE   NO

How about policy decisions to significantly change the products, programmes, or services delivered by the organizations for which your work?

 YES   NOT AN ISSUE   NO

(How about) decisions to change the policy concerning the routine pace of work or the amount of work performed in your workplace as a whole or some major part of it?

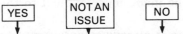 YES   NOT AN ISSUE   NO

(How about) policy decisions to *significantly* change the *basic* methods or procedures of work used in a major part of your workplace?

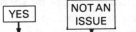 YES   NOT AN ISSUE   NO

(How about) decisions concerning the budget at the place where you work?

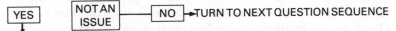 YES   NOT AN ISSUE —— NO ➞TURN TO NEXT QUESTION SEQUENCE

Do you participate in deciding the overall size of the budget?

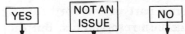 YES   NOT AN ISSUE   NO

Do you participate in general policy decisions about the distributions of funds within the overall budget of the place where you work?

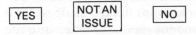 YES   NOT AN ISSUE   NO

Figure 10.3 Question filters and flows – simplified version of Wright's questions on decision-making

Source: Adapted from Wright, Institute of Social Research, Michigan

pigeonhole the respondent into certain places within a complex conceptual structure. By and large this process of selecting certain categories and rejecting others as applying to them is only apparent to the respondent at the level of individual questions, and I have already remarked on the importance of structured response categories in this respect. However, as far as interviewer training goes, second only to learning these question-and-answer packages is the task of mastering the sequences and flows in the questionnaire as a whole. These conceptual route maps are illustrated in an elementary way in the questions reproduced in Fig. 10.3, but, in relation to the structure of a complete questionnaire, involve working through or omitting whole passages of questions according to the answer received at any particular point. These flow paths are the main vehicle for carrying the broader conceptual assumptions and distinctions assumed in the theory under test. Usually they remain quite hidden from the respondent and only appear as marginal notes telling interviewers which question to ask next. Since the secret of translation is to convey the meaning of a concept by attending to its place in the whole, such assumptions about the conceptual skeleton of the interview should be made more explicit to the respondent.

In the best questionnaires there is already some attempt to monitor and check that respondents are satisfied that they are being processed down the correct conceptual channel by such devices as the 'repeated' and the 'rephrased' question. So asking questions like 'can I check again, as part of your job do you supervise or manage the work of other employees?' does succeed in alerting respondents to the fact that they have been and are about to be further channelled into a particular conceptual space. Such questions act as branching points in the conceptual structure, and so declare that some part of the forthcoming conceptual field is irrelevant for certain respondents. But they only do half the job, especially if the answer to such questions happens to be 'No', and the respondent is herded onto some new pasture. These strategic decisions are thus usually made without knowledge of whether the respondent sees the matter in quite the same way, interview subjects being typically quite unaware of the future conceptual consequences of the alternative answers they happen to have chosen.

314

The correction to this problem, put rather metaphorically, is that if we are going to pigeonhole people correctly it is important that we take them on a close inspection of the available pigeonholes in the first place. What I am suggesting is that instead of occasionally showing respondents a printed card to explain the more complex structured questions, more of the overall structure of the questionnaire should be revealed. The conceptual assumptions of the researcher are carried in the 'skip to' instructions and the directional arrows, in the colour-coded question groups, in the sectional headings, introductory and linking comments etc. The interview is a labelling process and should be checking all the time, 'this is to be your label, is it correct?' It is only by acknowledging the full range of devices which carry the conceptual structure under investigation, and thus getting the respondent more fully involved in the structure of the schedule as a whole, that conceptual convergence can be achieved.

One particular prejudice of mine in this respect is the matter of the initial explanation to respondents on the aims and purpose of the inquiry. Whilst respondents will attempt to dig this information out of every nook and cranny of the interview schedule, researchers by contrast are often quite lax in revealing the reason for the questions. Perhaps this is something to do with imitating the close-to-the-chest (if not downright deceitful) style of the experimental psychologist. Now whilst we should, indeed, fear the phenomenon of hypothesis-seeking behaviour on the part of respondents, this should not interfere with the business of fully revealing the conceptual structure of the inquiry to the subject. In general respondents have to make do with highly general initial statements of the purpose of the questionnaire (e.g. we are going to ask you some questions about economic life in Britain today), together with massively uninformative sign-posts and signals during its course (e.g. now some questions about work).

What I am saying again is that to get valid answers it is important to reveal as much of the conceptual structure as possible. Such thoughts raise again the strategic importance of the need to impart the conceptual structures assumed by the theory under test without revealing the detailed substantive hypotheses as a method of avoiding theory/data circularity.

Wright's questionnaire provides a fine example of how such a dividing line gets drawn. If we refer back to Figure 10.2b, it is certainly the case that the very essence of his theory is woven into the fine detail of every question posed to ascertain class position. The questionnaire thus renders his structuralist theory by stages into generative mechanisms, raw variables and mutual knowledge. Once again, however, the charge that the theory thus determines the evidence can be avoided since the data construction sequence above crucially omits the actual hypotheses under test. So, whilst we would hope that the respondents would be fully aware that they were being pigeonholed into social class positions by skill, credentials, organizational position, source of income etc., and some might even have an inkling that the investigation was trying to relate this to other matters such as income, they would have to be unusually perceptive to gather that their information was in aid of testing the following:

> *Hypothesis 1.* Income should be polarized between the working class and the bourgeoisie.
> *Hypothesis 2.* Average income among wage earners should increase monotonically as you move along each of the dimensions of exploitation from the working class to expert managers.
> *Hypothesis 3.* The pattern for unearned income should also be monotonically increasing along each of the dimensions of the class-structure matrix (Wright, 1985, p. 232).

Although I have posited that all communication depends on assumptions about the accepted-as-real, I have also acknowledged that it is created and confirmed in the course of social interaction. So whilst I have argued that the interview must be thought of as a deliberate and elaborate display of mutual knowledge, this is not to say that question construction can be utterly accurate and reliable in locating the external practices at issue. Lying in wait for my basic claim that institutional practices denote the key resource for identifying mutual knowledge are the well-known dilemmas over institutional categories, most memorably expressed in the dictum 'one person's "liberation movement" is another person's "terrorist organisation"' (see Giddens 1984, p. 337). Rather more pertinent to the discussion

316

here is the example of some of the classic difficulties of ascribing people to class positions on the basis of occupational characteristics. One such problem might be phrased 'one person's company directorship is a Tory MP's job on the side'. Double or multiple occupations have been regarded as a 'great source of difficulty' in census operations since 1861 (Bateson, 1984, p. 84). The point, however, is that, once acknowledged, the possibility of multiple occupations can become part of mutual knowledge and indeed space is usually given over in recording the possession of more than one job in most social surveys on this topic. Of course, this in itself does not solve the problem of class allocation; usually this becomes a matter of trying to distinguish 'main' and 'secondary' occupations, or having them ranked 'in order of importance', and then devising certain rules about which bits of information will appear in the class coding.

My basic reaction to the problem can thus be summarized as follows. Interview items must assume certain institutional practices which are part of people's mutual experience, and whilst there can never be a perfect sharing of the descriptive categories which express mutual knowledge, (a) discrepancies are not usually going to be of an order of magnitude which will affect the broad qualitative predictions which constitute sociological research hypotheses and (b) the worse dilemmas over institutional descriptive categories can be resolved by careful piloting and testing of the interview schedule. Lest this just sounds like the repeat of a lesson from Old Moser's Almanac, a final reminder that what I am claiming here does not apply to the measurement of people's inner belief and values, but only to mutual external knowledge. Recall further that I have said that mutual knowledge is not agreement about the meaning of words but concerns propositions and relationships about institutional practices.

The changing balance of linguistic requirements that such modifications bring to the interview can be illustrated by one final example. Consider the problem of the contradictory answer. Interview questions by their very nature pick up many discrete bits of information. As the example in Figure 10.2 shows the separate answers are often packaged together to give some overall classification to the respondent. These overall classifications will make assumptions about how particular institutional roles are packaged together. However, because the

317

language used to express such institutional knowledge cannot always be developed and assumed instantaneously and perfectly, we often have a situation where inconsistent replies occur. For instance Wright (1985, p. 317) discovered that 1 per cent of his sample said they were wage-earners employed by someone else, and yet it transpired they were owners or part-owners of the company for which they worked. In this case it is not the meaning of the terms 'self-employed' or 'employee' which define mutual knowledge; there are many financial and managerial reasons why owners might prefer to be designated as employees in their own businesses. The solution to the contradiction, again depending on sound pilot work with the question, is to find information relating to the actual relationship a person has with the company and so requires a whole series of further questions on the nature and extent of their ownership. Note that this dilemma would be irresolvable if what was at issue was the discovery of people's perceptions of the value of self-employment, or one assumed that respondents have equal conceptual rights in the interview. However, because this particular questionnaire has a clearly defined sense of what constitutes ownership, the task is essentially one applying the definition to the respondent's experiences. Wright goes so far as to 'correct' the self-designation of those 'employees' who are 'major shareholders' so that they are assigned to the ownership class. Again I would insist that the correction is not 'imposition' since the purpose of the survey is to understand the consequences of the relationship people enter rather than simply give them a name.

Social relations in the interview

Nothing is quite so polarized in the polarized world of methodological writing on the interview as the views on the nature of the social context required for the disclosure of accurate information from the respondent's lips. Broadly speaking there are two models of the social nature of the interview which follow closely the mainstream empirical and phenomenological strategies described above. The first stresses the importance of neutrality in interview performance; the interviewer's manner and appearance should do nothing to distort the free flow of information pertaining to the questions themselves. The ideal interviewer is thus a sort of Mrs Average, someone who is not too smart, not too scruffy, not too serious, not too silly, not too intelligent, not too dumb, not too anything. (She is a Mrs, incidentally because of the quaint cultural assumption about the inappropriateness of the approaches of male or young female strangers, plus not so quaint assumptions about cheap labour.) This goal of neutrality is celebrated most famously, if ironically, in Rose's (1945) metaphor for the interviewer as a 'combined phonograph and recording system'. As in the issue of question wording, this strictest formulation of the stimulus–response doctrine is never adhered to in practice because of the further (in)famous requirement of the standard interview, namely the achievement of 'rapport' between the respondent and researcher. Because we require considered answers and not simply verbal responses, subjects need some additional inducement to comply with what are often long, detailed and personal inquiries, and nothing works better in this respect than being friendly and courteous.

Ranged against this view we have the *interviewing-as-involvement school*. The idea here is that formal questions, however charmingly put, are only likely to induce superficial responses. However well and pleasantly spoken the inquiry, there is no disguising who is defining the issue (namely the interviewer-as-expert) and what is the status of the responses (namely, data). Rather more positively this strategy is an expression of the commitment to the phenomenological tenet that in order to understand a person's actions (including what they say in answer to a question) it is necessary to know their reasoning. Oakley (1981, p. 58) voices this instinct at the level of the emotional relationship with her much-quoted rallying cry that 'personal involvement is more than dangerous bias – it is the condition under which people come to know each other and to admit others into their lives'. What is needed in a genuine interview is thus not mere rapport but rather actual support for the respondent; subjects have to feel 'empowered' in order to reveal their true feelings (Mishler, 1987, Ch. 5). This goal is most memorably, and not one bit ironically, expressed by Oakley in the context of her investigation into motherhood, when she argues that what these particular respondents needed above all from her was 'sisterhood'.

The battle lines between these two camps have remained fairly static, though I would venture to say that the involvement school has been more vociferous of late. Oakley, in particular, has great fun at the expense of some of the utterly wooden advice on how neutrality/rapport is to be achieved, which she extracts from some of the thicker tomes on interviewing strategy. The following, on what to do should the interviewee have the impertinence to ask for the opinions of the interviewer is almost enough to make one prefer the fully robotized interviewer.

> In most cases, the rule remains that he is there to obtain
> information and to focus on the respondent, not himself.
> Usually, a few simple phrases will shift the emphasis back to
> the respondent . . . [e.g.] . . . 'I guess I haven't thought
> enough about it to give a good answer right now' . . .
> Sometimes the diversion can be accomplished by a
> head-shaking gesture which suggests 'That's a hard one!'
> while continuing with the interview (Goode and Hatt,
> quoted in Oakley, 1981, p. 36).

Adherents of control and neutrality in the interview situation are, of course, not without their arguments. By and large, these are the social counterparts of the question-wording problem above, which showed that whilst professing to the joint construction of meaning, the unstructured format actually allows researchers to impose and patronize like the best of us. Thus it could be said that there is a very fine line between 'involvement' and 'crusading', sympathy with women in their hopes and fears about pregnancy can all too easily transform them into underlabourers in the promotion of an epidural-hating, natural-childbirth-loving social movement. Similarly the need for personal involvement can be overdrawn. In Oakley's hands it renders the detached, scientific (and hence masculine) interviewing of women as a contradiction in terms. We are well down the path to solipsism here, and in a world in which only men can interview men, scientists understand scientists, fascists involve with fascists, and Oakley makes sense only to Oakley.

What tends to be missing from this debate, once again, is the question of how interview strategy relates to the issues studied. It is noticeable that the critical arguments mentioned above work at their best when they face the interviewer with a task beyond the capacity, or at least the strengths, of a particular interviewing method. The reason why Goode and Hatt's interviewers would appear such lemons shaking their heads and saying 'that's a hard one' is precisely because they would have surely just asked a similar question themselves in the context of an attitudinal inquiry. Conversely if, say, gas meter readers were seeking the distinctly 'factual' information about quarterly gas usage, then 'involvement' would not get them very far, nor, God forbid, would 'sisterhood' or 'brotherhood'. Better, I think, to ask the question straight, 'where's the meter?'

Now I have already located the subject matter of the realist interview in external mutual knowledge of institutional practices. Such interviews cannot and need not handle values, beliefs or, still less, 'emotions' which must be left to whatever method the phenomenologists/feminists can best devise. The question remains, what roles and situations will operate most successfully to create and sustain the mutual knowledge assumed in, and required to test, sociological theories? It will not surprise the reader to learn that I think that many of the traditional survey manuals become quite sound once the domain of inquiry is suitably limited. Thus when Oakley (p. 35) quotes Moser, derogatorily, as saying that 'pleasantness and a business-like nature is the ideal combination', I find it a statement impossible to fault from a scientific realist perspective. The same, apart from the consistent use of the masculine, goes for some of Goode and Hatt's earlier advice to the head-shaker who 'must introduce himself as though beginning a conversation but from the beginning the additional element of respect, of professional competence, should be maintained' (quoted in Oakley, p. 33).

None of these sentiments, however, really strikes at the social processes necessary to support the full cycle of data construction (Fig. 10.1c) and in particular the notion of conveying complex conceptual structures to the respondent, by stages, in the linguistic filters described in Fig. 10.2b. Curiously, one of the best descriptions I can find of how this is managed comes from the latest advocate of the 'involvement' position.

> respondents learn from how interviewers respond to their
> answers – restating or rephrasing the original question,
> accepting the answer and going on to the next question,

probing for further information – what particular meanings are intended by questions and wanted in their answers in a particular interview context. Respondents' acceptance of interviewers frameworks of meanings is a key factor in a 'successful' interview (Mishler, 1987, p. 54).

'Successful', here, goes into inverted commas because Mishler is thinking of studies of people's values and emotions in which such control would be tantamount to gross imposition. What he is describing here is the amazing capacity, that cannot be mistaken if you have ever conducted an interview, for respondents to 'latch on' to what the stranger in front of them is talking about. Channelling this willingness to learn is the way to successful interviewing, and Mishler goes on to give examples 'which demonstrate how an interviewer/physician "teaches" a respondent/patient to restrict answers only to the information the physician considers relevant'. Again, this is all shock-horror to Mishler, but music to my ears, since 'teaching' is surely the guiding metaphor for the conduct of the realist interview.

It is not appropriate here to go into further details about how such a role can be achieved in terms of manner, appearance, training etc. As for examples from the case studies, all I can do is pass quickly over the fact that unlike Wright (1985 p. 160) the social context I have in mind is hardly the stuff of the telephone interview. Instead I will end with my own rallying cry: the best interviewers will be good teachers. They must be prepared to take infinite pains to describe the nature of the information sought. They must be sensitive to the struggles the respondent may have in using what are ultimately the researchers' categories. They must be prepared to invite and field questions galore about the potential response categories and their significance. All of this must be done, however, in ways which remain faithful to the conceptual structures under test. These teachers, after all, have written the book, save for the gaps for data, and it is in their interest the respondents fill in the gaps as willingly and knowingly as possible.

Chapter Eleven

THE NEW RULES OF SOCIOLOGICAL MEASUREMENT

It is appropriate to conclude with a recapitulation of what I can only conceive of as the new rules of sociological measurement. Unlike other authors in this respect, my use of the phrase 'methodological rules' is not meant ironically. These rules are intended to constitute a programme for sociological research. They are not, of course, prescriptions to be followed blindly, without interpretation, which will somehow lead automatically to objective data. They are rules in the sense of all methodological rules described in Chapter 1, in that they are constraining as well as enabling, and they are the medium and outcome of the research that they recursively organize. Above all is the fact that, although they are reproduced as goals-to-be-striven-after, they are to be discovered in the routine logic-in-use of research practitioners.

I term them rules for sociological *measurement* because they cover only what is traditionally called quantitative research, and even here they concern only part of the procedures used in any investigation. However, these are 'measurement' rules in the broadest possible use of that term. These are not a series of narrow technical recommendations for creating variables but set down a method for the production of entire bodies of evidence which are necessary to genuinely substantiate sociological theory.

To sum up, the distinctive characteristics of our method are as follows:

Rule I.

Measurement parameters are forged in sociological theory. Variables must never be treated as discrete items but understood as part of a system regulated by some *generative mechanism*. Most sociological theory takes the form of comparison of the probabilities of certain types of action in certain social groupings. It follows that sociological measurement will chiefly consist of close specification of social categories and performing counting operations on these.

Rule II.

The raw material of empirical tests is the social regularity. *Regularities* occur because of the action of underlying *mechanisms* in particular *contexts*. All empirical hypotheses must pay equal attention to these three elements. Since it is assumed that the action of the generative mechanisms under investigation may be obscured by other social mechanisms, some method of controlling the latter is required. The statistical control of these confounding mechanisms is imperfect since it cannot attend to contextual variation and *comparative* and *longitudinal* research designs are called for to approximate to closed-system investigation.

Rule III

Empirical testing is at its most powerful in those disciplines employing *formal networks* of co-ordinated explanation. This allows for conceptual certitude as well as conceptual extension, so that precise linkages can be made between relatively speculative ideas and certain other concepts which are understood well enough to control and measure. Sociological theory must refrain as far as possible from ordinary language formulation and link certain of its basic notions to form an *abstract calculus* of formally defined concepts. Further extension of concepts, to portray a range of social systems, should take the form of hypothesis-making within generative formal models.

Rule IV.

Empirical testing is *adjudicatory* rather than verificatory. Empirical evidence must be constructed so that it relates to rival concepts or propositions rather than attempting to measure the 'real world' directly. This involves scouring rival schools of theory for *points of intersection* around which one can build a common empirical standard for comparison. The paradigm case for this in sociology will be disputes on social positions which one theory treats as separate categories, whereas another treats them homogeneously.

Rule V

Data construction in sociology is irretrievably social. Data production is thus difficult to control because it is stimulated by the totality of verbal and social cues in the interview. Meaning imposition is also a problem since the concepts under investigation are and should be those of the investigator. In order to alleviate these problems data should refer solely to institutional or *mutual knowledge.* Interviewers should adopt the role of *conceptual tutors* (but not hypotheses-disclosers) and respondents act as *learner/informants.*

Although each of these rules is drawn from parallels with physical science inquiry, I have made it quite clear that in social research each of them operates with a lower level of feasibility and at a distinct step-down in terms of precision. The empirical constraint on the acceptability of sociological theories will always be moderate because of certain in-built limitations associated with each of these strategies. The power of sociological measurement is constrained because of the probabilistic and loosely formalizable nature of all social theory, because of the indistinguishability of many rival theories, because of the moderate degree of control exerciseable via longitudinal and comparative investigation, because of the practical limitations on conceptual clarification in the interview and much else besides. Given this hedge of qualifications I have placed around the empirical strategy, more traditionally inclined quantitative methodologists might be inclined to say that with friends like

Pawson who needs enemies (strangely enough, I have heard this said).

To me, it is as objectionable to be doleful about the prospects of empirical inquiry on such grounds as it is to blast on with a 'high-tech' approach to measurement when the structure of sociological theory can never warrant it. Indeed it is obvious that since these rules themselves lay such great stress on conceptual forms, the empirical hurdle that they do provide must be seen as working alongside other criteria deemed appropriate for effective theory construction. The point is that even the modest empirical strategy that ensues can demonstrably overcome those phenomenological and relativist objections which have been deemed to undermine completely any possibility of quantitative empirical inquiry in sociology.

Even more to the point is the fact that these rules are crafted in the working methods of those who practise rather than preach about sociological research. The final arbitration on whether sociological method should be scientific, hermeneutic, critical or whatever can never be made as a point of high principle. Giddens (1976, p. 13) is quite wrong to assert that 'those who still wait for a (social-scientific) Newton are not only waiting for a train that won't arrive, they're in the wrong station altogether'. The fact is that, as well as perching on my cover, Newton (or rather the spirit of science as harnessed in these rules and methods) is alive and well in sociology.

BIBLIOGRAPHY

Abercrombie, N. and Urry, J. (1983), *Capital, Labour and the Middle Classes*, London, George Allen & Unwin

Althusser, R. and Herberlein, I. (1971), 'Validity and the multitrait – multimethod matrix', in Borgatta, E. and Bohrnstedt, G.(eds) *Sociological Methodology 1970*, San Francisco, Jossey-Bass

Atkinson, J.M. and Drew, P. (1979), *Order in Court*, London, Macmillan

Arber, S. *et al.* (1984), 'Evaluating alternative measures of social class: does gender make a difference?' Paper presented at the BSA Annual Conference, University of Bradford, April 1984

Arber, S. *et al.* (1986), 'The limitations of existing social class classifications for women', in *The Measurement of Social Class – Proceedings of a Conference*, Social Research Association

Bachelard, G. (1968), *The Philosophy of No*, New York, Orion Press

Bateson, N. (1984), *Data Construction in Social Surveys*, London, George Allen & Unwin

Bell, C. and Newby H. (eds) (1977), *Doing Sociological Research*, London, George Allen & Unwin

Bell, C. and Roberts, H. (eds) (1984), *Social Researching*, London, Routledge & Kegan Paul

Benton, T. (1977), *Philosophical Foundations of the Three Sociologies*, London, Routledge & Kegan Paul

Benton, T. (1984), *The Rise and Fall of Structural Marxism*, London, Macmillan

Berelson, B. and Steiner, G. (1964), *Human Behaviour: an Inventory of Scientific Findings*, New York, Harcourt

Berka, K. (1983), *Measurement*, Dordrecht, D. Reidel

Bhaskar, R. (1978), *A Realist Theory of Science*, Brighton, Harvester

Bhaskar, R. (1979), *The Possibility of Naturalism*, Brighton, Harvester (first published in 1975)

Blalock, H.M. (1968), 'The measurement problem: A gap between the languages of theory and research', in Blalock, H.M. and Blalock, A.B. (eds), *Methodology in Social Research*, New York, McGraw-Hill

327

Blalock, H.M. (1970), *An Introduction to Social Research*, New Jersey, Prentice-Hall

Blalock, H.M. (1972), *Causal Models in the Social Sciences*, London, Macmillan

Blalock, H.M. (ed.) (1975), *Measurement in the Social Sciences*, London, Macmillan

Blalock, H.M. (1982), *Conceptualization and Measurement in the Social Sciences*, Beverly Hills, Sage

Blalock, H.M. (1984), *Basic Dilemmas in the Social Sciences*, Beverly Hills, Sage

Blau, P. (1977), *Inequality and Heterogeneity*, New York, Free Press

Blau, P. and Duncan, O.D., *The American Occupational Structure*, New York, John Wiley

Blumer, H. (1956), 'Sociological analysis and the "variable"', *American Sociological Review*, vol. 21, pp. 633–60

Bohrnstedt, G.W. and Borgatta, E.B. (eds) (1981), *Social Measurement*, Beverly Hills, Sage

Boudon, R. (1973), *Mathematical Structures of Social Mobility*, Amsterdam, Elsevier

Boudon, R. (1974), *Education, Opportunity and Social Inequality*, New York, Wiley

Boudon, R. (1976), 'Comment on Hauser's review of education, opportunity and social inequality', *American Journal of Sociology*, vol. 81, pp. 1175–87

Boudon, R.(1979), *The Logic of Social Action*, London, Routledge & Kegan Paul (English translation 1981)

Boudon, R. (1982), *The Unintended Consequences of Social Action*, London, Macmillan

Bos, H. (1980), *Studies on Christian Huygens*, Lise, Swets and Zeitlinger

Brown, R. (1973), *Rules and Laws in Sociology*, London, Routledge & Kegan Paul

Bryant, C. (1987), Unpublished work-in-progress paper

Bulmer, M. (ed) (1975), *Working Class Images of Society*, London, Routledge & Kegan Paul

Burton, D. (1965), *An Introduction to Abstract Mathematical Systems*, Massachusetts, Addison-Wesley

Butlin, M. (1978), *William Blake*, London, Tate Gallery Publications

Calvert, P. (1982), *The Concept of Class*, London, Hutchinson

Campbell, N.R. (1928), *Measurement and Calculation*, London, Longmans, Green & Co

Care, N. (1973), 'On fixing social concepts', *Ethics*, vol. 84, pp. 10–21

Carley, M. (1981), *Social Measurement and Social Indicators*, London, George Allen & Unwin

Carter, L.F. (1971), 'Inadvertent sociological theory', *Social Forces*, vol. 50, pp. 12–25

Cicourel, A. (1964), *Method and Measurement in Sociology*, Glencoe, Free Press

Collins, H. (1975), 'The seven sexes: a study in the sociology of a phenomenon, or the replication of experiments in physics', *Sociology*, vol. 9, pp. 205–24

Collins, H. (1981), 'Son of seven sexes: the social destruction of a physical phenomenon', *Social Studies of Science*, vol. 11, pp 33-66

Connolly, W. (1983), *The Terms of Political Discourse*, Oxford, Martin Robertson

Costner, H. (1972), 'Theory, deduction and rules of correspondence', in Blalock, H.M. and Blalock, A. (eds), *Methodology in Social Research*, New York, McGraw-Hill

Cousins, J. and Brown, R. (1975), 'Patterns of paradox: shipbuilding workers' images of society', in Bulmer, M. (ed.), *Working Class Images of Society*, London, Routledge & Kegan Paul

Coxon, A. (1983), 'The misconstruction of occupational judgement', *British Journal of Sociology*, vol. 34, pp. 483-90

Coxon, A. and Jones, C.L. (1978), *Images of Occupational Prestige*, London, Macmillan

Coxon, A. and Jones, C.L. (1979a), *Class and Hierarchy*, London, Macmillan

Coxon, A. and Jones, C.L. (1979b), *Measurement and Meanings*, London, Macmillan

Coxon, A. and Jones, C.L. (1979c), 'Images and predication', *Quality and Quantity*, vol. 13, pp. 121-40

Crompton, R. (1980), 'Class mobility in Britain', *Sociology*, vol. 14, pp.117–19

Crowder, D. (1974), 'A critique of Duncan's stratification research', *Sociology*, vol. 8, pp. 19-45

Curtis, R. and Jackson, E. (1962), 'Multiple indicators in survey research', *American Journal of Sociology*, vol. 68, pp. 195-204

Davis, H.H. (1979), *Beyond Class Images*, London, Croom Helm

Davis, K. (1962), 'The role of class mobility in economic development', *Population Review*, vol. 6

de Vaus, D. (1986), *Surveys in Social Research*, London, George Allen & Unwin

Dijkstra, W. and van der Zouwen, J. (eds) (1982), *Response Behaviour in the Survey Interview*, New York, Academic Press

Duhem, P. (1906/1962), *The Aim and Structure of Physical Theory*, New York, Atheneum

Elias, N. (1978), *The Civilizing Process*, Oxford, Blackwell

Ellis, B. (1968), *Basic Concepts of Measurement*, Cambridge, Cambridge University Press

Fararo, T. (1984), *Mathematical Ideas and Sociological Theory* (Special issue of the *Journal of Mathematical Sociology*), New York, Gordon and Breach

Feather, N. (1961), *Mass, Length and Time*, Harmondsworth, Penguin

Feyerabend, P. (1975), *Against Method*, London, New Left Books

Ford, J. (1975), *Paradigms and Fairy Tales*, London, Routledge & Kegan Paul

Gallie, W.B. (1956), 'Essentially contested concepts', *Proceedings of the Aristotelian Society*, vol. 56. pp. 167-98

Georgescu-Roegen, N. (1971), *The Entropy Law and the Economic Process*, Cambridge, Mass., Harvard University Press

Giddens, A. (1976), *New Rules of Sociological Method*, London, Hutchinson

Giddens, A. (1984), *The Constitution of Society*, Cambridge, Polity Press

Gilbert, G.N. (1981), *Modelling Society*, London, George Allen & Unwin

Godel, K. (1931), 'Uber formal unentscheidbare satze der Principia Mathematica und verwandter systeme', *Monatshefte fur Mathematik und Physik*, vol. 38, pp. 173-98

Goldthorpe, J.H. (1973), 'A revolution in sociology?', *Sociology*, vol. 7, pp. 449-62

Goldthorpe, J.H. (1985), 'On economic development and social mobility', *British Journal of Sociology*, vol. 34, pp. 549-73

Goldthorpe, J.H. and Hope, K. (1974), *The Social Grading of Occupations*, Oxford, Clarendon Press

Goldthorpe, J.H. and Llewellyn, C. (1977) 'Class mobility in Britain: three theses examined', *British Journal of Sociology*, vol. 11, pp. 257-87

Goldthorpe, J.H. *et al.* (1980), *Social Mobility and Class Structure in Modern Britain*, Oxford, Clarendon Press

Goldthorpe, J.H. and Payne, C., (1986), 'Trends in intergenerational mobility in England and Wales, 1972-1982', *Sociology*, vol 20, pp. 1-22

Halsey, A.H. *et al.* (1980), *Origins and Destinations*, Oxford, Clarendon Press

Hammond, P.E. (ed.) (1964), *Sociologists at Work*, New York, Basic Books

Harré, R. (1972), *The Philosophies of Science*, Oxford, Oxford University Press

Harré, R. (1978), *Social Being*, Oxford, Blackwell

Harré, R. and Secord, P. (1972), *The Explanation of Social Behaviour*, Oxford, Blackwell

Harrison, B. (1979), *An Introduction to the Philosophy of Language*, London, Macmillan

Hauser, R. (1976), 'Review essay: on Boudon's model of social mobility', *American Journal of Sociology*, vol. 37, pp. 294-300

Hempel, C. (1966), *Philosophy of Natural Science*, New Jersey: Prentice-Hall

Heritage, J. (1978), 'Aspects of the Flexibilities of natural language use', *Sociology*, vol. 12, pp. 79-103

Hesse, M. (1974), *The Structure of Scientific Inference*, London, Macmillan

Hindess, B. (1973), *The Use of Official Statistics in Sociology*, London, Macmillan

Hindess, B. (1977), *Philosophy and Methodology in the Social Sciences*, Brighton, Harvester

Hindess, B. and Hirst, P. (1975), *Pre-Capitalist Modes of Production*, London, Routledge & Kegan Paul

Hindess, B. and Hirst, P. (1977), *Modes of Production and Social Formation*. London, Routledge & Kegan Paul

Hughes, J.A. (1976), *Sociological Analysis*, London, Nelson

Jacobson, A. and Lalu, N. (1974), 'An empirical and algebraic analysis of alternative techniques for measuring unobserved variables', in Blalock, H.M. (ed.), *Measurement in the Social Sciences*, New York, Aldine

Johnson, T. *et al.* (1984), *The Structure of Social Theory*, London, Macmillan

Kaplan, A. (1964), *The Conduct of Inquiry*, New York, Chandler

Keat, R. and Urry, J. (1975), *Social Theory as Science*, London, Routledge & Kegan Paul (second edition, 1981)

Kerr, C. *et al.* (1960), *Industrialism and Industrial Man*, Cambridge, Mass., Harvard University Press

Koyré, A. (1968), *Metaphysics and Measurement*, London, Chapman & Hall

Kuhn, T. (1961), 'The function of measurement in modern physical science', in Woolf, H. (ed.), *Quantification*, Indianapolis, Bobbs-Merill

Kuhn, T. (1970), *The Structure of Scientific Revolutions*, Chicago, University of Chicago Press

Kyburg, H. (1984), *Theory and Measurement*, Cambridge, Cambridge University Press

Lakatos, I. (1970), 'Falsification and the methodology of scientific research programmes', in Lakatos, I. and Musgrave, A. (eds), *Criticism and the Growth of Knowledge*, Cambridge, Cambridge University Press

Layder, D. (1985), 'Beyond empiricism? The promise of realism', *Philosophy of the Social Sciences*, vol. 15, pp. 255-74

Lazarsfeld, P.F. (1977), 'Evidence and inference in social research' in Bulmer, M. (ed.), *Sociological Research Methods*, London, Macmillan (originally published 1958)

Lieberson, S. (1985), *Making It Count*, Berkeley, University of California Press

Lipset, S. and Zetterberg, H. (1959), 'Social mobility in industrial society', in Lipset, S. and Bendix, R. (eds), *Social Mobility in Industrial Societies*, Berkeley, University of California Press

Lockwood, D. (1966), 'Sources of variation in working class images of society', *Sociological Review*, vol. 14, pp. 247-67

MacIntyre, A. (1973), 'The essential contestability of social concepts', *Ethics*, vol. 84, pp. 1-9

Marsh, C. (1982), *The Survey Method*, London, George Allen & Unwin

Marsh, C. (1986a), 'Social class and occupation', in Burgess, R. (ed.), *Key Variables in Social Investigation*, London, Routledge & Kegan Paul

Marsh, C. (1986b) 'Occupationally-based measures of social class' in *Measurement of Social Class: Proceedings of a Conference*, Social Research Association

Marsh, P. *et al*, (1978), *The Rules of Disorder*, London, Routledge and Kegan Paul

Marshall, G. *et al* (1988), *Social Class in Modern Britain*, London, Hutchinson

Martin, P. (1987), 'The concept of class', in Anderson, R. *et al* (eds), *Classic Disputes in Sociology*, London, George Allen and Unwin

Martin, R. and Fryer, R. (1975), 'The deferential worker?', in Bulmer, M. (ed.) *Working Class Images of Society*, London, Routledge and Kegan Paul

Masterman, M. (1970), 'The Nature of a Paradigm' in Lakatos, I. and Musgrave, A. (eds), *Criticism and the Growth of Knowledge*, Cambridge, Cambridge University Press

McHugh, P. *et al* (1974), *On the Beginnings of Social Enquiry*, London, Routledge & Kegan Paul

Mishler, E.G. (1986), *Research Interviewing: Context and Narrative* Cambridge, Mass., Harvard University Press

Murphy, J. (1981), 'Class inequality in education', *British Journal of Sociology*, vol. 32, pp. 182-201

Nagel, E. (1968), *The Structure of Science*, London, Routledge & Kegan Paul

Nagel, E. and Newman, R. (1959), *Godel's Proof*, London, Routledge & Kegan Paul

Oakley, Anne (1981), 'Interviewing women: a contradiction in terms', in Roberts, H. (ed.), *Doing Feminist Research*, London, Routledge & Kegan Paul

Open University (1975), *Instrumentation*, Milton Keynes, Open University Press

Open University (1979), *Classification and Measurement*, Milton Keynes, Open University Press

Oppenheim, F. (1981), *Political Concepts*, Oxford, Basil Blackwell

Outhwaite, W. (1988), *New Philosophies of Social Science*, London, Macmillan

Pahl, R. (1984), *Divisions of Labour*, Oxford, Blackwell

Papineau, D. (1978), *For Science in the Social Sciences*, London, Macmillan

Park, P. (1968), *Sociology Tomorrow*, New York, Pegasus

Parsons, T. (1938), 'The role of theory in social research', *American Sociological Review*, vol. 3, pp. 13-20

Pawson, R. (1978), 'Empiricist explanatory strategies: the case of causal modelling', *Sociological Review*, vol. 26, pp. 613–45

Pawson, R. (1980), 'Empiricist measurement strategies: a critique of the multiple indicator approach to measurement', *Quality and Quantity*, vol. 14, pp. 651–78

Pawson, R. (1982) 'Desperate measures', *British Journal of Sociology*, vol. 33, pp. 35–63

Pawson, R. (1983), 'Language and measurement: a reply to Coxon', *British Journal of Sociology*, vol. 34 pp. 491–7

Payne, G. *et al* (1981), *Sociology and Social Research*, London, Routledge
& Kegan Paul
Penn, R. (1981), 'The Nuffield class categorisation', *Sociology*, vol. 15,
pp. 265–71
Phillips, B. (1985), *Sociological Research Methods*, Homewood, Dorsey
Press
Popper, K. (1934/1959), *The Logic of Scientific Discovery*, London,
Hutchinson
Poulantzas, N. (1975), *Classes in Contemporary Capitalism*, London, New
Left Books
Quine, W. (1951), 'Two dogmas of empiricism', *Philosophical Review*,
vol. LX, pp. 20–43
Quine, W. (1960), *Word and Object*, Cambridge, Mass., MIT Press
Reason, D. (1979), 'On the essential futility of folk classification',
paper delivered at the Quantitative Sociology Group Conference,
Polytechnic of North London
Roberts, H. (ed.) (1981), *Doing Feminist Research*, London, Routledge &
Kegan Paul
Rogers, E.M. (1960), *Physics for the Inquiring Mind*, Princeton,
Princeton University Press
Rose, A. (1945), 'A rerearch note on experimentation in
interviewing', *American Journal of Sociology*, vol. 51, pp. 143–4
Rose, D. and Marshall, G. (1986), 'Constructing the (W)right classes',
Sociology vol. 20, pp. 440-55
Russel, B. (1910), *Principia Mathematica*, Cambridge, Cambridge
University Press
Sartori, G. (ed.) (1984), *Social Science Concepts*, Beverly Hills, Sage
Sartori, G. and Riggs, F. (1975) 'Tower of Babel: on the definition and
analysis of concepts', *International Studies Association*, Occasional
Papers, No. 6
Sayer, A. (1984), *Method in Social Science*, London, Hutchinson
Schon, D. (1963), *Displacements of Concepts*, London, Tavistock
Schuman, H. and Presser, S. (1981), *Questions and Answers in Attitude
Surveys*, New York, Academic Press
Schutz, A. (1962), *Collected Papers*, vol.I., Natanson, M. (ed.) The
Hague, Nijhoff
Silverman, D. (1985), *Qualitative Methodology and Sociology*, Aldershot,
Gower
Smith, H.W. (1975), *Strategies of Social Research*, New Jersey,
Prentice-Hall
Stevens, S.S. (1946), 'On the theory of scales', *Science*, vol. 103, pp.
677-80
Stevens, S.S. (1966), *Handbook of Experimental Psychology*, New York,
John Wiley
Stewart, A. *et al* (1980), *Social Stratification and Occupations*, London,
Macmillan
Stinchcombe, A. (1973), 'Theoretical domains and measurement',
Acta Sociologica, vol. 16, pp. 3-12

Sydenham, P. (1979), *Measuring Instruments*, Stevenage, Peregrinus
Taylorson, D. and Halfpenny, P. (forthcoming), *Measuring Social Class*, London, Tavistock
Thomas, D. (1979), *Naturalism and Social Science*, Cambridge, Cambridge University Press
Tudor, A. (1982), *Beyond Empiricism*, London, Routledge & Kegan Paul
Willer, D. (1984), 'Analysis and composition as theoretic procedures', in Fararo, T. (ed.), *Mathematical Ideas and Sociological Theory*, New York, Gordon & Breach
Willis, P. (1977), *Learning to Labour*, Farnborough, Saxon House
Wittgenstein, L. (1958), *Philosophical Investigations*, Oxford, Basil Blackwell
Wittgenstein, L. (1961), *Tractatus Logico-Philosophicus*, London, Routledge & Kegan Paul
Wright, E.O. (1978), *Class, Crisis and the State*, London, New Left Books
Wright, E.O. (1979), *Class Structure and Income Determination*, New York, Academic Press
Wright, E.O. (1985), *Classes*, London, Verso

INDEX

abstract calculus 228, 244, 254, 324
accepted-as-real 303–5
actualism 198–201, 207–12; *see also* empiricism, positivism
ad hoc (post hoc) explanation 160, 164–8, 250, 276
adjudicationism 255, 257, 264–86, 325
appearance/reality distinction 168, 179
auxiliary measurement theory 38, 58

Bhaskar, R. 6, 127, 129, 138–43, 149–51, 168, 197–205, 208, 217
Blalock, H.M. 37–8, 40, 53, 59–62, 71
Blumer, H. 12–13, 35
Bohrnstedt, G.W. and Borgatta, E.B. 38–42, 49
Boudon, R. 180–6, 190–5, 247–8, 250–3
box model 191–3, 245

causality: generative versus successionist 128; image-indicator causation 58–63; multi-causation 208; structural determinism 176
ceteris paribus 67, 201
Cicourel, A.V. 12–13, 46
circularity 109–16, 289, 315
class *see* social class
classification 89–90
clerical proletarianization 282
closure: actualist versus realist 198–207; conceptual 226; experimental 137–44; immobility 167; statistical versus contextual 207–24, 252

comparative and longitudinal inquiry 219–24, 324
concept, conceptualization: *a priori* 42–6; as cognitive structure 90;
concepts and observables 52–73; confused 238; filter 309–11; reinterpretation 277–81; transformation 283; *see also* contestabilism, formalism, operationalism, reconstructionism
concomitance 160–4, 179, 186
conditional (probabalistic) explanation 188, 195, 251, 284, 325
consistency criterion 58, 67–70
contestabilism 227, 229, 233–7
context, contextualization 66, 72, 206, 212–17
control *see* closure, interview
Costner, H. 57–9, 62, 67–70

data construction 295, 307, 325
'direct' observation 41, 60, 62, 71, 114, 117, 131, 199
double hermeneutic 18, 19, 24
dual language (two language) model 132–3
duality of structure: applied to method 31, 323; applied to social constitution 193

empiricism 19, 39–42, 266–7, 291; empiricist backlash 1, 17; post-empiricist 9, 10, 127; *see also* actualism, positivism
entrenchment 147–9, 232
experiment: logic 201; production

335